Computers and Privacy
in the Next Decade

Proceedings of the Workshop on
Computers and Privacy in the Next Decade
Sponsored by the Special Committee on the Right to Privacy
of the
American Federation of Information Processing Societies, Inc.
Asilomar Conference Grounds
Pacific Grove, California
25–28 February 1979

Computers and Privacy in the Next Decade

EDITED BY

Lance J. Hoffman

Department of Electrical Engineering and Computer Science
School of Engineering and Applied Science
George Washington University
Washington, D.C.

1980

ACADEMIC PRESS

A Subsidiary of Harcourt Brace Jovanovich, Publishers

New York   London   Toronto   Sydney   San Francisco

This material is based upon work supported by the National Science
Foundation under Grant MCS 78-25753. Any opinions, findings, and
conclusions or recommendations expressed in this publication are those
of the author(s) and do not necessarily reflect the views of the National
Science Foundation.

54145

#60925/0

JC
596.2
U5
C65
C.2

ACADEMIC PRESS, INC.
111 Fifth Avenue, New York, New York 10003

United Kingdom Edition published by
ACADEMIC PRESS, INC. (LONDON) LTD.
24/28 Oval Road, London NW1 7DX

Library of Congress Cataloging in Publication Data

Main entry under title:

Computers and privacy in the next decade.

"The material presented herein is the product of
two meetings supported by a National Science Foundation
grant to the American Federation of Information
Processing Societies."
    Includes bibliographies.
    1. Privacy, Right of——United States——Congresses.
2. Computers——Access control——Congresses. I. Hoffman,
Lance J. II. American Federation of Information
Processing Societies.
JC596.2.U5C65   341.44'8'0973   80—11388
ISBN 0—12—352060—6

PRINTED IN THE UNITED STATES OF AMERICA

80 81 82 83   9 8 7 6 5 4 3 2 1

To Lara

Contents

I

A Privacy Agenda for the 1980s

II

Invited Papers and Comments

List of Contributors and Participants

Numbers in parentheses indicate the pages on which the authors' contributions begin.

Paul Armer (43), *Charles Babbage Institute, 701 Welch Road, Suite 224, Palo Alto, California 94304*

Carole Parsons Bailey (45), *5 Squirrel Hill Lane, West Hartford, Connecticut 06107*

Martha Barnett, *Holland & Knight, 92 Lake Wire Drive, Lakeland, Florida 33802*

Alan Bennett, *Senate Committee on Governmental Affairs, 3300 Dirksen Senate Office Building, Washington, D.C. 20510*

Robert Blanc, *National Bureau of Standards, Administration A209, Washington, D.C. 20234*

Robert P. Campbell, *Advanced Information Management, Inc., 14860 Daytona Court, Woodbridge, Virginia 22193*

William Cavaney, *Defense Privacy Board, Pomponio Plaza Building, 1735 N. Lynn Street, Arlington, Virginia 22209*

Robert Lee Chartrand (125), *Science Policy Research Division, Congressional Research Service, Library of Congress, Washington, D.C. 20540*

Jerome J. Daunt (187), *7506 Allen Ave., Falls Church, Virginia 22046*

Irene Emsellem, *Senate Judiciary Committee, 2226 Dirksen Senate Office Building, Washington, D.C. 20510*

Gordon C. Everest (141), *Department of Management Sciences, University of Minnesota, Minneapolis, Minnesota 55455*

Oswald H. Ganley (133), *Information Resources Program, Harvard University, Cambridge, Massachusetts 02138*

Hans Peter Gassmann (109), *Directorate for Science, Technology, and Industry, Organization for Economic Cooperation and Development, 2 Rue André Pascal, 75775 Paris, France*

Robert C. Goldstein (51), *Faculty of Commerce, University of British Columbia, Vancouver, British Columbia, Canada V6T 1W5*

H. Rex Harston, *Department of Computer Science, Virginia Polytechnic Institute and State University, Blacksburg, Virginia 24061*

Lance J. Hoffman (3), *Department of Electrical Engineering and Computer Science, The George Washington University, Washington, D.C. 20052*

Lucy A. Hummer (137), *Room 4427A, State Department, Washington, D.C. 20520*

Portia Isaacson (35), *Electronic Data Systems, 7171 Forest Lane, Dallas, Texas 75230*

David A. Johnston (163), *Legislative Service Committee, Statehouse, Columbus, Ohio 43215*

Charles W. Joiner (183), *ABA's Section on Individual Rights and Responsibilities Committee on Privacy, 251 Federal Courthouse, Detroit, Michigan 48226*

Carol G. Kaplan (195), *Privacy and Security Staff, Bureau of Justice Statistics, 633 Indiana Avenue, N.W., Washington, D.C. 20531*

Rob Kling, *Computer Science Department, University of California, Irvine, Irvine, California 92664*

Steve E. Kolodney (31), *SEARCH Group, Inc., 1620 35th Avenue, Sacremento, California, 95822*

Kenneth C. Laudon (89), *Department of Sociology, John Jay College of Criminal Justice, New York, New York 10019*

Marcia MacNaughton, *Office of Technology Assessment, 600 Pennsylvania Avenue, S.E., Washington, D.C. 20530*

Douglas McAdam (65),* *Department of Sociology, State University of New York at Stony Brook, Stony Brook, New York 11794*

Granger Morgan, *Department of Electrical Engineering, Carnegie-Mellon University, Pittsburgh, Pennsylvania 15213*

Abbe Mowshowitz† (97), *Department of Computer Science, University of British Columbia, Vancouver, British Columbia, Canada V6T 1W5*

Susan Hubbell Nycum (39), *Chickering and Gregory, 3 Embarcadero Center, Suite 2300, San Francisco, California 94111*

Elmer R. Oettinger (151), *Institute of Government, University of North Carolina, Chapel Hill, North Carolina 27514*

James B. Rule (65), *Department of Sociology, State University of New York at Stony Brook, Stony Brook, New York 11794*

Naomi Seligman, *McCafferty, Seligman & von Simon, Inc., 220 East 61st Street, New York, New York 10021*

Irwin J. Sitkin (61), *Aetna Life and Casualty, Corporate Data Processing and Administrative Services, 151 Farmington Avenue, Hartford, Connecticut 06156*

*Present Address: Department of Sociology, George Mason University, Fairfax, Virginia 22030.
†Present Address: Interfaculteit Bedrijfskunde, Poortweg 6, 2612PA Delft, The Netherlands.

Robert Ellis Smith, *Privacy Journal, P.O. Box 8844, Washington, D.C. 20003*

Oliver R. Smoot (57), *Computer and Business Equipment Manufacturers' Association, 1828 L Street, N.W., Washington, D.C. 20036*

Theodore D. Sterling (103), *Computing Science Department, Simon Fraser University, Burnaby, British Columbia, Canada V5A 156*

Linda Sterns (65), *Department of Sociology, State University of New York at Stony Brook, Stony Brook, New York 11794*

George B. Trubow (23), *John Marshall Law School, 315 South Plymouth Court, Chicago, Illinois 60604*

Rein Turn (119), *Computer Science Department, California State University, Northridge, California 91330*

David Uglow (65), *Department of Sociology, State University of New York at Stony Brook, Stony Brook, New York 11794*

Willis H. Ware (9), *The Rand Corporation, 1700 Main Street, Santa Monica, California 90406*

Marilyn T. Welles, *Automated Sciences Group, Inc., 8555 16th Street, Silver Spring, Maryland 20910*

Fred Weingarten,* *Division of Computer Research, National Science Foundation, Washington, D.C. 20550*

Alan F. Westin (167), *Department of Public Law and Government, Columbia University, New York, New York 10027*

---

*Present Address: Consultant, 5701 Harwick, Bethesda Maryland.

Preface

Alan Westin has characterized three phases of awareness and action on the privacy/data bank issue: the early warning phase, the study phase, and the regulatory phase. I would like to suggest that these phases are parts of a series of historical waves.

The controversy over the proposed national data bank in 1967 was one of the first events in the early warning phase of the first wave. We then moved on to the study phase, and here the most notable reports were those of the National Academy of Sciences Project on Computer Data banks, the Report of the HEW Secretary's Advisory Commission on Automated Personal Data Systems, and the report of the Privacy Protection Study Commission.

The study phase overlapped the regulatory phase, where the most significant actions so far have been the passage of the Privacy Act of 1974 and the new executive branch initiatives on regulatory action.

At the same time, we are in the early warning phase, historically, for the next wave; its herald is the inexpensive microcomputer system.

We have learned a lot about computers, organizations, and privacy in the last decade; hopefully, we shall be able to take advantage of some of our past experience in facing up to the challenges and problems that will arise in the next decade. It remains to be seen whether computers are any different than automobiles or nuclear energy with respect to unanticipated effects or the problems involved in putting a new technology into place.

The material presented herein is the product of two meetings supported by National Science Foundation Grant MCS 78-25753 to the American Federation of Information Processing Societies. The goals of the project are to highlight the most pressing issues in the field and to suggest creative methods of attack on the research issues involved. Special thanks are due to Dr. Fred Weingarten, then at the National Science Foundation, for his foresight and encouragement in sponsoring this work.

I

A Privacy Agenda for the 1980s

A Research Agenda for Privacy in the Next Decade

Lance J. Hoffman

Introduction

"Privacy" is a complex notion involving the social contract between individuals and the society in which they live. It invites clashes between individuals and institutions, and between privacy protection and free access to information. This paper presents an agenda which attempts to outline research priorities that can lead to reasonable resolutions of these conflicts. However, even if all its projects are undertaken, the agenda suggested here cannot permanently resolve these problems, since values are in constant flux and differ across societies and across historical time periods.

Most of the projects listed can be undertaken from philosophical, psychological, press, behavioral, economic, legal, sociological, computer–communications, or public interest vantage points. Each of these perspectives contribute to a comprehensive dialogue. Research is needed both from a historical viewpoint (where we have been) and from a policy research viewpoint (where we ought to go).

The major areas on our research agenda are historical research, needed institutional mechanisms, needed technological mechanisms, policy questions, privacy versus alienation, area-by-area analysis of laws and regulations, and assessment of new technological developments.

Historical Research

The time has come for experience with the first wave of privacy legislation—both federal and state—to be systematically evaluated. The Privacy Protection Study Commission, operating under tight time constraints, did this to a limited extent. Researchers today, however, have the benefit of

3

COMPUTERS AND PRIVACY
IN THE NEXT DECADE

several more years of experience with the relevant laws and administrative procedures.

An interdisciplinary group of experts should examine the experiences to date of government and private organizations that have had to comply with privacy constraints and Freedom of Information Act or public record requests. The effects of federal and state legislation on system development, information exchange, and interagency information flows should be understood and evaluated. The parts of the legislation which have worked well should be identified, as should the parts which have remained unused.

Finally, the implications of omnibus versus specific legislation can be studied, as can the use of privacy as a shield for restraint of trade or for other interests.

Needed Institutional Mechanisms

The 1979 Asilomar workshop on computers and privacy emphasized the utility of interaction among and between various disciplines. Multidisciplinary deliberations should be conducted on a broad scale. A continuing group should meet periodically to exchange information and discuss current national and international questions related to privacy and information policy. This group should have a broad membership (including the public) and one of its tasks should be a continual updating of the research agenda. This group (or a separate entity) could be a clearinghouse of information on privacy, information policy, and public opinion.

Informed critics have long been concerned with the vulnerability of computer systems which affect people. Electronic funds transfer systems have been cited as an example of an area where not enough is known about potential risks. Therefore, research concerning the development of "early warning systems" to alert policymakers and technologists to potential risks and harm is called for.

Needed Technological Mechanisms

One of the weakest areas in computer systems is the auditing mechanism. Knowledge of appropriate techniques is improving, but probably not faster than the increase in computer crime, nor faster than the complexity of computing systems that must be understood by auditors. Additional research into improved auditing techniques and their associated costs is important.

Technological mechanisms may have to be developed to allow a "free port" capability to deal with transborder data flows carried over international networks. These mechanisms should be responsive to international guidelines for transborder data flow under development by various groups such as the Organization for Economic Cooperation and Development (OECD). Differences among guidelines must, of course, be resolved.

There has been a good deal of technical work on computer program verification and the proving of security "kernels." An independent assessment of the importance of verifying or proving security-related aspects of computer software and of the work done so far in this area is now called for.

Policy Questions

Deserving of research are the public policy implications of the licensing of data bank operators at the federal or state level, certification of computer personnel, certification of computer programs, and voluntary controls. Appropriate balance in total tracking (womb-to-tomb) systems; purging, sealing, and retention policies for public and private records; and universal identifier/social security number problems require further study.

Although there has been speculation and some theoretical work on formula-based decision making, we have no empirical data on the actions of or alternatives available to persons denied benefits (such as credit) on the basis of point-scoring formulas.

The appropriateness or inappropriateness of the use of truth verification technology (polygraphs, voice stress analyzers, etc.), its effect on the individuals and the rest of society, the technical requirements for appropriate truth verifiers, and which (if any) currently available devices meet these requirements are all ripe areas for future research.

Privacy versus Alienation

The term "privacy" more and more is used as a catchall to denote, in addition to traditional concepts, the sense of alienation or estrangement of the individual from society (especially government). More accurate terms to express the various notions often addressed under the privacy rubric are necessary if these notions are to be properly studied and public policy developed.

Area-by-Area Analysis of Laws and Regulations

Analysis of laws and regulations relating to specific functional areas should be carried out in the context of the historical research and public policy considerations described above. Operational needs should be weighed against privacy requirements in such areas as taxation, financial, insurance, research, social service, employment, and educational records and vital statistics.

Criminal justice records, in particular, present important issues which have yet to be resolved. More detailed studies of the effects of technology, law, and public policy on the missions of criminal justice agencies are required. Data access relationships among the various components of the criminal justice community (including FBI–state agency relationships) should be studied, keeping in mind that different operating requirements prevail in local, state, and federal milieus and in intelligence and criminal history systems. While some initial work has been done or is in progress (e.g., Law Enforcement Assistance Administration studies and the Office of Technology Assessment study of the FBI National Crime Information Center), much more should be done in a broader context to satisfactorily answer policy questions in criminal justice.

Assessment of New Technological Developments

New technological developments should be assessed continuously for policy and regulatory implications. Regulating citizens band radio, for instance, is child's play compared with the difficulties of imposing a Code of Fair Information Practices on individuals using personal computers; many of these devices may soon be "data havens." The implications of new identification methodologies and the likely interconnections among computers, cable television, and other media are some of the technological and policy questions to be explored in the light of the foregoing discussion.

Summary

In this paper I have attempted to highlight some of the pressing research problems related to computers, privacy, and information policy in the next decade, and to provide some suggestions for researchers in relevant fields. More detailed discussions of selected privacy issues appear in Part II of this volume.

Acknowledgments

It is a pleasure to acknowledge that the ideas presented in this paper grew out of discussions with Oswald Ganley, H. Rex Hartson, Charles Joiner, Carol Kaplan, Elmer Oettinger, George Trubow, Rein Turn, Willis H. Ware, and Alan Westin. George Trubow, in particular, provided an extremely valuable reading and criticism of an earlier draft of this paper. However, any errors or omissions are the sole responsibility of the author.

II

Invited Papers and Comments

Privacy and Information Technology— The Years Ahead

Willis H. Ware

The congressional threat in the early 1970s to mandate universal use of the Social Security number as a personal identifier led then-secretary of the Department of Health, Education and Welfare (HEW) Elliott Richardson to form his Secretary's Special Advisory Group, which produced the now well-known report "Records, Computers, and the Rights of Citizens," a document whose 30,000 copies have been very influential. The work of the HEW group contributed several important intellectual ideas—among others, the notion that privacy was a matter of mutual concern between record subject and record keeper and the notion that a code of fair information practices should govern how record keepers would deal with their information and their subjects. The HEW report in turn provided the intellectual foundation for the Federal Privacy Act of 1974 which in turn created the Privacy Protection Study Commission. The work of the commission culminated in its final report and five appendixes in mid 1977; the report itself was delivered to Congress and the president on July 13, 1977. It extended the intellectual framework of the HEW effort, generalized it, put it in a broader and more appropriate perspective, and examined many record-keeping areas of the private sector. For example, the negative notion of harm to a data subject, as expressed by the HEW group, was replaced by the positive concept of fairness in record-keeping matters. Furthermore, the commission spoke to the question of information collection and its intrusiveness, a subject which the HEW group had not dealt with. In some sense these two reports are the old and new testaments of privacy. There has also been a number of government-funded studies, for example, the Westin examination of medical record keeping.

Privacy and Record Keeping

In the most general way, what do I see privacy to be? First of all, this country is far too large, too complex, and is involved in far too many national and

9

COMPUTERS AND PRIVACY
IN THE NEXT DECADE

international activities, to be run with pencils, papers, and green eyeshades. Without realizing it in any explicit way, the country has made an irrevocable commitment to computers. There is no way back, and should electrons suddenly misbehave one morning, the country would be largely at a standstill. Primarily because of size, but also in part from complexity, the institutions of government and industry must collect and deal with information about people. We all know that it is essentially impossible for an individual to exist, function, and participate in today's society without interacting with a multitude of record systems.

The collision between a legitimate need of public and private institutions for information about people with the rights, privileges, concerns, and position of the individual is the nub of privacy. A decade ago, the chips were all in the hands of the record keepers; individuals had little standing to contest what information was collected, how it was used, with whom it was shared, and especially what government did with it. Beginning with the Fair Credit Reporting Act (FCRA), continuing with other legislative actions of the 1970s, and culminating with the Privacy Act of 1974, the odds have gradually shifted toward the individual. Another way to characterize privacy is to observe that it represents the social thrust of seeking an appropriate balance between legitimate needs of institutions for information about people and the standing of the individual.

Privacy is not a flashy and visible social issue like energy or pollution. It is not as noticeable and its effects are subtle and everywhere. The sense of this comment—namely pervasiveness and subtlety—tends to characterize most situations that involve information, its flow, use, control, or management. We have all seen corporate executives, members of government, and other individuals shy away from the mystique of computers and not even try to understand them and their effects. The situation is changing, of course, and getting better in some places, but there still are organizations that do not accurately perceive with full insight the role of information in their affairs. Regrettably, information issues often get only lip service and little action. Thus privacy tends to be low on the priority list for attention.

To distinguish among privacy, security, and confidentiality, let me offer definitions of them which I believe reflect contemporary usage.

Privacy. The social expectation that an individual (and by extension, a group of individuals, or an institution, or all society) must (1) be able to participate in determining how information about him is used or communicated to others, and be assured that such information is properly protected against inappropriate use; (2) be assured of openness, forthrightness, and fairness in relations with any record-keeping organization that maintains data about him; and (3) be protected against unwelcome, unfair, improper, or excessive collection or dissemination of information or data about him.

Security. The totality of safeguards required to (1) protect a computer-based system, including its physical hardware, personnel, and data against deliberate or accidental damage from a defined threat; (2) protect the system against denial-of-use by its rightful owners; and (3) protect data and/or computer programs (and/or system privileges) against divulgence to or use by unauthorized persons.

Confidentiality. This entails (1) status accorded to data or information indicating that it is sensitive for some reason, therefore needs to be protected against theft or improper use, and must be disseminated only to individuals or organizations authorized (or privileged) to have it; (2) by extension, status (sometimes assured by law) accorded to data or information that reflects an understood agreement between the person furnishing the data and the person or organization holding it that prescribes the protection to be provided and the dissemination and use to be permitted; (3) a legally recognized relation between certain individuals (e.g., lawyer–client) that privileges communications between them from disclosure in court. (Sometimes, confidential information is legally required to be given in exchange for some benefit, privilege, right, or opportunity; sometimes it is voluntarily given.)

Thus, confidentiality is an attribute of information characterizing its need for protection. Computer security represents the technical and administrative means for providing such protection and controlling access to information. Privacy is largely a legally oriented and procedural matter of how information is used. It is clear, I think, that computer security is a necessary, but not sufficient, precursor for accommodating privacy. Unless a record system can protect its information and control access to it, there is little hope that privacy protection can be accorded.

Computers and the Nation

I would like next to make some general observations about the interaction of computer technology with affairs of the country. The United States has made its irrevocable commitment to computers. It has not examined or studied the impact of it; nor, I would assert, does the United States understand in the fullest scope what that commitment implies for the future. Let me suggest some thoughts.

Computer-based record-keeping systems—like any sytem—will have to deal with errors and correct them. Moreover, decisions about people made on the basis of information in the record system may have to be modified after the fact for a variety of reasons. The record system may have a legal responsibility to retain information about people for specified durations of time, or for specified purposes. There may be legal or business requirements to audit the functioning and performance of a record-keeping system, and in many cases such a system will have to bill for its services. Therefore, information about people will exist within a record-keeping system for varying amounts of time, no matter what the system may happen to be.

Data Banks

We refer to some information as being in a data bank. However, some of it will exist for only a moderately short period of time (for example, in a transaction-oriented system); thus we might think of data pools that are part of the system design and necessary to its functioning. Sometimes data will accumulate in puddles for varying periods of time, simply because of the way the designers have implemented the flow processes. Inevitably such data banks, pools, or puddles will become attractive targets for government agencies, blackmailers, foreign opponents, law enforcement, and perhaps even lawyers in court actions. Why? Because more and more of one's life will be documented in the record, as opposed to either not being documented at all or being documented in a large number of geographically dispersed places.

Thus, it will be very inviting to examine such collections of data and to establish factual behavior as opposed to conjectural behavior whose validity has to be established by laborious processes of evidence. It will be tempting to prospect in them for possible criminal acts, malicious mischief, or just plain curiosity. Therefore, it will be a problem for most systems—possibly all, especially nationwide ones—to provide very thorough protective mechanisms and access controls. Normally, in the computer security context, one thinks predominantly of the master file in the system, but I submit that the pools and puddles also need consideration by the designer, particularly since they can exist in the way stations of the system or its communications complex, as well as in the central facilities.

Controlling Access

Second, there is the so-called gatekeeping issue in the context of record systems. The phrase is used to characterize the role of the record in controlling access to services, privileges, opportunities, or benefits, for example, credit or education. Because the content of the record effectively determines whether an individual has access to something, it can easily become involved with discriminatory questions. To illustrate, there has been in the real estate business a procedure known as redlining, which consists simply of drawing a red line around some geographical area to indicate that real estate transactions within it would be considered undesirable. Think how subtle that process can become in a computerized system. In granting credit, a process known as point scoring is sometimes used. In effect, it tries to weigh certain characteristics of human behavior and arrive at a composite measure for an individual that indicates whether or not he is eligible for credit. To put it more precisely, it is an algorithmic approach to granting credit where the parameters of the algorithm reflect the statistical or factual behavior of individuals along many dimensions, for example, age, duration of employment, owner versus renter, length of time in residence, and salary. Point scoring amounts to an automated decision-making process about people, using the content of the record for the decision.

Therefore, we have a discriminatory practice of blocking groups of individuals from some benefit or service. Yet, there is the obvious requirement for business to make good decisions about individuals, lest risks not be adequately controlled. There is obviously a very hazy interface and probably a smooth transition from generalized discriminatory practices to well-based, sound business practices. In the hazy interface between them, I can imagine that someday very interesting case law will have to be developed.

Regulation

Let me turn now to regulatory issues. Why do we regulate in this country? There are many reasons, among them: We must manage for the public good a scarce resource, for example, electromagnetic spectrum space; we wish to bring about standards and uniformity of practice for better public service, for example, telephone company technology; we wish to protect the public against natural monopolies—again the phone company example; we wish to safeguard the public where there is a hazard—the airlines and their interaction with the Federal Aviation Administration. Examine for a moment the role of the Federal Communications Commission (FCC), but first distinguish carefully between communication and information processing.

To me, communication is only a transportation network for information. The goal of any communication process is to deliver to the recipient exactly the same information—in particular without error—that was entered by the sender. Information content is to pass through the transportation network unchanged, although its representation may change many times in transit. Sometimes it is delivered to the recipient in different representation than that of origin. For example, a telegram may be handwritten by the sender but is delivered to the recipient typed. Enroute, representation of the information in a telegram changes from that of written paper, to that of keystrokes, to that of electrical signals, to that of electromagnetic energy, and eventually to that of printed page. Thus, the essence of communication, as I see it, is to deliver the originating information error-free to the recipient in a representation suitable for his purposes. However, the whole purpose of computing or information processing is to change information by creating new information, destroying information, juxtaposing information, or segmenting information, to name just a few ways.

Basically, the FCC is in business because it allocates a limited natural resource for public good and guards against monopolistic practices. As part of that, it creates standards and deals with interface issues in an effort to assure the quality of service for everyone. The FCC does not deal particularly with the content of communications, except in the broadcast mode where it is the public morals watchdog. For point-to-point communication, the FCC does not generally concern itself with content other than to worry weakly about publicly distasteful things such as obscenity or pornography. I think this observation is very pertinent to new classes of service that are ahead, for example, electronic message systems. We will need to distinguish with care between the role of the FCC in controlling and regulating the technical arrangements for communication versus the information content of communication, which clearly involves constitutional rights and guarantees.

Generally speaking, the distinction between information and its representation is not normally made, and I suspect that in the future we will have to care more about such a subtle matter. Parenthetically, I would assert that the only reason the FCC conducted its first computer inquiry was because the classical communication industry wanted to change in a basic way; namely, it wished to go from a simple transportation network to one that involved information processing as part of that network. Owing to the commonality of plant and facilities to provide both services, the FCC inevitably became involved, because the country simply had no appropriate other mechanism to deal with the question.

Computer Mystique

Next, I would like to deal with a very general and almost philosophical matter. I will pose it as a question. Do we get ourselves into trouble by believing that computery is mysteriously different? Do we create unnecessary trouble for ourselves by believing that it is not subject to practices and knowhow that we have developed in the past and understand? Should we perceive instead that a computer-oriented situation is similar to things with which we do have experience and seek to identify only those new dimensions which it introduces or only those parameters on which it is truly different. In the latter category, of course, could be such things as timeliness of response or remote and prompt access.

It strikes me that software is the classical example of this point. In the beginning, we thought it could not be managed. We thought it was somehow so different that we persuaded ourselves that it was essentially a creative artform that could not be subject to the usual management principles and practices. We now understand that the same management principles do apply, but there is a crucial new dimension of the matter, complexity. We have, therefore, developed such things as inspections, walkthroughs, programming teams, structured programming, and other techniques that, fitted into classical management structures, did deal with the complexity issue. We have belatedly learned that software can be managed, that it is not fundamentally different, but it does have a few essential new attributes.

I am suggesting that in dealing with a computer-oriented matter, we should look for useful analogs of past situations that we have learned to deal with. I am suggesting that we should stop arguing that computers are different in some mystical way. Rather, we should take the view that computers do somehow relate to our past experience and knowhow, but can be in a few limited dimensions dramatically different. Such a point of view would then let us concentrate our attention and energies on the differences and deal with them, rather than trying to solve a huge overwhelming problem from square zero. With hindsight, I would assert that the HEW committee stumbled across a useful analog, although it did not perceive it as such at the time. A few people in a late-evening discussion noted the similarity between the record-keeping question and fair labor practices, and thus was conceived the code of fair information practices.

Information Ownership

Finally, I would like to touch briefly on the information ownership question, which it seems to me has come to the surface very sharply in the whole copyright issue. Historically, one owned information because he owned the representation of it, for example, a book. Moreover, one protected not information but some representation of it. The situation began to get fuzzy when printed materials found their way into computer systems, and, for the first time, the question of representation versus information began to appear, although I have never heard it discussed clearly in such a way. My intuition tells me that in the years ahead we will have to distinguish conceptually with care—perhaps even in our legislation—between information and how it happens to be represented.

Transborder Data Flow

I would like to tie some of these thoughts to the subjects that are discussed in other papers. First, let us talk about the transborder data flow (TBDF) question. It strikes me that this is an instance in which we believed the situation was grossly different in some fundamental way and unlike anything from the past. The discussion of TBDF has not been an intellectually precise, clearly defined matter, but rather has tended to involve a potpourri of things, including semantic issues, matters of nationalism, issues relating to national security, cultural heritage, and economic barriers, etc. It is not necessary to ask why this was, but it is useful to observe that complex issues often start out intellectually confused.

It has struck me that there are useful analogs that ought to be examined to help us create an appropriate environment in which to allow personal data to flow across national borders. One is the federal–state relationship in this country. I would point, for example, to the Fair Credit Reporting Act in which the federal law gives a floor of protection and states may go further if they wish. Conceivably, we could agree internationally on a satisfactory floor of privacy protection with the option for individual countries to go further if it was seen essential.

Another useful analog, it seems to me, is international travel, in which people fall under the legal jurisdiction of the country they are in, rather than of the home country. There are, to be sure, mechanisms whereby representatives of the home country attempt to assist the traveler. But should the traveler commit a crime against the law of a country he is in, he is as liable as though he were a citizen of that country. However, not everything about an individual travels with him and so there is a peculiar dichotomy in which the individual and some of his possessions are under the legal jurisdiction of one country but the rest of his possessions remain under the legal jurisdiction of his country of residence. International lawyers have long since figured out how to straddle this difficulty, and in the overview things seem to work smoothly. Another useful analog would appear to be the international postal conventions, in which first-class mail presumably travels safely, securely, and unopened across national borders; there are various agreements about how things are to be done. Other suggestions that come to mind are international agreements on the flow of goods, on the exchange of law-enforcement information, and on the conduct of telecommunications.

If one extrapolates such a line of argument to privacy safeguards, one can come out with trying technical issues. If, for example, some information about an individual is subject to the legal jurisdiction of his home country and other is subject to the legal jurisdiction of a country he is visiting, then everything in the record may have to be very carefully flagged as to source of jurisdiction and access to it controlled accordingly. What is worse, of course, is that information collected in one country may be comingled with information collected about an individual in a second country and stored all in the same computer system under yet a third legal jurisdiction. This is probably one of the new twists that international flow of data creates, but I would point to the embassy concept, in which a given country extends its national jurisdiction to a small part of real estate in some second country. Perhaps we can usefully extrapolate such a concept to information. As a matter of collateral observation, I note that as reported in a recent issue of *Computerworld*, the most recent OECD guidelines seem to mesh with my line of argument. For example, the first guideline says "Take all necessary steps to ensure continuous and secure transborder movement of personal data." That is tantamount to saying that people should be allowed to move smoothly—not necessarily without controls—across national borders. The next guideline suggests that transborder data flow should not be prevented or restricted unless such movements are contrary to laws on domestic processing of personal data or certain other conditions. It strikes me that this is analogous to immigration regulations which in effect say that everybody is welcome but we will try to keep out the undesirables or those which in some way have already acted contrary to law. Without going further, I would suggest that the TBDF issue seems to be evolving toward treating information as we treat people or goods, but singling out for special treatment those new and important dimensions that computer-based things introduce.

Personal Computing

The business of personal computing is booming, as we all know; and I wonder whether personal computers will not develop many of the attributes that amateur radio has. Are we not going to have buddy networks and personal message services, and networks of home computers that collectively cooperate for some purpose? All it takes to bring such things to pass is some agreement among the participants about character sets, formats, and interface protocols. The whole notion of personal computers being involved with others via the common carrier network of the country will be especially enticing if one can get access to low-cost, packet-switched, and perhaps overnight service. If packet-switched radio techniques come into common use, then we might expect to see a blending between personal computing buffs and the amateur radio buffs. The government, as we all know, depends on amateur radio operators for emergency communication services, and it is conceivable that the government might even take steps to organize the personal computer fraternity into some kind of national asset for emergency or disaster service.

When, not if, such networks come into existence, there now arises the possibility of a message service that circumvents, or at least competes with, anything that commercial industry or the post office might offer. Who knows what interesting regulatory tariff questions, or political-jurisdictional arguments might appear?

In another dimension, personal computing will serve the very important purpose of improving the information IQ of the general public. One might have made a similar argument about amateur radio and public awareness of the related technology, but there is a crucial difference. The buy-in threshold for amateur radio is really quite high. Among other things, one needs to acquire substantial technical knowledge and to learn Morse code, and the financial investment can be severe. In contrast, the buy-in threshold to personal computing is very modest or even low. There is no need to understand technology. Once the financial investment of several hundred dollars has been made, the user is on his way to do useful things. Therefore, I would anticipate that personal computing will spread much more rapidly and much more broadly than other technology-based public hobbies. There are a number of payoffs to this significant contribution.

1. Given the pervasiveness of information and the value of information to exercise of power, one can imagine that as the technology prospers, the segment of society that understands it and can exploit it will gradually amass power and control. Thus, technology can be a force for concentrating societal power in the hands of a small segment. A high information IQ on the part of the public will help to offset this trend.

2. The mystery of computer-based systems and the general unawareness of how they function and of their nature just has to have had some effect on computer crime. Thus, I would argue that improving the information IQ of the public (and thereby executives as well as customers) will exert some deterrent against computer crime.

3. On the other hand personal computing will create a large number of knowledgeable people, many of whom are bound to be innovative, intellectually sharp, and technically informed. There could be a new class of individuals to pose a threat of computer crime. A boom in personal computing may well stimulate computer security concerns vigorously.

4. The comfort index of the typical citizen who unavoidably must interact with the many record-keeping systems that surround him will be increased. In this regard, those involved with computing are not a typical cross-section of the public. Even with their knowledge of computer technology and relative ease with record-keeping systems, computer-oriented people sometimes nonetheless encounter a traumatic experience. Most of the population stand in awe of computer devices and do not have the foggiest idea of how to deal with systems that contain them. It is important that the information IQ of the public be increased because every citizen will have to deal with and be prepared to confront an increasingly large number of such systems.

Electronic Message Systems

I will now turn to the subject of electronic message sytems (EMS), point of sale systems, and the like. Obviously, every one of them will have the data pool and data puddle problem touched on earlier. Every one will have auditing requirements, error control, and remedial action requirements, and where financial matters are involved, there may be legal requirements for retention of data. Obviously, appropriate safeguards of kinds perhaps not yet conceived will have to be an integral part of every such system. Appropriate legislation is also clearly needed. In regard to the electronic message systems, the issue of information versus its representation is particularly pertinent.

In the postal system as we now know it, the representation of information is not changed as it transits the system. The physical object put into the system by the sender arrives at its destination in the same physical condition—give or take a little damage that the U.S. Postal Service may have inflicted. In an EMS the representation of the information will almost certainly be changed. Perhaps the information content of the original document will be transmitted by facsimile means to an exact replica at the other end; or perhaps as in the telegraph network, the information content of the original document will be converted to electrical impulses that eventually produce a new representation of the information at the other end. In any event, unlike mail delivery as we now know it, the error problem during transmission will be new to the post office; it is hoped that it will do better with the matter than the classical telegraph facilities of the country have in the past.

I recently read that one of the undecided issues of an EMS run by the Postal Service is whether the government should monitor all such traffic. If such were to prove the case, there would materialize overnight a huge market for encryption devices, or at least an enormous interest in the digital encryption standard (DES). The hobby shops would have DES chips and devices within weeks. Similarly, if personal computing leads to message services among individuals, the computers themselves could be used to provide encryption protection for the traffic. One way or another, though, I suspect that users of an EMS will demand the privacy and sanctity that first-class mail supposedly provides.

Cost

I would like to deal with the issue of cost. Security safeguards, control over information use, and control of access are extremely important in their own right. Aside from personal privacy, such issues are of importance to fraud, embezzlement, malicious mischief, harrassment, threats, and a whole host of other things important to organizations and the management of business risks. Having done an adequate job on computer security as I have defined it, it is a very short and easy step to accommodate privacy. The HEW group made an observation that has proved, I believe, to be prophetic; it was said that more management attention, discussion, and trauma would be spent in responding to privacy than dollars.

While the issue of cost cannot be ignored, it is essential to sort out with care just what costs are ascribable to privacy controls and/or legislation versus what costs are really pertinent to safeguarding computer systems and their information for sound business and organizational reasons. Cost would not likely be a matter of debate and excitement except for the suddenness of the change that has occurred. For example, we all readily and without thought accept the cost of maintaining municipal fire departments and paying premiums on fire insurance, but I suspect we would not have been so casual about such matters had the costs of protecting against fire appeared on the scene over a few years. Society has accepted the cost of providing protection against many threats gradually over at least a century and perhaps longer. In contrast, the whole privacy issue has emerged in less than a decade, and the cost consequences of it have become visible only in the last few years. Thus, in my view, it is the suddenness of the change that is magnifying concerns about cost, and in the long run, I submit that cost will gradually become a nonissue. What society wants, society agrees to pay for. We wanted trips to the moon and we wanted an elaborate interstate network of roads; we paid the many billions of dollars to get them. Correspondingly, society will come to accept the nominal cost of privacy as part of the protections that it wishes.

Miscellaneous Topics

Finally, I submit remarks on a few scattered points. In regard to variability among state laws that deal with privacy, I would note that for the public sector the matter is really not a significant issue. If the voters of a particular state choose to implement a very onerous, restrictive, and overly costly law against their own government, it is a matter of whatever such voters wish. Effects on adjacent or other states are minimal and perhaps even zero; there will be some interface problems, perhaps, on the federal scale. However, the matter becomes of major importance for the private sector. When the voters of one state can enact laws that seriously impact on the behavior of people or the cost imposed on them in other or even all states, then the issue of variability is paramount. In some respects, the variability issue among states resembles the TBDF matter. If we can agree on the easy passage of people, goods, and transportation across state borders, then we ought to be able to come to analogous agreements in regard to information.

In this regard, the FCRA is illuminating because it provided for the possibility that states could enact additional safeguards. As it has turned out, only a few states did so and the additional restrictions were so minor that it has not proved to be a problem for credit reporting bureaus who operate interstate.

I would take the view, therefore, that in regard to private-sector privacy legislation, either the federal government has to be preemptive or it has to lay down some principles to assure that one state's actions do not impair all others. We must be careful not to create internally the analog of the TBDF issue as it was in 1977, and that we are now struggling to resolve. Internationally there are only a dozen or so players. Domestically there would be 50 players, and while I would not care to guess how the complexity of the situation would scale with the number of involved parties, it could get to be troublesome.

In another direction, I would like to observe that of the issues we are addressing, there are some near-term ones. Among them I would note that electronic funds transfer systems are likely to take off in the next few years; as we all know, the U.S. Postal Service is talking about supplying electronic message services. Personal computing is upon us, but there are longer-term issues. What if our estimate of the growth of personal computing is far too low? Suppose it escalates at five or ten times what we now think will happen? As Richard Hamming has observed, a factor-of-ten change in something introduces fundamentally new effects; in the case of the personal computer what might they be?

We are also looking into an era of the automated office, or more generally, the automated workplace. What are the implications of such advances for the work scene? For labor relations? For management consequences? For job satisfaction? Or even the family structure, should such advances keep people at home while doing their work? Word processing is growing, but not overly rapidly, and it too might grow at a significantly larger rate. Computer-based message systems are mostly in the experimental or research phase and have not been widely used in commercial or government organizations. What are the implications of the two for management issues, job satisfactions, and the like? The technologists who monitor progress predict that cheap storage is just around the corner. What will it mean when everyone has his own extensive data base attached to his own personal computer that in turn has ready access to the telecommunications network of the country?

It would be nice to be ahead of the power curve in the future, so far as effects such as suggested are concerned. Ideally, the country would have some oversight mechanism that would watch the progress of information technology and would be alert to the implications of its progress for society, its structure, and behavior. The computer fraternity has helped to play the role so far and perhaps in the future it will be sufficient, but perhaps not. The Congress and the country really should have a trigger mechanism to alert us to the consequences of information technology, to the privacy implications of proposed legislation, and to developing risks. Again, the computer fraternity has helped to play the role to some extent in the past and its involvement is growing; but our relations with the pressure points in Washington tend not to be extensive or well-developed. Those of the computer industry are not lobbyists; often they are not well received because they tend to be overwhelmed by the details of technology and to talk of them. They fail to rise above the narrow matters and to perceive the global social issues. Thus, they tend to have a real communication gap and a real acceptance problem. In part, this is related to the mystique of computing but in part to the fact that those involved in computing simply have not accumulated decades upon decades of relating to the government scene as have other industries, technologies, or institutional groups.

To be sure, more members of Congress have a familiarity with computing technology; newer congressional staff people are coming from college with training and awareness. One can find more and more managers, some highly placed, that can knowledgeably discuss the intricacies of computer matters. The National Telecommunications and Information Administration has been created. Is government learning rapidly enough how to deal with the broad scope of computer matters? Or is technology running ahead faster than government is progressing? That is the question for the future.

Microcomputers: Legal Approaches and Ethical Implications

George B. Trubow

In keeping with the subject of this workshop, "computers and privacy," I approach my topic with regard to the use of microcomputers for the storage and retrieval of personal information, that is, any information that describes or can be referenced to an identifiable person. Thus, what makes information personal is not its content but its reference.

The microcomputer (micro) is a comparatively recent phenomenon. There is not much case law dealing with privacy and computers in general, and one might question the propriety of a lawyer discussing ethics; accordingly, perhaps there is little for me to say. There are, however, important policy questions to be resolved if informational privacy is to be preserved in the era of the micro, and I can at least identify those questions. I note what I believe are the more significant issues of law or ethics that face us, and these points are expanded upon in other papers. An interdisciplinary dialogue can be extremely useful at this early stage of policy analysis about privacy and micros.

What Is the Microcomputer?

The micro (often called the personal or home computer) looks like a small electric typewriter attached to a television screen. The keyboard allows one to communicate with the system and to manipulate the data that it stores; the cathode tube displays the information. I leave it to others to describe the technical capabilities of the micro; I merely note that, by some measures, micros now available may be considered to have a capacity equivalent to the basic computer models used by business and government in the 1960s, and soon micros will duplicate the large computers of the 1970s. Computer power once wrapped in hardware that filled a large room is now contained in a

23

contraption the size of a commodious breadbox. The cost of such a system is comparatively small. Radio Shack advertises a very respectable personal computer for about $600, and we can soon expect cheaper and more powerful models. More sophisticated micro systems for business and professional use now can be purchased for $5000–$15,000, as compared to costs of $100,000 and more paid recently for hardware of similar capacity. These factors of size and cost make it possible for almost anyone who wants a computer system to have one.

What Information Uses for the Microcomputer?

Many business and government information functions previously considered too small to justify automation can now be converted easily and cheaply to electronic manipulation. One result will be the decentralization of data bases throughout any given business or government organization; another will be that even the most insignificant information can be automated.

The vast array of potential business and professional uses of the micro is open to speculation. A recent report covering the market potential for micros in medical systems during the 1980s estimates that more than $1.3 billion will be spent; a long list of the possible medical uses include the maintenance of patient records. What about other personal service professions and occupations? The lawyer and accountant can keep complete files about client affairs. The priest can keep comprehensive and detailed information about each of his parishioners. The teacher may maintain easily accessible files on each student, current and past. Insurance agents and social workers can improve their ability to provide service by keeping comprehensive files crammed with detailed personal information about their clients.

Apart from a burgeoning use of micros in business and government, job-related information may be kept by an individual in his computer at home. Data that an employee may not be permitted to keep or use routinely in his job many be maintained privately on his micro. A bank's financial officers, for instance, could develop relatively complete dossiers of customer financial history and status. A police detective could at home maintain intelligence and investigative files that might not be permitted in the department computer. One might keep in his micro information about a colleague's job performance that might not be recorded in the employer's personnel files. Each of us, thinking reflectively about his own job and function, can imagine interesting and creative uses for information about co-workers or clients that could be maintained in personal computers. One possibility is that home computers may become havens for information not allowed at the office. I shall discuss that problem later.

A separate dimension of the micro involves consumer use for personal and household affairs. The micro at home could store budget and tax information, grocery inventories, and the like. We imagine lists for Christmas cards, anniversary gifts (who gave what to whom), parties and guests (who went where, what was worn and eaten, with attention to a guest's likes, dislikes, and allergies). One could keep track of the social circulation of friends and others. The micro could be an automated diary, permitting one to record in detail where he went, whom he met, what he heard and saw. Automated indexing and cross-referencing could be a great asset to the biographer, or to the snoop. (Incidentally, how interesting it might be to keep a record of petty slights or affronts, given or received.)

In addition to uses wherein the computer owner generates the information, micros may be linked to other data bases. Other papers in this book will consider electronic funds transfers and electronic mail, wherein the micro will be an important ingredient. Public record information is becoming increasingly automated. An individual could, at relatively minor cost, have extensive public records copied for him on a cassette or disc which he could take home and use in his micro. Information which heretofore has been relatively inaccessible despite its public nature, may become easily available to any citizen in his own home. Perhaps it may be necessary to reevaluate what and why information is considered "public record."

These few examples hardly begin to explore the potential for new dimensions of micro use. Some have suggested that micro innovation will be relatively unimportant for personal use since the average individual will not know how to create new programs or uses. The assumption is that only large computer manufacturers or suppliers have qualified personnel who advise government and business at higher rates than an individual can afford. The advent of the retail computer store, which may be owned or staffed by experienced and qualified experts, controverts that notion. The average individual who makes a purchase from his computer retailer may get expert help as part of the price, or at nominal additional cost. The hobby computer will be used by the "computer freak" experimentally to develop an increasing range of functions and uses; hundreds and thousands of people will become engaged in research regarding computer application. Hobby clubs will provide forums for the exchange of information and expertise, and the development of new techniques for gathering and using information. Colleges and universities throughout the nation are annually graduating hundreds of students who have been taught BASIC, the common micro language, and who have been introduced to computer science. More and more people are becoming able to use and experiment with micros.

In the past, relatively reliable personnel have been selected by government and business to manage information systems which, by and large, were kept for legitimate purposes. Cost has limited the acquisition and use of information, and employees usually may not play with computers for their own purposes. Even with such constraints, there have been many instances wherein employees have defaulted in their responsibilities and have improperly used information. There will be virtually no limitations on those who operate personal computers, however. Almost anyone can have one; who knows the kinds of information that may be stored and the uses that may be devised for it?

Legal and Ethical Dilemmas

Most issues of information privacy are not created by computers, although the complexity of the issues is markedly enhanced by computer capability. Answers as to who ought to have access to what personal information are not supplied by technology; but because micros can make available to the average citizen vast quantities of information with an ease never before contemplated, new and perplexing questions arise about information use. The main reason for these new problems is that micros permit a data base to be moved from a government or business office into the home. As a result, privacy involves clashes not only between the individual and government or business, but between individuals. Consider for a moment the legal basis for constraints on information.

By its consitutional authority Congress has regulated information used by federal agencies, and the commerce clause has permitted regulation of information used in certain businesses. However, the First Amendment prevents federal or state government from otherwise regulating speech or the press. Limitations on the individual citizen regarding acquisition or use of information come from common law, and not the Constitution.

Tort law penalizes defamation or invasion of privacy. Defamation is concerned with false information that damages reputation; violations of privacy, either by intruding into private affairs or publishing private facts, involve truthful information as well. In the former, one has a cause of action against another who pokes into "secluded" or private places where solitude or confidentiality might be expected. For instance, to read another's diary without permission could be classified as an invasion of privacy by intrusion. Publication of private facts involves disclosure of personal information about another when the information is not of public record or newsworthy. That the information was truthful was not a common law defense; it was enough that relatively widespread publicity was given to a private fact not of public concern. Common law privacy protection, however, has not dealt specifically with personal information held by another. The possession of information by an individual is generally unregulated.

Furthermore, there is some suggestion in recent Supreme Court opinions that the First Amendment may collide with, and perhaps destroy, the tort of publication of truthful private facts. For instance, suppose that Jones has some very sensitive personal and private information about me, and he is planning to tell others. Even were the information false, the publication could not be enjoined because to do so would violate the First Amendment (state action is found because I seek an injunction in a state court). What if I bring an action for damages after Jones publishes the truthful but private facts? He (and the press) could argue that his speech would be unlawfully limited if damages can be recovered in court for the publication of truth because this will chill freedom of speech and press. So far, this possibility has been carefully avoided, although clearly recognized, by the Supreme Court. (Damages for defamation have been allowed because the Constitution has not been interpreted to protect lies.) The constitutional conflict between privacy (found only in the "penumbra" of the Constitution) and free speech (specifically protected by the First Amendment) awaits resolution. If the confidentiality expectation surrounding private facts is eliminated, then the individual will have no remedy against another who publishes damaging but truthful personal information. Publication without justifiable motives may be some basis for removing the First Amendment shield, but few privacy buffs are hopeful. What principles, then, can be employed to protect an individual's information privacy from violation by another individual?

Fair Information Practices and the Individual

Attention to personal information in computers has focused mainly on the duties of government and some businesses. Almost no thought has been given to the obligation of the individual regarding use of personal information about others. Principles of "fair information practice" were espoused in the well-known Department of Health, Education and Welfare report on computers and privacy; the Privacy Act of 1974, the 1977 report of the Privacy Protection Study Commission, and the Financial Privacy Act of 1978, all incorporate similar notions regarding government and business use of personal information. An examination of these basic principles in the context of the individual who has a personal computer at home reveals the inadequacies of current policy.

1. *No personal information should be maintained in secret.* The existence of a personal information system should be advertised, even though access may be denied. Should a householder be expected to post notice on his front door or in a newspaper concerning the nature of any personal information about others that he may store in his home computer?

2. *Give the data subject access to files about himself, and an opportunity to amend and correct those files.* As to information held by federal government and regulated business, the subject of a file may see what is in it, and ask that wrong information be corrected or that an explanatory statement be added. Should this practice be forced upon the individual who has a micro at home? Clearly here is a privacy clash between the person who has a micro and one whose name and vital statistics may be stored in it.

3. *Keep data relevant, accurate, timely, and complete.* Government and business are expected to keep information reasonably current and accurate when it is used for decisions affecting individuals. To what extent can or should this obligation apply to an individual with respect to information in his personal micro?

4. *Use information only for the purposes for which it was collected.* This principle makes sense as applied to government and business, but what about the individual in his own home? Should he be prohibited from certain uses of personal information about others?

5. *Keep information safe from unauthorized access or alteration.* Important or sensitive information should be adequately protected. What security burdens can or should be placed upon the individual with respect to his personal computer?

These principles seek to give the individual some control over information pertaining to him, but they make most sense as applied to government and regulated business. The first task is to determine what principles should govern the maintenance and use of personal information by individuals. An even more formidable task will be to devise ways to monitor and enforce the principles.

Regarding the "data havens" previously suggested, another problem is presented with respect to adequate monitoring of government or business. One may use information in his micro at home to make job-related decisions that may not, however, reflect the use of improper data. Will trusted employees be asked to hide data at home? What about employees who may do that on their own? We shudder at the notion that simply because one works for regulated business or government his home routinely may be invaded for a search for personal information about others. Furthermore, even if one has information that is not supposed to be used in job-related decisions, what prevents him from keeping it in his personal capacity?

Thus far, I have pointed to some factors that suggest a bleak outlook for privacy in the era of the microcomputer. Policies must be developed to provide some control to an individual with respect to information about himself kept by other individuals, if current notions of information privacy are to be preserved. Orwell cautioned us against "Big Brother." Perhaps a more uncontrollable threat is "Little Brother" next door. The next portion of this paper should suggest some solutions to these critical problems. Unfortunately, the text for that section is not yet prepared; I hope to have a draft ready well before 1984.

Comment on "Microcomputers: Legal Approaches and Ethical Implications"

Steve E. Kolodney

It is always a pleasure to participate in a program with George Trubow because I invariably learn something from him. This exchange is no exception, and I would like to thank Professor Trubow for his perceptive paper, which raises many disquieting questions about computers becoming household appliances.

As a new technology emerges, there is a tendency for the best minds to perceive all manner of problems that might arise from its adoption by society. This is both prudent and proper. However, in order to anticipate the future, one must construct models that are built on estimates and assumptions. Should key assumptions be wrong, then the model is faulty and the outcome becomes improbable. Trubow's argument presumes that the computer revolution is likely to result in individuals operating their own personal data-processing systems for private purposes. I do not believe this will eventuate, at least not in the forseeable future.

Before examining why, let me draw some distinctions in terminology. The term "microprocessor" is used to describe the basic silicon chip that is at the heart of the microcomputer technology; "microcomputer" is the microprocessor interfaced with timing, memory, and power supply; and "microcomputer system" describes the microcomputer coupled with input–output and data storage devices.

Perceptible Trends

Microprocessors are already a part of everyday life. Digital watches and calculators are made possible by these chips. Soon, thermostats, burglar alarms, smoke detectors, and many other monitoring devices will be

31

COMPUTERS AND PRIVACY
IN THE NEXT DECADE

controlled by such devices. In fact, microprocessors are rapidly replacing many of the electromechanical mechanisms that we have come to depend on.

The emergence of the general purpose microprocessor, most notably the INTEL 8080, promised to make data processing available at prices that individuals could afford. Soon cottage industries were turning out "systems" for home use and for the hobbyist. The personal computer was hailed as the next step in the evolution of consumer electronics. In anticipation of this market, computer stores began to appear across the country. There, one can buy the latest systems, peripheral equipment, and an assortment of software. More and more companies, often one-man operations, began to offer new products in support of the burgeoning market.

Today there is a body of literature aimed at the personal computer market, and expositions continue to draw large crowds. Yet, change is occurring.

Computer stores which once catered to hobbyists are now directing their efforts toward small businesses or are becoming software houses. Micro-computer systems are being configured with printers, larger memory, and hard disk storage at a price no longer within the reach of most individuals. Soft-ware packages stress small business applications and operating systems more suitable to the business environment. Many of the hobby clubs no longer meet.

The general-purpose microcomputer market is shifting from the household to the small business and government agency. Many individuals who were the first to purchase their own systems have proven to be entrepreneurs who are developing software for sale to others. Very few people are using their systems to catalogue recipes or automate Christmas card lists. How then will this technology be used by individuals?

Personal Microcomputers

Alan Kay of the Xerox Research Center has been working on a vision he calls Dynabook, a creative plaything costing no more than $400, which would be used by people throughout their lifetimes. Dynabook would permit a child to draw pictures or write stories and save the results for retrieval at a later time. Throughout one's life, Dynabook would be a companion—a responsive device whose use would depend on the creativity of its owner. In essence, Dynabook would serve as a diary of growth and change, but hardly a machine dedicated to keeping files about others.

Terminals are probably the next major home market. A recent study by Frost and Sullivan, market analysts, suggests that microcomputer-based terminals will be used to transact personal business between households and banks. Already, cable television companies are experimenting with using home terminals to poll their audience on a variety of economic, political, and social issues, and individuals are participating in televised classes via computer terminals. Shortly, individuals may be shopping for household goods from catalogues, using terminals to place their orders. Also, members of organizations may soon attend meetings by remaining in their homes and interacting through terminals.

Microcomputers may eventually be used in the home in conjunction with sophisticated communications systems. With expanding usage of satellite communications, we might expect each home to serve as a transmitting–receiving ground station: The microprocessor will be at the heart of the technology. Today, the Office of Technology Assessment, U.S. Congress, is studying the policy implications of electronic mail and electronic funds transfer. Major work in encryption being carried out at the Massachusetts Institute of Technology and Stanford University should result in electronic signatures and coded correspondence that defy forgery or interception.

Finally, the greatest usage of microcomputers will continue to be in video games and other amusements. Games will become progressively more interactive, to the point that the player will actually program the computer against which he is competing. The evolution of these games over the past few years has established this trend firmly. In addition to games that employ television tubes, new games will be self-contained and very complex, pitting players against one another or against the computer. All in all, computers in the home will be used primarily for amusement and entertainment, and to a lesser extent to transact business and to communicate.

Conversely, there are many indications that personal computers will not routinely be used to process self-generated data. First, interaction with the computer requires software. Operating systems are confusing, and today's programming languages require aptitude and training. While it is certainly true that languages will improve and that individuals may literally "talk" to the computer, the development of applications for the home computer will still be time-consuming and require creativity.

Second, once an application has been developed, the problem of data will remain. Some suggest a market for data bases. For a subscription fee, you might receive a weekly (daily) tape or disk of professional football statistics or grocery prices which could be manipulated to produce certain desired reports. Lacking this, the individual would have to create and enter his own data. Even if one only followed a dozen securities, for instance, entering their daily prices could soon become a nuisance.

Ethical Implications

The foregoing suggests a model or scenario very different from that proposed by Trubow. If correct, the ethical implications, too, will be different. No doubt future generations will grow up with microprocessors and microcomputers all around them. As a result, they will be comfortable with the technology and knowledgeable about its use.

Leisure hours will be consumed by competitive activity in the form of complex and interactive games. People will compose music by computer or participate in conferences and classes being held in distant places. More and more personal business will be transacted at home.

All of these are positive aspects of the advent of microcomputers. Since I do not foresee widespread usage of personal computers for routine data processing, I do not envision a host of corresponding legal or ethical issues surrounding the individual's use of the technology. Consequently, it seems to me that the government need not be overly concerned with abuses in this area.

However, microprocessors and the next generation of microcomputers will make data processing a vital part of most businesses. The proliferation of the technology will make existing problems more widespread and enforcement nearly impossible. Perhaps new approaches to the collection, storage, and dissemination of individual data used by such organizations are now in order.

The Personal Computer versus Personal Privacy

Portia Isaacson

Microcomputers will soon be in our homes, our businesses, our churches, and our schools by the millions. These microcomputers will be used to access, create, store, process, and transmit massive quantitites of information much more cheaply than it could have ever been done before. Much of this information will be about people.

Let us compare information stored in microcomputers to the same information stored on paper in filing cabinets. The microcomputer form of the information is easier to access selectively, may be cheaper to reproduce and to mail, can be transmitted over the telephone more rapidly, can be accessed as a node in a network, and can be more readily entered into other data bases.

Much information about people is presently being kept on microcomputers. For example, my computer store has sold computers to a psychologist who keeps his patient medical files on the computer, to a personnel agency that keeps applicant information on the computer, to several CPAs who keep client data on the computer, and to savings and loan companies that keep loan applicant financial information on the computer.

Current Microcomputers Uses

Millions of microcomputers create an enormous demand for information. Already, data bases are being offered by mail order to owners of microcomputers. Public information utilities which offer information over telephone lines to home computers are also emerging to satisfy this need. For example, the *New York Times* Data Bank is a huge data base of information abstracted from the *New York Times* and a number of other publications. Access to the data base is offered for a fee, although it is presently so high that it discourages

35

COMPUTERS AND PRIVACY
IN THE NEXT DECADE

public access. However, future technology will certainly drive this cost down as commonly available microcomputers create a volume demand that spreads the cost over more subscribers. Such data bases will certainly proliferate. When the data base access volume becomes great enough, it may no longer be necessary to publish the newspaper to make the collection of the information economically justifiable. We will have a new kind of electronic publication. Will electronic publications create privacy issues? It is already possible to interrogate the *New York Times* data base for all the information collected on a particular person over the last 10 years. That same information could not have reasonably been acquired before the data base, since to get it would have required exhaustive manual searching of millions of pages of information. Now it can be had at the push of a button! Are our present laws sufficient to protect the individual's right to privacy in the age of the electronic newspaper? I doubt it.

Home computers may be used to access myriad information services such as Viewdata system in the United Kingdom. The U.K. Post Office, which also operates the telephone system, has implemented the Viewdata system, now called Prestel in the United Kingdom. Massive stores of information, such as news, airline schedules, want ads, public welfare information, and educational information, is housed in a central computer system. A page of this information can be requested from a home or a business via a small calculatorlike terminal connected to the telephone line. The requested page is returned over the telephone line to a receiving TV set with a special Viewdata modification where it is displayed in full color. The U.K. Post Office is paid by the information requestor for use of the telephone line on a per minute basis as in a normal voice call in the United Kingdom. Furthermore, the information provider, such as a travel agency, pays the U.K. Post Office to offer its data base on the Viewdata system. The information provider can charge the customer for viewing a page. The charge is added to the telephone bill of the requestor; the U.K. Post Office does the necessary accounting and pays the information provider. A limited electronic mail capability is planned, which will allow the display of messages on the Viewdata TV. This capability will be especially useful for the deaf who cannot use the normal telephone.

There are several privacy issues related to a Viewdata-type system. Should the offering organization be allowed to keep records of who accesses what information and discreetly offer that information for sale? Should information about people be offered via Viewdata (e.g., an electronic *People* magazine)? Should credit reports be offered via a Viewdata-type system? Who will police the Viewdata system?

Community Memory has been the dream of a San Francisco group for years. Community Memory functions as an electronic community bulletin board. Entries can be made, updated, and deleted from terminals placed around town or from home computers. The information in the Community Memory can be browsed or can be retrieved using keywords assigned by the person entering the information. There are at least a dozen such systems now operating, typically by computer hobby clubs. Usually they are called community bulletin boards. These electronic bulletin boards contain whatever information is entered, including information about people. Typically, the person entering the information is not identifiable. Clearly another name for the community bulletin board is the community bathroom wall. How will we handle electronic gossip in the information age?

Microcomputers and the Future

The proliferation of microcomputers means that more people will know how to use computers. Not all these people will be honest. Present data bases containing private information will be more commonly accessed by unauthorized parties. There will be more motivation to steal information because of the greater market for computer readable data. An information black market may be created. Worse yet, there may be unauthorized changes made to data bases. An "electronic hit" service might be offered where, for a fee, a person is virtually destroyed through data base modifications.

Microcomputers will encourage decentralization of data bases in corporations. Such decentralization may make privacy policies more difficult to enforce.

Personal computers will be used by individuals to keep information about other people. Bridge club lists, party lists, and little black books will be kept on personal computers. Word processing will be used to maintain diaries, autobiographies, and notes on acquaintances. What sort of privacy policy will be appropriate for personal information systems? I certainly do not want to notify each person whose name I place on my Valentine card list. Also, just because my diary is on my computer does not mean I should give people access to information about them. We must be very careful before extending privacy regulations meant for business and government to individuals.

In the future home, today's home computer, TV set, radio, and telephone will have evolved into an information center that will entertain, educate, do accounting, and allow access to massive stores of information. Unfortunately, that same device could be used to transmit, without our knowledge, sensitive personal data and even to monitor personal activities. Who will police the producers of consumer computers and mass-market software marketers to see that Trojan horse techniques are not used to bug our personal information systems of the future?

Privacy in Electronic Funds Transfer, Point of Sale, and Electronic Mail Systems in the Next Decade

Susan Hubbell Nycum

Introduction

In preparing for this discussion of the status of privacy in electronic funds transfer (EFT), point of sale (POS), and electronic mail systems in the 1980s, I became acutely conscious of the following: Ten years ago I had not even heard of these systems—as a concept perhaps, but only as one of a list of "why doesn't someone write a system to. . . ." Furthermore, 10 years ago I had not yet met any of the workshop participants. Only one or two were known to me by reputation. These facts give me pause. If the technological developments in the 1980s move as quickly as in this past decade, my views may appear, by 1989, to be ridiculously shortsighted.

I do not think this will happen, for the following reason. Technological progress in these systems will not be the driving force in their implementation and use from now on, people will. The questions to be resolved will be societal, regulatory, legal, and economic. Of these, only economic forces have any history or experience in moving quickly. The experience has been that these others are reactive in nature, deliberate, and even slow to respond to stimulus. Thus, I feel fairly confident in saying that some version of what we know now will be the systems in place in 1989. I should say that there is absolutely no question in my mind that these systems will continue to exist in 1989. Some may hope they will be discontinued for societal or economic reasons, but I feel we are in an irreversible pattern. Electronic funds transfer, for example, cannot be shut down. The snowball is rolling downhill, and the existing momentum is already too great to halt it. Thus the technological environment in which privacy will be considered is, in my view, recognizable today. I suspect the trend of lower hardware costs and miniaturization will result in an increase in distributed data bases. I hypothesize that by 1989 we will see the electronic equivalent of individual filing cabinets, but importantly, with immediate access to each other and their contents regardless of geographic location.

COMPUTERS AND PRIVACY
IN THE NEXT DECADE

Privacy and Electronic Information Storage

What does the foregoing mean to privacy? Privacy as a societal and particularly consumer concern, appears to me to have several stages of focus, some
of which have already occurred.

Stage One is the definition of privacy, explicitly or intuitively. What is it that
is involved? Alan Westin has done the best job of defining what is at stake in
electronic systems. That privacy concern (the right to control the dissemination of information about oneself) is very different from nineteenth-century
privacy concerns (the right to be left alone). It is essential at the outset that the
privacy rights of specific interest be identified. In my judgment the privacy
right at issue in EFT and POS systems is the right to control the dissemination
of information about oneself, while the principal concern in electronic mail is
freedom from surveillance of one's nonpublic messages.

Stage Two is to value that right. This is not a judgment that can be made in
the abstract; it is viable only in the context of tradeoffs (e.g., with freedom of
information, with efficiency of operation, with delivery of new services). Very
few studies have been done on how the consumer values his own individual
privacy, but a societal value has been associated with privacy, akin to the value
of First Amendment freedoms.

Stage Three is to assess the vulnerability of privacy in automated systems,
generally and specifically in the types of systems described above. Some of this
assessment has been done by the Privacy Protection Study Commission
(PPSC) and by the National Commission on Electronic Funds Transfer
(NCEFT). That assessment will have to be ongoing and much more thorough
regarding the specific systems.

Stage Four is to assess the threats to privacy in the automatic systems. Some
of these threats are identical to threats in manual systems, and some are
different. These issues in electronic mail systems are the least explored; they
are better understood with reference to POS and EFT, since these are plowed
grounds.

Stage Five is to assess the risk to privacy occasioned by the presence of
vulnerability and by the likelihood of a threat becoming an act. This assessment is still in process.

Stage Six is to identify the measures necessary to implement that which will
(or should) reduce the risks to an acceptable level. This assessment is in
process.

Stage Seven is implementation of those measures. This stage is at its
beginning.

Stage Eight is monitoring for compliance and for change in any of the
phenomena critical to Stages One through Seven. This must be ongoing.

Based on the foregoing list, my prediction is that privacy in EFT, POS, and electronic mail systems in the 1980s will appear to the consumer to track that which he enjoyed in preautomated systems. I predict that the privacy in fact afforded the consumer for the most part will be greater than he actually enjoyed in the 1970s.

Why? Because society will become aware and concerned, and because vested interests will provide to society what it wants at the price it will pay—in dollars and in choices among alternatives (e.g., Proposition 13, environmental protection, automotive safety, energy conservation).

Electronic Mail

The historical sanctity of the privacy of mail in this country is epitomized in the famous "gentlemen do not read other gentlemen's mail" approach to communiques by the Japanese concerning Pearl Harbor. Invasions of privacy of the mail, while known to exist, are poorly tolerated. I feel that the consumer or user expectations for privacy in government or government providers of mail services are so basic to the fabric of the United States that the designers and implementors of electronic mail systems will place high priority on privacy, and society will insist on it almost regardless of cost.

Electronic Funds Transfer

Electronic funds transfer systems, where directed by traditional financial institutions (banks, thrifts, and credit unions), will also enjoy a high level of privacy. Banks really have traditionally been privacy conscious. For example, it was a Bay Area banker who first challenged the Bank Secrecy Act [*Calif. Bankers Assn.* v. *Schultz*, 416 U.S. 21, 85 (1974)]. Banks have dragged their feet in complying with IRS summonses and have been, if anything, overcautious in following the dictates of the Financial Institutions Regulatory and Interest Rate Control Act of 1978 (FIRA).

Point of Sale

· My philosophical concern for the future of privacy is, considered in the context of EFT, POS, and electronic mail, within the point-of-sale systems. Note that FIRA regulates POS from the financial institution end of the transaction. My reading of the final reports of the PPSC and the NCEFT that assessed the testimony before them, coupled with other input, including personal experience as a consumer and a business lawyer, gives me the least confidence in these systems from a privacy perspective.

Manual system sales transactions have never been havens of privacy, and there is no expectation that the storekeeper is acting as a quasi-fiduciary for the user the way his mailman or his banker is perceived.

I believe consumer protectionists know this, and I think they will be active in urging the assignment of a high priority to privacy in all aspects of POS systems not only because these systems interface closely with banks and provide a source of leakage of private financial information but because dossiers comprising one's buying habits and places of purchase can lead to serious privacy invasions.

Future Regulation

As I look to 1989, I see Congress and the regulators moving swiftly to resolve consumer privacy protection matters in EFT, such as has already led to passage of FIRA and promulgation of regulations thereunder. Yet FIRA excludes functions that also comprise the bundle of activities that are EFT, such as check verification and guarantee, and interbank transfers. Inclusion of the remainder of these activities (jettisoned during negotiations over the bill) will take time, certainly into the early part of this decade. Related questions must be answered, some of which have deep and fundamental significance, such as federalism (How and to what extent should the states be permitted to regulate EFT?) and competition (Is sharing more or less competitive?). What is branching in an EFT environment? To what extent should government participate in offering EFT services? These will be resolved over time, and I feel that by the end of this decade EFT, as we think of it now, will be operational. The public will have accepted the services, vendors will have succeeded or failed, and users will be out of the red on the costs, many of which the consumer will pay directly. Security will be well understood, even though some gigantic and embarassing losses will have occurred. The results of a survey in 1990 to all parties would, I feel, indicate that if given the choice only a few would revert to pre-EFT measures.

I foresee the same or a similarly paced future for electronic mail—and on a shorter time frame overall than has been the case for EFT. Consumers were not demanding EFT, it has had to be "sold" to them by the purveyors of financial services. But consumers are demanding an improvement in mail service, and electronic mail has popular and business appeal. Ironically, here it is the postal service that must be convinced.

Private electronic mail services such as the mailbox provision on ARPANET and teleconferencing systems, do not in my view carry any greater expectations of privacy than do the private file capabilities of open shop computing facilities. As long as the capability exists for providing that level of protection—which should be very sophisticated by 1989, given the concern being expressed for and resource allocations being made for security research—then the availability for use of facilities for transmittal and storage of various kinds of messages should be wide enough to be useful.

Comment on "Privacy in Electronic Funds Transfer, Point of Sale, and Electronic Mail Systems in the Next Decade"

Paul Armer

The paper on which I have been asked to comment is most optimistic about the future of privacy in electronic funds transfer (EFT), point of sale (POS), and electronic mail systems. I wish that I could agree with it, but I cannot.

On what does Susan Nycum base her optimism? My reading of the paper comes up with the following reasons:

1. Societal awareness and concern.
2. Vested interests provide to society what it wants at the price it will pay.
3. Invasions of privacy of mail are poorly tolerated.
4. Consumer expectations for privacy in mail services are so basic that implementors will place high priority on privacy.
5. Society will insist on it (i.e., privacy in mail systems) almost regardless of cost.
6. Banks have been privacy conscious in the past.
7. A Bay Area banker first challenged the Bank Secrecy Act.
8. Consumer protectionists know that POS systems are apt to be leaky, and therefore they will be active in urging high priority for privacy.

Somehow, Nycum and I must live in different worlds; I find none of her reasons for optimism the least bit compelling. I will grant that Item 7 above is true, but find no reason in logic to take heart from it.

If I had more time, I might respond to each of her reasons in turn and tell you why I either disagree with it or why I find it such a slender reed that it gives *me* little reason for optimism. Consequently, I will make one general comment and respond to one of her reasons.

The general comment that I want to make is that Nycum's paper fails to recognize that the greatest threat to privacy in the arenas she has addressed is the government. I have spoken out so often on the dangers of EFT being used

COMPUTERS AND PRIVACY
IN THE NEXT DECADE

for surveillance purposes that it does not bear repeating here. It is a message that I have been trying to spread for over a decade.

The one reason advanced in the paper on which I want to concentrate is that vested interests provide to society what it wants at the price it will pay (Item 2 on the above list). I am a sincere believer in the forces of the marketplace—I wish the government would do a lot less regulation than it does. However, the marketplace is not worth very much when it comes to a number of problems. And, in general, privacy is one of those problems.

"Let the marketplace decide" is one of the arguments often advanced by pushers of EFT and I am surprised that Nycum is advancing it. It has been nicely addressed (from my biased viewpoint I would say refuted) in the piece which James B. Rule did for the Office of Telecommunications Policy on EFT. It should be read; it is a classic. Rob Kling likes to point out to those who want to let the marketplace decide that we do not handle drugs like cocaine in that way. Economists know that "externalities" cannot be taken into account by the marketplace. By its definition, an externality is external to the market. In the 1960s one did not have a choice between an automobile that put out a great deal of pollution and one that put out less, but at a higher price. In the 1970s, cars pollute less because of laws and regulations, not because the public would buy only the cars that put out less pollutants.

I am not saying that the marketplace will never do anything for privacy—indeed it may (e.g., by offering cryptographic systems so good that even the government cannot read them).

A great deal remains to be done, and it will not be an easy battle. I am a pessimist, particularly with respect to the threat from the government.

Comment on "Privacy in Electronic Funds Transfer, Point of Sale, and Electronic Mail Systems in the Next Decade"

Carole Parsons Bailey

My comments will be brief. I have long admired Susan Nycum's work and the difficult task she has performed for this conference only reinforces my high estimate of her competence and intellectual courage.

I also agree with many of the points she makes. Surely the future of electronic funds transfer (EFT), point of sale (POS), and electronic mail systems will hinge far more on our ability to define and resolve some tough social and economic issues than on our ability to develop and market smaller, faster, and more versatile computers. I also see no reason to doubt that many of the systems we see being tested today will have become commonplace by 1989. The snowball *is* rolling downhill, and the existing momentum *is* too great to be halted.

Overall, however, I am much less sanguine than Nycum seems to be about where the snowball may land—about what may eventually lie at the bottom of the hill. If her analysis is flawed (and while respecting it immensely I do believe it is), the flaw, I think, is in its optimism about the willingness and ability of our society's economic and political institutions to recognize the privacy implications of the kinds of systems we are talking about, and, most importantly, to do so before, rather than after, serious problems arise.

Nycum's paper implies, for example, that the stage of defining what privacy means is now behind us. I would like to believe that is so, but, unfortunately, much of my own experience suggests the contrary. Talk to government and business leaders about the privacy issue today and even the supposedly knowledgeable ones will give you a variety of explanations as to what the problem is and what its solution involves. Indeed, as I understand Nycum's paper, it, too, contains more than one privacy definition. The "Westinian" claim to control the dissemination of information about oneself is said to be the right at issue in EFT and POS systems, while "freedom from surveillance of one's nonpublic messages" is said to be the one to be protected in electronic

45

mail systems. Then, when the paper begins to discuss system vulnerability and the likelihood of a threat becoming an act, it flirts with defining privacy as a system security concern.

To the initiated, of course, the claim, and the concern over freedom from surveillance, and security are reconcilable dimensions of something we call "privacy protection policy," and we can assign each its proper place in any scheme of legislated, or otherwise mandated, safeguards. However, we are not public policymakers coming to the privacy issue afresh, and, in my opinion, we are being unrealistic if we look to the future assuming that we and public policymakers share a common understanding of what the key policy objectives are, or should be, and of what in the main needs to be done to achieve them.

Furthermore, although I, too, believe that the recent enactment of federal EFT and bank privacy legislation is a healthy sign of legislative interest where legislative interest is needed, I am troubled both by the process from which the legislation emerged and by the results the process produced. I find, for example, that for the first time since the privacy issue surfaced in the mid 1960s, Congress has passed a law that is targeted on a particular technology, and, in addition, has set up a privacy regulatory agency, the Federal Reserve Board, to interpret what the law means. For anyone who has struggled through the privacy debates of the 1960s, and also for anyone who has been trying to persuade our European colleagues not to target data protection legislation against the computer, and not to turn the implementation of such legislation over to a powerful regulatory agency, the Electronic Funds Transfer Act (EFTA) of 1978 has to seem ironic.

In the defense of the law's technocentric approach, I suppose someone might read back to me a favorite Alexander Pope couplet:

> For forms of government let fools contest,
> Whate'er is best administered is best.

The question in this case, however, is what is "best administered." It worries me, for example, to see a statute apply to a funds transfer initiated by punching buttons on a telephone but not to one initiated by calling the bank and talking to a clerk who punches the buttons on a computer terminal. From the consumer's point of view, the technological distinction is minor, if not meaningless. From a financial institution's point of view, there are now some new tradeoffs to be considered in deciding whether and how to move toward electronically activated banking by telephone.

Perhaps I am seeing ghosts. Perhaps, as Nycum suggests, Congress will continue to work on the items that were dropped from the EFT legislation in order to get it enacted before the end of the last session (1978). Our experience with similar "information policy" legislation, however, suggests that many years can elapse before such a statute is amended. The fastest record, 7 years, was set by the Freedom of Information Act (FOIA), and one may remember that the FOIA was amended immediately after, and largely in response to, a constitutional crisis.

Another problem that the EFT legislation poses is how it will fit with the Fair Credit Reporting Act (FCRA), the Fair Credit Billing Act (FCBA), and its own companion title on government access to consumer financial records. The law is elegantly drafted to avoid any overt conflict with the first two, the FCRA and the FCBA. Yet we know from the Privacy Protection Study Commission's (PPSC) analysis that there are disjunctures between the FRCA and FCBA that make life unnecessarily difficult for the consumer and now we have still another complicated set of notice and correction procedures laid on top of them—to what practical consequence for the consumer, no one, so far as I can tell, is prepared to say.

This also is true with regard to the EFTA's companion title on government access. That law applies not to information generated by certain types of transactions executed in a particular way, but to "financial records" of customers that are held by a defined class of institutions. Thus, one must ask if the law applies to all customer records generated by EFT or POS transactions, or just to some of them. And if only to some, which are excluded?

The point of this litany is not to portray the EFT statute as a foolish one. Indeed, it may be ideally framed for its particular purposes. My sense of it, however, is that it is not very well integrated with other laws that preceded it or coincided with it, and, if I am right, I believe it should therefore be seen less as a cause for celebration than as a cause for concern about difficulties that may lie ahead in the legislative arenas of the 1980s.

To make EFT and POS systems work efficiently while safeguarding personal privacy efficiently might we not have to overhaul the FCRA, the FCBA, the EFTA (and perhaps also the Truth in Lending Act)? And if we do need such a systematic overhaul, where will the impetus for it come from, and how will we select the most effective means to achieve its objectives?

Nycum suggests that the impetus will come from consumers themselves, but if that is to be, consumers are going to have to behave differently than they have in the past. Perhaps the impetus will come from leading institutions in the private sector. For that to happen, however, one suspects that the privacy issue will have to be insulated from quarrels over EFT's impact on the structure of financial service markets in this country, and, again, one is talking about a break with historical precedent.

How will we select the most effective means to achieve the rewritten statutes' objectives? Will we simply try to streamline and to integrate the fair information practice and confidentiality requirements of a half dozen separately enacted laws, or will we attempt to rethink our strategies for assuring that privacy intersts are regularly respected? Will we, for example, continue to put the burden of assuring compliance on the consumer, or on one or more regulatory agencies, or will we look for ways for business and government organizations to discover that they can do well by doing good?

Consider our conventional approach to civil remedies. It has been customary to punish the organization that fails to comply with a privacy protection statute by allowing the aggrieved individual to sue for monetary damages. Today, however, a growing number of thoughtful people, particularly in the private sector, believe that civil suits for actual and punitive damages may be a counterproductive way to induce institutional users of computer and telecommunications technology to develop services that are optimally respectful of customer interests. The argument turns on a tradeoff between the cost of developing and operating such services and the cost of defending against claims that the services have in some way been harmful to particular individuals. The latter cost, it is argued, arises mainly from the fees and administrative expenses associated with court cases of long duration; not from the damage settlements that are actually made. It is a cost, moreover, that is said to be more or less great in proportion to the complexity and rigidity of the legal requirements imposed on a service. If the requirements are detailed and inflexible, the likelihood increases that someone will find grounds for suit, regardless of whether the objectives the requirements seek to implement are being met. This creates a situation in which organizations that strive to act in a socially responsible way are as vulnerable as those that do not—a situation in which they are, in effect, deprived of the ability to make the tradeoff between service responsiveness and legal defensibility in the way they would prefer.

The proposed solution to this problem is to devise a remedies strategy that causes the burden to fall primarily on those who fail to comply with a statutory or regulatory requirement—rather than on everyone who happens to be subject to it. For example, the PPSC recommended that when a credit grantor, depository institution, or insurer fails to comply with an individual's request to see and copy records about himself, the individual should be able to obtain a federal court order directing that the records be produced. If, in the resulting litigation, the individual substantially prevails he should also be entitled to court costs and attorney's fees, but not to any other form of compensation. Accepting the argument that the chief costs of such litigation are fees and administrative expenses, the PPSC reasoned that an organization providing an information-based service would most prudently spend its money on operating procedures that avoid such suits, and that it would, in fact, do so if given the opportunity.

This approach to remedies is based on the belief that widespread compliance rather than punishment for alleged failure to comply should be the objective. It cannot be used in all instances, of course; in some circumstances the damage resulting from failure to comply is significant and must be recognized. Nevertheless, many today seem to think it makes a great deal of sense as a leading remedies strategy in the information policy area where the adequacy of an organization's procedures is often at issue. Furthermore, it can have substantial benefits for ordinary individuals. Not only does it promise greater institutional responsiveness to their interests, but it also allows them to take action to compel compliance with legal requirements without having to demonstrate that they have sustained any injury other than denial of service features legitimately due them.

The EFTA makes an interesting step in this direction. Although damages, including treble damages, are available under several provisions, Section 915(e) allows a financial institution to reduce its liability by coming forward, admitting its mistake, and voluntarily making it up to the affected individual. By requiring the financial institution to pay actual damages voluntarily, Section 915(e) does not fully solve the problem, since it leaves open the question of how the extent of damages is to be determined. It does, however, take a large step toward inducing financial institutions to comply with the spirit rather than the letter of the law, and thus to institute procedures that will benefit the majority of consumers rather than just the perseverant few who take their grievances to court. This, I would submit, is a hopeful step and one that ought to be preserved in any overhaul of other statutes to which the EFT one relates.

The question of doing well by doing good also comes up in one other area that I beleive we should seriously consider, namely, in our societal decisions as to who should own and operate the facilities that will make nationwide EFT, POS, and electronic mail services possible. It seems to me that the surveillance problem is going to be much more manageable if the private sector rather than government runs the automated clearinghouses, the POS interconnect facilities, and the facilities for sending mail electronically. In our 10-year effort to get the fair information practice philosophy acceptably articulated, we have tended to overlook the extent to which institutional pluralism can be an important safeguard for personal privacy in our society. Given the fact that organizations wield substantial power in American society, and given the fact that individuals have relationships with a multiplicity of often competing organizations, it seems prudent to consider how one can shape the development of EFT, POS, and electronic mail systems so as to reinforce the ability and willingness of nongovernmental organizations to go to bat for the people they serve when government looks as if it may not be acting as responsibly as it should.

How to make that happen is a discussion all to itself. For the moment, however, suffice it to say that as we look to the 1980s, the advocates of strong privacy protection safeguards are going to have to be much more concerned than they have been about the structure of authority and responsibility in which the kinds of systems we are talking about are couched. Indeed, if they do not become concerned, they may find that giving people access and correction rights, and even some control over the disclosure of information about themselves, will turn out to be an ineffective means of assuring that privacy is adequately protected.

Privacy Cost Research: An Agenda

Robert C. Goldstein

Introduction

The cost of implementing computer-privacy proposals has been of concern for some time, especially to organizations with large personal information systems. Model-based research has been conducted which produced some useful cost data and, more importantly, developed a structure for thinking about privacy cost issues. A by-product of this early research has been the identification of a number of areas where additional work is needed. This paper discusses these possibilities for future research under three headings:

1. Research on Privacy Cost Models.
2. Using Cost Models.
3. Research Suggested by the Models to Date.

Background

The issue of cost has been an important one ever since the beginning of the current interest in the computer–privacy problem. Many of the "standard" privacy provisions appear, on the basis of intuition, to be quite costly. Organizations operating large personal data systems are, quite naturally, concerned with maintaining their economic and technical viability. However, even strong supporters of privacy proposals have had to recognize that the passage of unworkable legislation would very likely be followed by its tacit neglect. Thus, there is a real need for ways to evaluate the costs associated with these privacy proposals prior to embedding them in legislation. In addition, cost data could be very helpful in indicating useful directions for additional privacy-oriented hardware and software development.

51

COMPUTERS AND PRIVACY
IN THE NEXT DECADE

A rather simple cost model was developed in 1973 and used as the basis for a number of studies (Goldstein, 1974). Much insight into the behavior of the cost issue was gained from this work, although because of the preliminary nature of the model, some care was required in interpreting the specific numerical results. This early work provided indications of the particular aspects of privacy legislation that were likely to be expensive and indications of the extent of the impact on particular organizational resources. One regulatory provision that was widely believed to be very expensive, the logging of all data accesses, was predicted to require relatively modest resources, and this has since been confirmed by experience. Another rather surprising result suggested that there would be minimal impact on automated information handling, and that the brunt would fall on manual activities. The apparent explanation for this is that the most burdensome regulatory provisions deal with things that are not readily automated.

This early experience revealed a number of shortcomings in the model. As a result, a second-generation version was developed that is capable of representing a wider range of interesting cases as well as more accurately describing the interaction between information-handling procedures and privacy regulations (Goldstein, 1979). However, there are still a number of areas where improvements can be made. In addition, there are other lines of research related to the use of a cost model, or suggested by experience with it, that appear fruitful. The remainder of this paper outlines some of these.

The next section discusses a number of possibilities for improving privacy cost models. This is followed by a section on research questions that could be addressed if a good cost model were available. The final section identifies some problems that, while not specifically related to the cost of privacy, have been spotlighted by the privacy-cost research.

Research on Privacy Cost Models

Many aspects of the privacy cost problem were not adequately dealt with, even in Goldstein's second model. This occurred either because of constraints on the available time and resources or because better ways of dealing with the problems were not known.

Without doubt, the single most important shortcoming is the lack of information on the model validity. This shortcoming could potentially be attacked in two ways. The first is the usual approach to validating models, in which the estimates produced are compared to actual measurements on real organizations operating in a regulated environment. I do not believe that this approach will be very useful at present because it is doubtful that there actually are any organizations fully complying with the current privacy legislation.

Furthermore, most of the privacy compliance measures that do exist were probably implemented as add-ons to systems originally designed before the regulations were imposed. While cost measurements in this environment would be interesting, they would not be particularly useful for validating a model.

The second possible approach to validation is a piecemeal one. Many of the individual activities postulated by the privacy-cost models are already being carried out by some organizations for other purposes. For example, transaction logging is performed by some realtime systems to facilitate recovery following system crashes. Measurements in these environments could be used to confirm or alter specific equations in the models. This approach is also attractive because it could be done selectively. Attention could be concentrated on validating those aspects of the model that appear, on the basis of preliminary results, to account for large fractions of the total cost.

A second area where there appears to be an immediate opportunity for improvement is in the representation of security issues. The present model deals with security in a rather superficial way. However, a considerable body of other research exists in this area and the integration of this work with a privacy-cost model would provide a greater degree of accuracy for relatively little investment.

Another direction in which model development might move would be toward specialization for particular industries or types of information. This topic is relevant because of the apparent trend in the United States toward regulating information handling on a categorical, industry-by-industry basis. This regulatory strategy appears to be motivated by past experience and by information-handling policies in various industries, rather than by any assertion that the problems are inherently different. In fact, the modeling efforts to date have failed to identify any important industry variables except, perhaps, the sensitivity of the data and their use. However, if this regulatory trend continues, it would be useful to examine the issue in more detail to see if there are any industry or information-type factors that should be considered.

Perhaps the most ambitious extension to current models that might be contemplated would be aimed at the inclusion of *indirect* costs of privacy regulation. The existing models attempt only to identify the direct costs associated with implementing the regulatory provisions. No consideration is given to such indirect effects as delays in obtaining personal information, or possibly even prohibitions on certain uses of data. In many situations, the need to make decisions on the basis of reduced information may be presumed to result in less than optimal decisions, and there must be some cost associated with this. In general, any restriction on the flow of information may be expected either to create additional costs or to reduce efficiency in some way. It is quite possible that these indirect costs are far greater than the ones dealt with by current models.

Of course, if one is going to extend a model into this area, it seems obvious that one should try to include the *benefits* of privacy regulation as well. These questions delve into areas far removed from technical data processing considerations that were the primary subject of the original modeling work.

Research Using Cost Models

The two major players in the privacy-legislation game are lawmakers and operators of personal data systems, and each faces questions that a validated model could help to answer. While there seems to be fairly general agreement concerning the objectives of privacy legislation (judging from the degree of similarity among the many proposed bills), there are a number of areas where alternative ways of achieving an objective are known. Cost information could be quite useful in choosing among alternatives that were deemed to be equally effective in meeting objectives. Such information could also be used to compare alternatives that were not equivalent, as part of a traditional cost–benefit analysis to determine whether an additional measure of protection is justified. I am not aware of any previous use of a cost model for selecting among alternative versions of legislation, and it appears to be a very useful and interesting application.

Once the basic nature of the regulation is known, organizations operating personal data systems have an incentive to determine the lowest cost method of compliance. Compliance costs will be affected by many variables that can be manipulated by management such as the degree of centralization in information handling and the extent and type of automation that is employed. The cost of compliance will also depend on the sensitivity of the data, and in some cases, it may actually be cost effective to eliminate some sensitive information from the data base in order to permit less expensive compliance techniques. The evaluation of alternatives such as these is another valid use of a good cost model.

The two preceding areas are both concerned with solving particular real problems. A more general application of cost models could be found in the study of the effects of privacy regulation on economic entities larger than the individual firm. It would be interesting, for example, to examine the effect on particular industries, such as credit reporting or insurance. In fact, in a totally rational world, the decision to enact such legislation would take into account the total cost to the entire economy. Extending the existing models to deal with larger economic entities is an interesting problem that has not yet been addressed.

A final area of potential applicability for cost models is in the identification of desirable new hardware and software capabilities. The cost equations in the existing models assume the current state of technology. They could easily be altered to reflect improvements that were known to be in the offing to obtain cost estimates relevant to specific forthcoming technologies. Alternatively, one could use the model to experiment with purely conjectural technologies in order to identify development areas that would have a major impact on privacy costs. On the basis of work done to date, the greatest payoff would seem to come from the automation of tasks that are currently assumed to require manual performance. For example, if some type of automated inquiry terminal could be used to handle the various privacy-related requests that data subjects are authorized to make, the cost of handling such requests would drop dramatically. Achieving these cost reductions, however, depends not only on developing a suitable inquiry terminal, but on making it readily available to the population of inquirers. The problem is not simple, but neither does it appear beyond solution.

Research Suggested by the Models to Date

Experimentation with the existing models has identified several areas not specifically dealing with cost that need to be better understood. Perhaps the most important of these is the question of data quality. "Data quality" is the term used to refer to the provision in most privacy laws that specifies standards of accuracy, completeness, relevance, and timeliness. The problem arises from the fact that these standards are usually expressed in a highly nonoperational manner. This leads to two specific questions: (1) What level of data quality is required? (2) What specific techniques can be used to establish and maintain it?

The level of data quality is usually related to a criterion of fairness in decision making. What does this really mean? How much error can a record have before a decision based on it will be "unfair." While at first glance this may not appear to be amenable to scientific investigation, there is some interesting work in the accounting area that may be relevant. Studies have been conducted to determine how much of varous kinds of errors can appear in financial statements before incorrect conclusions will be drawn (Gibbons, 1976). Similar experiments could be performed with personal information in specific decision contexts, such as job or credit applications.

Once we know what level of data quality is required, we need to develop ways of maintaining it at reasonable cost. Preliminary work with the existing models suggests that data quality issues have the capability for generating very high operating costs, since they seem to imply either a continual monitoring of the data base contents or a specific check prior to releasing any information. Since this latter approach would probably lead to intolerable delays in responding to inquiries, some variation on the former will probably be needed.

It seems possible that the testing of records for quality can be automated once suitable criteria have been developed. For example, it may be possible to attach a critical time limit to data items of various types used for particular purposes. Each time a record was retrieved, the system could check to see if any of the fields had expired, in which case they might have to be suppressed in the report, or perhaps flagged to indicate possible unreliability. In addition, some 'type of continuous scan might be performed by the sytem on a time-available basis to identify records that needed to be rechecked. Note that to make this an efficient process, records should be selected not only on age criteria, but also on likelihood of being needed. It would be pointless to spend resources continually updating dead records. Since the actual rechecking would appear to be a manual task in most cases (and hence both expensive and time consuming) algorithms for picking the right candidates at the right time might be very valuable.

A second operational problem identified during the course of the cost research is in the area of personal identification. All of the legislation, as well as the cost-modeling work, assumes that the identity of the data subject and inquirer are both known. In today's data-processing world, neither of these has a particularly high probability of being true. Much research is currently underway to develop better ways of identifying terminal users to a computer, and it is likely that this problem will be adequately solved reasonably soon. The problem of identifying data subjects, on the other hand, appears to involve difficult political and social issues. There is considerable fear that any proposal to require unique, reliable, personal identification will lay the groundwork for invasion of many individual rights, including privacy. However, in the course of this debate, it is important to bear in mind that, without some such identification scheme, it is difficult to see how existing and proposed privacy laws can be implemented with any degree of reliability.

References

Gibbins, M. Persuasive communication and accounting. Unpublished doctoral dissertation, Cornell University, 1976.

Goldstein, R.C. *The cost of privacy*. Wellesley, Mass.: Honeywell Information Systems, 1974.

Goldstein, R.C. *An event model of privacy costs*. West Lafayette, Indiana: Purdue University Information Privacy Research Center, 1979.

Comment on "Privacy Cost Research: An Agenda"

Oliver R. Smoot

Perspective on Cost Models

Cost model use is frustrating. Cost modeling is accepted widely in the Department of Defense, NASA, and major businesses, but not in regulatory debates. Even the reaction to privacy cost experiments has been negative. However, these studies and models are indispensible. Willis Ware's analogy of privacy issues to preventing auto pollution in the 1930s is most instructive. The automobile, in all its forms, and its fueling cycle are simple compared to flows of personal information. We need good models or we shall write bad rules.

Just as in automobile pollution control, where we must address the individual automobile's chemical cycles apart from issues of society's dependence on hydrocarbon-fueled transportation, so, too, we must carefully separate the issues invoked by the word "privacy." Specifically, both privacy costs and security costs must be addressed, each in its own way.

Research on Cost Models

Goldstein raises important technical and substantive issues in the first part of his paper. He reports that the costs will differ between systems where privacy requirements are "added on" to existing systems and newly implemented systems. While true, newly implemented significant systems are a fast decreasing proportion of all systems. We do not expect manufacturers or users ever again to undertake lightly installing completely new systems. More information functions, both large and small, are automated with each passing year; therefore, the technical approaches will become further settled.

57

COMPUTERS AND PRIVACY
IN THE NEXT DECADE

Thus, the piecemeal approach will be the norm for validation. We should encourage initiation of validation experiments now. Perhaps the special-interest groups in the ACM and DPMA concerned with privacy issues can be encouraged to establish projects for validation and act as clearinghouses for reporting results.

The security aspects of cost models brings us up against a crucial matter. Security cost models (or parts of models) must be constructed soon, and must be good. All privacy cost models will lose their credibility if they depend on security models perceived to be invalid by data processing management. This is because data processing management will be more amenable to using cost models, but they will be correspondingly more critical of any shortcomings.

The suggestion that information-handling problems may not differ inherently from one information function to another is startling since its calls into question the conclusions of the Privacy Protection Study Commission.

The issue of including *indirect costs* seems to me to be more related to the issue of including *benefits* than is apparent in Goldstein's paper. Frankly, I would proceed with caution in this area, as in all other extensions. The benefits issue raises the question of whether some actions, for example, computer security, are not simply overdue good information-management techniques. Indirect costs calculation should similarly be broadened to include indirect benefits.

In conclusion, my priorities are (1) validation, (2) computer security, (3) direct benefits, and (4) indirect benefits and costs.

Research Using Cost Models

The alternative strategy for regulation and the inclusion of new technologies, which are discussed in Goldstein's section with this title, both raise a basic issue: Must we not strive for the most functionally stable statements possible in drafting all privacy legislation? Furthermore, must we not do so without delegating the implementation to a regulatory body? If the intent of privacy legislation is to prevent Orwell's "1984" in 1984 or 1994, must we not think in the most durable terms possible. The Privacy Act of 1974 provides some guides in this direction, for example, in specifying that agencies "establish appropriate administration, technical and physical safeguards to insure the security and confidentiality of records. . . ." This mandate, directed at the federal agencies, has resulted in a variety of responses (and nonresponses). Would these be appropriate words for the private sector? What sanctions would be necessary and sufficient? If one believes this charge to be too vague, what alternatives are there that could prevalidate all of the variety in private-sector business practices, using both current and coming technology?

Research Suggested by the Model

The data quality issue, expressed technically in Goldstein's paper, has explosive political overtones. This is the heart of most debates over requirements for notice, access, review, correction, and validation. Quantitative data could be of assistance in resolving some of these issues, but could get lost rapidly in debates over point scoring, redlining, etc.

Goldstein's last sentence deserves a paper in itself. If reliable data-subject identification is a prerequisite to reliable privacy-law implementation, past experience indicates that organizations will suffer in favor of the individual. Privacy, however, is different because we cannot adopt organization liability approaches as are used in other areas (e.g., banking). If someone forges your name to a check and the bank does not catch it, the bank loses the money, not you. But, if false identification is used to obtain your hospital records, does it matter that the hospital is liable to you? The information is now out, circulating, gone. A suit against the hospital will legally make you whole. If such suits become oppressive, what will institutions do? Will a universal identifier be a concomitant to effective privacy protection?

Comment on "Privacy Cost Research: An Agenda"

Irwin J. Sitkin

Privacy Cost

It seems to me that the great majority of business people (and maybe even some politicians) are justifiably concerned about expenses associated with implementing proposed privacy legislation, and I agree with Goldstein that it would be super if any such real or potential costs could be identified and evaluated *prior* to any desired behavioral change being cast into concrete as the law of the land. The Privacy Protection Study Commission (PPSC) considered cost as the fourth of "five competing *societal values* that must be taken into account for formulating public policy to protect personal privacy" (PPSC, 1977). The five factors are (1) First Amendment interests, (2) freedom of information interests (3) the societal interest in law enforcement, (4) cost, and (5) federal–state relations. Cost *minimization* was clearly one of hte PPSC objectives with, as an example, several commissioners convinced that open ing an insurance company's underwriting files to inspection by policyholders would provide a powerful motive for encouraging the underwriters to record accurately only pertinent information and to maintain their records in as timely and as complete a manner as possible. But, at the same time, the PPSC recognized that encouraging policyholders to pore over underwriting files for information that could serve as the basis for defamation actions was certainly not a way to minimize cost. The intent was to encourage organizations to invest in better systems rather than to increase expense for costly litigation over *past* practices and honest mistakes (PPSC, 1977).

In the bank record area, the access right was limited to adverse decision situations because people already receive monthly statements with information on their bank accounts (PPSC, 1977).

In a similar vein, the PPSC also believed that granting an individual rights

61

within existing legal frameworks was far more efficient and significantly less costly than embarking on an ambitious new regulatory approach. Accordingly, they recommended policy measures which would effectively increase *ongoing* implementation costs by subjecting organizations to judicial or administrative sanctions when the organization did not comply with the requirements. The bottom line was an expectation that organizations taking affirmative steps to comply with the PPSC's recommendations would have little expense beyond the cost of educating employees, initially revising some procedures and forms, and creating appropriate policy guidance (PPSC, 1977).

Clearly, while cost is a consideration, it is not the primary one; even the PPSC listed it fourth out of five.

Societal Issues

My experience suggests that when dealing with societal issues (or as Goldstein says, "political and social issues") many decisions made by business people and politicians are based on intuitive judgments, that is, people making decisions "for" people; and I doubt that Goldstein or anyone else will be able to model that. Even if a model could be developed after the fact, it still would not provide much insight into future costs. Goldstein's difficulty in modeling direct costs is nothing compared to what he will find when he tries to model indirect costs; and I must question whether such an investment in time and energy is really worthwhile.

Example of the Effect of Privacy Protection Proposals

Shortly after the PPSC came out with its report, Bill Bailey (President of Aetna Life & Casualty and a PPSC member) met with several senior Aetna managers and Aetna's privacy council to discuss plans for implementing the PPSC recommendations. Although there was little doubt about what was going to be done, one of the underwriting vice presidents at the meeting sincerely urged reconsideration, delay, or, at the very least, caution before rushing off to implement the recommendations, supporting his case with comments about the significant costs involved. Bailey listened intently, and then asked the vice president, rather directly, if he would comply with the regulations were they law. Upon hearing the expected positive response, Bailey then indicated that he preferred to have Aetna treat the PPSC's insurance recommendations (that did not require immunity) as if they were law. With our marching orders clearly stated, we at Aetna then went on to develop our implementation plans, not because a law required us to but rather because it was the right thing to do. Of course, while we were quite sensitive to the added costs embedded in our options, there was little effort devoted to describing them precisely or to pinpointing the value added to our product. Our "gut" sense, of course, is that having a privacy program will make us an inherently more desirable company to do business with.

We concluded early on, as I think Goldstein has, that there would be minimal impact on automated information, policy, and claim-handling systems, and that the most burdensome regulatory provisions would be those dealing with systems and procedures that were not automated. On the other hand, I doubt Goldstein's statement that logging all data accesses has since been confirmed to require modest resources. We at Aetna felt, and still feel that logging would be an expensive burden, and, if required, it would be more burdensome on our automated systems than on our manual systems.

Failure of Modeling

The fact that modeling efforts to date have failed to identify any important industry variables, coupled with the inability to validate the models, reinforces the nagging questions in my mind concerning whether these issues profitably lend themselves to modeling at all. Reinforcing this concern were Goldstein's comments in his discussion about indirect costs, which indicated that delays or prohibitions in obtaining personal information might result in having to make decisions on the basis of reduced information. I agree with that observation, but he suggests this may be presumed to result in less than optimal decisions and to account for some indirect cost. However, in discussions with Aetna underwriters (who were, as you can well imagine, concerned about what information they might be prohibited from using, or worse, prohibited from obtaining), we and they came to realize that they really did not need all that information about who slept with whom, what the neighbors thought, etc. Once over the "what's really relevant information" hurdle even the underwriters began to see the possible *benefits* of not having to store and process all that unnecessary information. Someone even quipped that the underwriters might make better decisions having less information to clutter their minds! Again, these are subjective feelings. Not only is it difficult to estimate the costs of assuring privacy, but it is next to impossible to determine the cost of the harm that comes to individuals from not having privacy protection (in terms of loss of a job, credit, insurance, etc.). So even if one could figure out the cost of implementation, one still could not develop a cost–benefit analysis.

Data Base Monitoring

Goldstein, in discussing the data quality issues, pointedly argues that expense can be minimized by continually monitoring data base contents. However, I am still not persuaded that testing for "quality" can be fully automated. For me it is still GIGO—garbage in, garbage out. People ensure the quality of data, through standards, attention to detail, pride in the job, the carrot, the stick, or whatever motivates them to do a "quality" job.

Now I am not saying Goldstein should give up, because I do agree that model-based research *is* useful in developing a structure for thinking about privacy cost issues, and I also agree that there *is* a real need for ways to evaluate the *real* costs associated with privacy proposals. I do feel, however, that while validated models might help set a law's direction, it really comes down to people making intuitive judgments about societal values.

Reference

Privacy Protection Study Commission. *Personal privacy in an information society*. Washington, D.C.: U.S. Government Printing Office, 1977.

Preserving Individual Autonomy in an Information-Oriented Society*

James B. Rule
Douglas McAdam
Linda Stearns
David Uglow

To locate our viewpoint among the variety of approaches to these issues, let us say that our emphasis has been less strictly technological and less optimistic. That is, we tend to see the most profound changes in relations between personal information and individual autonomy as effects of changes in social relationships, rather than as those of technological change. Furthermore, we see the social changes as so far-reaching as to defy easy resolution through the reform of personal data management. Thus stated, we realize, these characterizations amount to little more than a confession of bias. The implications of such biases for concrete analysis, however, should be amply apparent in what follows.

Some Sociological Background

Modern Americans inhabit a social environment virtually composed of formal organizations. The main source of the privacy controversies of the 1960s and 1970s has been the demands of formal organizations for information on the people with whom these organizations must deal. Each major life juncture seems to entail involvement of some formal organization. Birth, immunization, education, military service, marriage and divorce, the use of

*Portions of this contribution are from *The Politics of Privacy* by James Rule, Douglas McAdam, Linda Stearns, and David Uglow, © 1980 by James B. Rule; reprinted by arrangement with the New American Library, Inc., New York, New York. Our collaboration on the book grew out of our work together on a study of ordinary Americans' experiences with and understandings of personal data systems, supported by the National Science Foundation, Division of Mathematical and Computer Sciences.

65

COMPUTERS AND PRIVACY
IN THE NEXT DECADE
ISBN 0-12-352060-6

credit and insurance, homeownership, medical care, and, ultimately, death—these and countless other key life events require the participation of formal organizations. Such participation almost always seems to require intake of information on the persons concerned. Sometimes these intakes serve the purposes of certification of a key life transition such as a birth, immunization or treatment for a disease, or educational attainments. Elsewhere information helps the organization concerned to distinguish what treatment is to be accorded the individual concerned. In any event, the flow of personal information between organizations and individuals clearly affects the interests of the people concerned. The privacy issues of the 1960s and 1970s have amounted to conflicts over uses made by formal organizations of documentary information on the people with whom these organizations must deal.

Simply to characterize this new reality as reflecting the "appetite" of organizations for personal information would be accurate, but would miss much of the significance of these changes.* The growth of modern, bureaucratic personal data systems attests to the formation of new *relationships* between ordinary Americans and formal organizations. The organizations concerned hardly developed their present appetite for personal data as an end in itself. Rather, they did so in order to satisfy demands for authoritative action concerning the people depicted in the records. People expect certain organizations to deal intelligently with a heterogeneous array of people. These dealings are as multifarious in content as are the organizations themselves. In every case the organization is expected to render to each person his or her "due," that is, the "correct" form of bureaucratic action, in light of all relevant information on that person's past history and current statuses (see Rule, 1974, especially pp. 320–326). Clearly, such discriminating decision making can only take place by reliance on detailed recorded information on the persons concerned.

Income taxation, for example, entails assessment of precise liability for each taxpayer reckoned in terms of income, dependency status, assets and losses during the tax year, and a host of other circumstances. Given that the payment of taxes is a distasteful obligation, and that most persons strive to avoid paying any more than necessary, no system of enforcement could avoid collecting and using voluminous data on the persons concerned. Such data not only enable the organization concerned (the IRS, in this case) to assess the obligation to pay, but they also provide the basis on which to adjudicate disputes with taxpayers over their obligation, and to locate those taxpayers judged delinquent or suspect.

---

*For discussion of a number of these issues, see Edward Shils' (1975) remarks on the "cognitive passion" of government and related demands on privacy in "Privacy and Power" in his book of collected essays.

The same observations could be offered for most other bureaucratic personal data systems which have sprung up since the last century. Consumer-credit data files, for example, enable credit-granting organizations to assess precisely how much credit should be extended to the person concerned. Insurance reporting systems afford insurance companies sophisticated bases for discriminating judgments about whether to insure people, and if so, at what rates. Law-enforcement records enable these organizations to distinguish their treatment of the literally millions of persons with whom they deal every year, according to the kinds of action which such people deserve.

Although one may not normally think of it this way, this organizational monitoring of persons is of a piece with broad ranges of other bureaucratic activity. Sociologists have often characterized formal organizations as systems for coping with uncertainty in their environments (Perrow, 1972; Thompson, 1967). All organizations must keep track of more or less unpredictable aspects of their environments—making plans, adjustments, rearrangements, and the like, so as to achieve their desired results. If the critical goal is selling automobiles at a profit, then the organization must attend to variations in supplies of raw materials, costs of power, fluctuations in demand, availability of labor, and a host of other things in order to remain viable. If the goal is the administration of a church diocese, central management must monitor the attitudes of the clergy, the faithfulness of the communicants, the costs of maintaining the physical plant, the attitudes of the larger community toward the church, and many other potential sources of uncertainty. Formal organizations are not the only social forms which facilitate human action in the face of otherwise uncertain conditions. However, only formal organizations in the modern sense devote themselves so systematically and self-consciously to searching for unpredictable or disruptive elements in the environment, and attempting to master them so as to achieve desired results.

For the organizational activities of interest here, the environment is people; the uncertainties to be mastered are ambiguities as to which people deserve what organizational responses. Modern income taxation systems are charged with enforcing an obligation according to complex principles, in the light of circumstances which differ in every case. Not only must such systems apply these principles to heterogeneous cases; they must also reckon with people's often strenuous efforts to withhold information. To confront this "blooming, buzzing confusion" of people's financial affairs and to enforce a modicum of compliance entails real mastery of uncertainty. The same holds true for other organizations that systematically demand and use personal information in dealing with very large publics. They can no more do without authoritative information on the people with whom they deal than can General Motors meet its goals without data about the costs of raw materials, the demand for finished automobiles, costs of transportation, and the thousands of uncertain circumstances that make formal organizations necessary in the first place.

Systems of detailed personal records do not appear *whenever* organizations deal with large numbers of people. Instead, they develop under conditions of complex obligations and extended mutual dependency between organizations and their publics. In *Private Lives and Public Surveillance*, Rule (1974) characterized these conditions as most propitious:

1. When an agency must regularly deal with a clientele too large and anonymous to be kept track of on a basis of face-to-face acquaintance;
2. When these dealings entail the enforcement of rules advantageous to the agency and potentially burdensome to the clientele;
3. When these enforcement activities involve decision-making about how to act towards the clientele. . . ;
4. When the decisions must be made discriminatingly, according to precise details of each person's past history or present situation;
5. When the agency must associate every client with what it considers the full details of his past history, especially so as to forestall people's evading the consequences of their past behavior [p. 29].

Thus, Yankee Stadium will require no detailed documentation on ticket purchasers, despite variation in ticket prices and seat assignment. When organizations enter into relationships enduring over time, whose outcomes must be geared to details of people's lives, the recourse to personal data systems as bases for action is very likely.

Thus the growth of vast, bureaucratic personal data systems, both computerized and conventional, often marks the development of characteristically modern forms of *social control*. By this we mean direct patterns of influence by organizations over the behaviors of individuals. Such influence may be benign, as in systems for administering medical care, or coercive, as in the development of dossiers on political enemies. The systematic collection and monitoring of personal information for purposes of social control we term *surveillance*—again, whether the purposes are friendly or not. The development of efficient systems of mass surveillance and control is one of the distinctive sociological features of advanced societies. Never before our own era have large organizations been able to remain in direct interaction with literally millions of persons, both keeping abreast of their affairs and reaching out with authoritative bureaucratic action in response to such monitoring.

The Extension of Surveillance

We believe that these rather abstract concepts earn their keep by helping us to formulate a question of fundamental interest: How far can we expect the development of modern surveillance and control to go? What forms of previously private information are most likely to come into demand as grist for the mills of bureaucratic surveillance? What forms of behavior are most likely to be subjected to centralized organizational control through the use of such information?

Much organizational interest in the details of people's private lives relates to the effort to curtail one or another form of deviant behavior. Credit systems serve largely to counteract disruptive effects from those unwilling or unable to pay; police record systems serve to aid in the control of crime and criminals. Thus, new forms of surveillance are especially likely when they promise to enable organizations to root out some troublesome form of misbehavior. Innovations in surveillance which promise to identify potential shoplifters to department stores, or terrorists to airlines, or illegal aliens to immigration authorities, then, are bound to attract intense interest from the organizations involved.

The nature of deviant activity, however, may be only indirectly related to the personal data sought for its control. This makes it especially difficult to foretell what forms of personal information are most likely to come into demand. When organizations take the record of past deviant behavior to predict future propensities for such behavior, the link is clear enough. No one is surprised that the police use criminal records from the past to anticipate and act against future criminality. But organizations also seek to predict the future behavior of those with whom they deal by studying nonintuitive statistical correlates of such behavior. Thus, if the IRS came to suspect that tax evasion was highly associated with venereal disease, that agency would probably seek the same sweeping power to delve through people's medical records that it now enjoys relative to their bank accounts. One ought not to smile too quickly at this seemingly far-fetched example. Social science research has turned up associations no less improbable than this one. Furthermore when a given form of deviant behavior offends particularly powerful interests, the efforts to seek out information on its possible correlates may become intense.

But the interest in understanding and thereby controlling deviant behavior is not the only occasion for the extension of bureaucratic surveillance. Many efforts to document details of persons' private lives arise in an attempt to document and define what one might term "fine-grained" bureaucratic obligations. The enormous amounts of personal documentation required for medical insurance and social security, for example, serve largely to establish eligibility for those services. The growing importance of these bureaucratically determined benefits is hardly less important in fueling the spread of surveillance than the effort to suppress deviance in the ordinary sense. The point is, both bureaucracies and the publics to which they respond expect exact distinctions to be drawn between the guilty and the innocent, between those likely to prove guilty and those not so likely, between the eligible and the ineligible, and among different forms and degrees of eligibility among the same people over time. When distinctions can be drawn in the treatments owing to different members of the public, one can expect efforts to document the bases for these distinctions and hence to render them grist for the mills of bureaucratic action.

In virtually all innovations in mass surveillance, the pressure of public demand plays an important part. One can point to few systems of collection and use of detailed personal information in America which were foisted on a wholly unwilling public simply for narrow bureaucratic purposes. On the contrary, people often want and even demand the fine-grained decision making afforded by personal data systems. Criminal record systems could not exist without the demands of the great majority of the public for keeping rigorous track of criminals. Credit systems would be impossible without the considerable public enthusiasm for the comforts of easy, convenient credit. People may feel that their privacy is threatened by the demands for personal information characteristic of the modern world; but they often seem willing enough to yield personal data in specific instances where desired services are at stake.

Indeed, available evidence suggests that people's desire to see "justice" done, in one way or another, accounts for much of the popular demand for extension of surveillance. People seek their own just desserts, in terms of the credit privileges, insurance rates, tax liability, passport use, or whatever, to which they feel themselves entitled. At the same time, the public also demands effective discriminations *against* welfare cheaters, poor credit risks, dangerous drivers, tax evaders, criminals, and the like. These discriminations in the treatment of persons by organizations can only be achieved by recourse to personal data keeping. The instinct of demanding justice in the allocation of scarce resources is of course as old as social life itself. However, the capabilities of modern organizations have made it possible for organizations to apply such principles in decision-making relations with literally millions of persons.

Often, it is difficult to say whether popular demands represent the cause or the effect of the growing sophistication of organization in surveillance and control. The result, in either event, is a secular trend toward increasingly effective bureaucratic attention to and demand for such information. Thus we confess real doubt about observations such as the following by Alan Westin (1967):

> A close survey of the positions adopted by leading ideological and civic groups toward issues of surveillance and privacy since 1945 indicates that there is now a general identification of privacy with liberty, and that concern over unlimited governmental or private surveillance runs the ideological spectrum from the Daughters of the American Revolution to the New Student Left, and from the *National Review* to the *Nation*. . . . The cry that "Big Brother is Watching" is now raised by any person or group protesting against what he or it considers unfair surveillance. . . . Anxious articles and editorials about restoring norms of privacy have

appeared in business, labor, legal, and academic journals, and many civic groups have adopted policy resolutions deploring erosions of privacy [p. 378].

It all sounds good. No one, after all, is likely to come out *against* privacy. But a close look at the clamor for more of it suggests that its proponents do not all have the same thing in mind. The Daughters of the American Revolution may well deplore, let us say, government snooping into the tax-exempt status of conservative educational organizations, but they are likely to be the first to demand more vigorous invasion of the privacy of groups like the New Student Left. *The Nation* may well deplore invasions of the privacy, for example, of welfare mothers; but it would be quick to support FBI investigation of right-wing militant groups.

People do indeed protest what they consider "unfair surveillance," often in the same breath with which they demand more vigorous surveillance for purposes which they support. Nearly everyone can point to some form of surveillance with which they are unhappy, either because it strikes them as ineffective or because the form of control at which it aims seems undesirable in itself. The more fundamental public reflex, however, seems to be to insist that discrimination based on detailed personal data be made whenever the ends of such discrimination seem desirable. Public and private bureaucracies are usually only too willing to accommodate these demands, where indeed they have not encouraged them to begin with. The long-term effect can only be further pressure against individual privacy and autonomy, in the sense in which most people use these terms.

Given the forces fostering the growth of surveillance, we can identify no "natural limit" to the incorporation of personal information into the attentions of personal data systems. That is, we can conceive of no form of personal information which might not, under certain conditions, come to serve the purposes of bureaucracies aiming at some form of social control. Such forms of control may be brutal or humane; they may be instituted autocratically or with the widest popular participation. But so long as we term the "efficiency criterion" continues to guide bureaucratic innovation in these respects, the potential for extension of surveillance to more and more areas of life is endless. The theoretical endpoint of such trends is a world in which every thought and action of everyone registers at once with a centralized monitoring agency. To note this extreme is scarcely to announce its imminent attainment; but the implications of this theoretical endpoint for present developments bear reflection nonetheless.

Certainly no area of human life is inherently too private to attract the application of bureaucratic surveillance. Indeed, the most sensitive and personal aspects of life are often most associated with the social uncertainties which make systematic monitoring and control attractive. People yield all sorts of embarrassing or otherwise sensitive information to medical personnel as one of the costs of modern medical care. Similarly, then provide documentary accounting of the disorders and treatments involved to insurance bureaucracies as a requirement for reimbursement for such treatment. As connections arise between forms of personal information and possibilities for urgently desired social control, demands for the data in question are sure to follow.

Thus, a fundamental trend in modern, highly developed societies is the progressive centralization of social control in large bureaucracies, and the incorporation of more and more personal information in these bureaucratic systems to guide the workings of control. Other trends mitigate these effects to some extent. As the demands of centralized bureaucracies grown in these respects, those of local forms of surveillance and control—the family, the community, or the kinship system, for example—may subside (see Rule, 1974, pp. 331–332, 342–343). But no one can doubt that the growth of bureaucratic surveillance and control constrain individual autonomy and privacy in the sense in which most people use these terms. The value issues raised by the workings of a relative handful of mammoth systems of surveillance and control are bound to be weightier than those associated with the independent workings of many dispersed, local systems.

The Protection of Privacy and Its Limitations

In due course, the growing powers concentrated in bureaucratic systems of personal data management began to arouse considerable public anxiety. Who sets the purposes of bureaucratic surveillance? Can the systems be trusted?

The privacy issue, as it took shape in the late 1960s, represented a minefield for America's political and administrative elites. Dissatisfaction over organizational handling of personal data threatened to place important prerogatives up for grabs. On the one hand, ability to collect, store, and use personal information had become a major resource for key American bureaucracies, both public and private. On the other hand, some of the early objections to these practices sounded serious indeed. Given rising public mistrust of the official exercise of power, culminating, ultimately, in the Watergate affair, the nascent privacy protection movement of the late 1960s might have led to fundamental attacks upon established power positions. Whether this would occur depended on the meaning attributed to the protection of privacy in the emergent public understanding of that notion.

In fact, no frontal collision has occurred between an aroused public opinion and organizations engaged in what we term surveillance. The emergent official interpretation of privacy protection has forestalled any such confrontation. In this view, the noxious or dangerous feature of bureaucratic surveillance systems appear not as things inherent in their nature, but as failures to work "correctly"; and "correct," in this context, means consistent with the longer-term bureaucratic ends governing the systems. This convenient accomodation, from the standpoint of established forces, has made it possible to pursue the "reform" of these systems in ways which enhance, rather than threaten, their key interests. It would be difficult to overestimate the significance of this interpretation.

The domestication of the privacy issue has many parallels in the history of attempted regulation of noxious practices by powerful institutions in America.* In these instances, lost opportunities for thorough reshaping of the practices involved pass so subtly and quietly as to be virtually unnoticed. In the case of privacy, as with many another issue, the fateful turning points came not in the heat of public debate, but at that subtle point where key assumptions are taken for granted.

Of enormous importance in these developments was the early penchant to focus on notorious abuses of personal data management. Congressional hearings, journalistic and popular writings, and scholarly treatments of the emergent issue all tended to dramatize certain categories of particularly ugly misuses of personal information. They publicized cases of credit bureaus causing damage by maintaining and reporting erroneous information, or they focused on instances of erroneous or misleading arrest data unjustly affecting a person's access, let us say, to employment, or they centered attention on cases of an early education record unfairly stigmatizing a child throughout his or her school career.

The more resourceful representatives of organizations engaged in surveillance basically accepted critics' objections to such abuses and the legitimacy of efforts to correct these. In so doing, however, they helped to shift the debate over privacy protection to one over elimination of particular sets of abusive practices. This was construed to mean making surveillance systems work *better*, on the assumption that both organizations and the individuals depicted in the systems shared an interest in achieving the ends for which the systems were created. By concentrating attention on abuses of personal record-keeping so extreme that they served neither individuals nor organizations, participants in this debate shut out examination of the larger desirability of the growing power of surveillance systems *in general.*

Perhaps even more important, by fostering an interpretation of privacy protection in these terms, both the critics and the defenders of surveillance

---

*For those familiar with the work of Theodore Lowi, the similarity between this interpretation and his ideas will quickly be apparent. (See Lowi, 1971, especially the Prologue and Chapter 1.)

practices could avoid the really difficult and painful questions: How much surveillance is a desirable thing? How far should the development or bureaucratic monitoring of otherwise private affairs be extended? Instead of engaging these enormously difficult and contentious questions, the privacy planners eventually evolved what we term the efficiency criterion. By this criterion, privacy is deemed protected if three conditions are met in managing personal data: (1) that the data be kept accurate, complete, up-to-date, and subject to review and correction by the persons concerned; (2) that the uses of filed data proceed according to rules of due process that data subjects can know and, if necessary, invoke; and (3) that the organizations collecting and using personal data do so only insofar as necessary to attain their their appropriate organizational goals. Under these principles, organizations can claim to protect the privacy of the persons with whom they deal, even as they accumulate more and more data on those persons and greater and greater power over their lives. It would be difficult to imagine a more advantageous interpretation of privacy protection, from the standpoint of surveillance organizations.

However, the terms of this emergent compromise neglect something very important. The growth of modern bureaucratic surveillance, we have argued, represents a social trend of enormous significance in itself. That significance extends far beyond the issues surrounding abuse of particular systems in their present form. It demands consideration of the directions of social change implicit in present practices and of the alternatives to increasing reliance on surveillance.

A hard look at these matters reveals many reasons for seeking limits to the extension of bureaucratic surveillance—not simply as a source of unfairness or inefficiency, but as a bad thing in itself. The simplest of these reasons is what we have termed "aesthetic" reactions against intensive surveillance. No one really wants to live in a world where every previously private moment becomes a subject of bureaucratic scrutiny. There is something inherently desirable, at least for most people, about maintaining realms where experiences are shared only by the parties to them (see Fried, 1968). Even when the ends of surveillance are impeccable and even when the agencies concerned carry out their monitoring with full rectitude and discretion, the monitoring of *every* moment would strike most people as unacceptable.

To be sure, present surveillance systems have hardly brought us to the point of total monitoring. But again, the logic of change in these systems suggests no natural limit to their further extension. So long as the efficiency criterion continues to guide the development of these systems, their attentions will continue to spread over larger and larger areas of what had been private experience. At some point, nearly everyone would acknowledge, such extension passes the point of moral or aesthetic acceptability. Where that point lies is not an objective matter. It can only be identified through earnest debate and thoughtful reflection on the values of privacy and autonomy versus those of efficiency. There are no grounds for assuming that such debate and reflection would yield consensus among all thoughtful parties, but this hardly justifies ignoring the incontestable fact that modern surveillance systems promise eventually to reach the limits of acceptability by everyone's standards. Where that point occurs is a matter that ought to be explored in any thoughtful treatment of the privacy issue. Yet the official response to these matters evades these difficult issues, rather than encouraging us to confront them.

Another reason for limiting the unrestricted growth of bureaucratic surveillance lies in the value of preserving what one might term a desirable "looseness" in social relations. Other differences notwithstanding, many, if not most, surveillance systems work to make people responsible for their pasts. Criminal records ensure that people do not escape the repercussions of their criminal acts; insurance reporting works to link disreputable people to their community reputations; credit reporting helps credit grantors to hold people responsible for their past credit-using behavior.

Most Americans probably feel that these processes are legitimate and desirable; at least in some measure. However, most people probably also feel that there ought to be limits to the extent to which people's records are held against them. Statements like the following (House Committee on Government Operations, 1968) from a spokesman for the country's largest insurance and employment reporting firm do leave one a little uneasy:

> It is a fact that the interchange of business information and the availability of record information imposes a discipline on the American citizen. He becomes more responsible for his performance whether as a driver of his car, as an employee in his job performance, or as a payor to his creditors. But this discipline is a necessary one if we are to enjoy the fruits of our economy and the present freedom of our private enterprise.

It is a system of soliciting and reporting accounts of people's lives from friends, neighbors, co-workers really essential to the enjoyment of freedom? More generally, is it desirable that people always be held fully responsible for all of what prospective employers, creditors, or insurors would consider their past shortcomings? (See Greenawalt, 1975.) It is true that the conventional wisdom in America endorses the notion that people must "reap as they sow," but popular sentiment also endorses the worth of "a fresh start" or "a clean slate." Systematic forgetting of a person's pasts, even when troublesome from the standpoint of bureaucratic efficiency, may reflect a social value of considerable importance. Whether the values of efficiency or those of "wiping the slate clean" ought to prevail in any particular setting is bound to be a contentious issue.

We hardly insist on any particular resolution of the issue; indeed, the nature of the choices seems to us to preclude any programmatic solution, apart from piecemeal compromises on a case-by-case basis. We do, however, insist that the issue be confronted directly, and that the interests of efficiency alone not serve as a satisfactory basis for such confrontation. Again, the official response to the privacy issue has most often obscured these agonizing choices, precisely when they need to be dramatized.

A third compelling reason for limiting the growth of bureaucratic surveillance has to do with the effects of these systems on social power relations. The growth of modern surveillance inevitably brings about cumulative change in relations between what Shils (1975) would term "centers" of social power and the "peripheries." Surveillance makes it possible for those at the centers to monitor the activities of large populations and "reach out" with forceful actions to shape and control those behaviors. Often, of course, the purposes for which surveillance capacities are originally developed may be strictly mundane, or indeed purely humanitarian. That is, the social control which the systems afford may entail nothing more objectionable than enforcing tax obligations or providing health care. However, once these surveillance capabilities are in place, there is always some risk of their appropriation for purposes of repression by centralized powers. Under these conditions, it may matter rather little what were the original intentions of those who created the system, or even whether the system is governmental or private. Changes in political climates, for example, may leave bank or credit card files more open to government snooping than even some government records. The results of increasing the power of centralized institutions over those who make up the peripheries cannot always be foreseen.

These powers need not always be exercised in order to have their undesirable effects. We must recall the chilling effect which stems from people's knowledge of the data-monitoring capabilities of centralized institutions (see Wessel, 1974). Events of the 1970s have certainly altered many American's views of what centralized institutions, especially government ones, are capable of in these respects. Now it is much more difficult than it once was to dismiss the possibility that one's phone is being tapped, or that one's tax returns may be used for unfriendly political purposes, or that one's life has become the subject of a CIA file. The realization that these activities *might* take place, whether they really do or not in any particular instance, has potentially destructive effects on the openness of social systems to innovation and dissent. Clearly, the best way to avoid these effects is to cut back the instrumentalities which convey such threats.

Virtually everyone would acknowledge some point at which surveillance by bureaucracies simply becomes too thoroughgoing, even when carried out with total discretion for seemingly unimpeachable purposes. What if, instead of electronic funds transfer (EFT) systems, someone were to propose a "wireless funds transfer" system, in which people were equipped with miniature radios, to be carried or worn at all times, capable of authorizing debits from their accounts. Such a system would obviously offer even greater convenience than EFT, since one would always have total access to one's resources. Most people, however, would begin to feel uneasy, we suspect, about any system that provided such intimate and potentially unerring contact between private persons and centralized powers. At some point, a measure of insulation between what Shils terms center and periphery becomes a highly desirable thing in itself.

Consider a medical surveillance system designed to provide timely intelligence on threats to people's physical or mental health. Suppose that a tiny radio transmitter could be implanted under one's skin, to send continuous signals to a central computer for recording and monitoring. The cumulative record of such things as heartbeat, blood sugar, electroencephalogram, and the like could provide a data base for predicting all sorts of dangerous conditions, ranging from heart attacks to psychopathic outbursts. Indeed, if participation in the monitoring were required of everyone, the expanded data base would afford insights to benefit the sick and the well alike. Furthermore, if the system embodied a way of pinpointing the location of each user, heart attack victims and others involved in emergencies could count on prompt help. Continuous monitoring and analysis of data, under a system like this, could make it possible to transmit timely warnings, perhaps through the radio transmitter itself, to people who, in light of their records, were in danger of ill health or antisocial behavior. From one point of view, a system like this would represent the ultimate in preventive health care.

No one, we imagine, would find fault with the ultimate ends of such an undertaking—improving the quality of health care, and providing such care in the widest and most timely way. Nor would most people deny that public institutions have an authentic interest in establishing control over the uncertainties of public health. After all, the burdens of ill-health invariably fall in one way or another on society as a whole. There would be no insuperable difficulty in ensuring privacy in the conventional sense in a system like this. Procedural guarantees could well ensure such things as confidentiality, access rights, and due process in the use of data.

We suspect, however, that none of these redeeming possibilities would suffice to make such an arrangement acceptable to most people. Even if administered with the most scrupulous guaranteees on behalf of impeccable ends, a system like this would strike most of us as excessive. Such examples cause us to smile, or, if we take them seriously, to shudder, because these arrangements simply go too far in breaking down barriers that insulate individuals from larger institutions. Aesthetically, such arrangements, revolt us because they would destroy the sense of aloneness and autonomy which most people count essential ingredients of life. Strategically, the powers that such systems would confer on an overbearing regime are so sweeping that the risks implicit in their existence are simply better not taken. Even without repressive intent, the administration of such a system could hardly remain indefinitely free of pressures to share its capabilities for surveillance and control with other systems. The accretion of extraneous social control functions in the case of Social Security would be trivial compared to the demands made on sysems like the ones imagined here.

Spokesmen for programs of privacy protection through due process in personal data management have generally characterized their intent as that of "restoring the balance" between individuals and data-keeping insititutions (for further discussion see Westin, 1967; Miller, 1971; PPSC, 1977). Although the details are never very clearly specified, the idea seems to be that procedural guarantees like those discussed above eliminate dangers potentially arising from misuse of personal data systems. But in the light of larger patterns of social change, the notion of "balancing" the prerogatives of data-keeeping organizations and those of individuals, or of weighing the demands of privacy against the need for information, seems superficial. Procedural reforms may indeed provide an arena where individuals can assert their interests in the uses of their personal documentation; but these safeguards are matters of social convention. They endure only as long as the political and social climate in which they arise. In a more profound sense, the balance between individuals and centralized organizations is permanently altered once such systems are in place. Certainly one would always prefer procedural safeguards to their absence wherever personal data systems exist. However, it is misleading to argue that such safeguards somehow return the balance of social power to its status before the establishment of centralized institutions.

Let us remember that bureaucratic structures have no *purposes* of their own. Formal organizations develop capabilities to do certain kinds of things and of mastering given forms of uncertainty, but the ends that these skills serve are not dictated by the tools. A list of names and addresses, an array of pertinent information, or a bureaucratic mechanism for collecting and ordering such data, once in place, exists for the benefit of whoever controls them at any given time. The purposes leading to the founding of such a system need not necessarily shape their continued working. Creating pluralistic rules of the game by which individuals are accorded some influence over treatment of their data is desirable in itself, but it has no effect beyond the point where participants stop playing by the rules.

Again, there need be no question of the sincerity of the intentions of the founders of these systems, or of the seriousness with which procedural safeguards are originally instated. The point is simply that political and social climates change, and that the inherent capabilities of organizational forms typically outlive the frame of mind of those who bring them into existence. David J. Seipp (1978) has found a remarkable quote from a spokesman for the FBI back in 1931. Asked whether the Bureau would consider resorting to wiretapping, he replied,

> No sir. We have a very definite rule in the bureau that any employee engaging in wiretapping will be dismissed from the service of the bureau. . . . While it may not be illegal, I think it is unethical, and it is not permitted under the regulations by the Attorney General [p. 108].

The speaker was a young J. Edgar Hoover, replying to a query in a Congressional Committee on Expenditures hearing.

What constitutes "acceptable practice" does change, then; and the tempting availability of sophisticated personal-data-monitoring techniques may bring about recourse to practices previously foresworn. This makes it risky to place too much confidence in the self-restraint of any institution. Consider the following quote (Westin, 1967) from the middle 1960s:

> The history of police-force use of eavesdropping is sufficiently stained with misconduct throughout the nation that use of physical surveillance devices at the state level should be strictly limited to district attorneys' offices and state attorney generals' offices, and at the federal level to the FBI and military agencies [p. 376].

Obviously, any attempt to safeguard individual privacy and autonomy while leaving the powers of personal-data collection intact must identify some institution as a trustworthy repository of such powers. In light of events since the 1960s, however, the choice of the FBI and the military for this role can only be described as quaint.

The Alternative: A Looser, More Private World

We suspect that most people, confronted with the foregoing concerns, would hardly remain indifferent. No one really likes the idea of endless growth of bureaucratic surveillance, but what alternative can there be?

The fact that it may be difficult to conceive of realistic alternatives reflects the important gaps in most discussion of the privacy issue. A key assumption in these interpretations is that of organizations' needs for personal data. The underlying logic in this approach seems to go something like this:

1 The needs of organizations for personal data are relentlessly rising.
2. The continued satisfaction of these needs is a condition for a more bountiful, more efficient, more "advanced" social world.

3. The only policy is to satisfy such needs while making organizational demands for data as fair and as palatable to the public as possible.

Obviously, we share the view that modern formal organizations have characteristic reasons for relying on personal documentation, but the lock-step argument noted above caricatures the thoughtful analysis of this reliance which the issue requires. The message seemes to be that we can choose only between increasing loss of personal information to bureaucratic surveillance and a return to some sort of organizational "Stone Age." Yet a searching look at the needs of organizations for personal information suggests that they hardly represent a *sine qua non* of organizational life. In fact, one can identify a range of alternatives to increasingly intense use of personal data in organizational decision-making; these alternatives have not received the attention which they deserve.

Organizatons collect personal information largely in order to sustain discriminating decision-making processes concerning the persons depicted by the data. In an effort to produce just the proper treatment of each individual, and hence to forestall squandering resources on improper treatments, organizations seek more and more pertinent data to afford closer and closer discrimination among cases. However, what represents an improper application of resources is not eternally given; it is a social convention that might well be reconsidered in the interests of protecting privacy and autonomy. If organzations were not expected to make such fine discriminations in their treatments of persons, the need for rigorous data-collection would be greatly eased. The alternative to endless erosion of personal privacy and autonomy through increased surveillance lies in lessening discriminations among people in the application of organizational resources.

Today organizations, both governmental and private, invest enormous resources in pursuing what has been termed fine-grained discrimination. What we are proposing is a reallocation of resources to develop and underwrite less discriminatory, and hence less information-intensive, ways of dealing with people. What we face here is not simply a choice between meeting the information needs of organizations and seeing these organizations grind to a halt. Instead, the choice lies between meeting the costs of discriminating and paying the costs of relaxing such discrimination. For every degree of intimacy of surveillance relinquished by organizations, benefits accrue in privacy and autonomy.

Pursuit of less information-intensive alternatives would entail fundamental change in expectations about the treatments which organizations owe to their publics. It would mean minimizing differences in how people are treated in light of their records, and hence minimizing the necessity for developing such records. Instead of sharpening their discriminations, organizations would be expected to provide a baseline of adequate resources for all, with minimal differences according to cases.

Again, the alternatives here are not binary choices, but choices among many possible degrees of discrimination and the commensurately rising demands on privacy. Such tradeoffs are easily noted, for example, in income taxation. From its relatively simple beginnings, the U.S. income tax system has become a giant consumer of personal data. The rise in the range and frequency of data intake, of course, corresponds directly to the growing multiplicity of personal circumstances which tax laws take into account in assessing liability. A major impetus for such growth, one supposes, is public demand for "just consideration" of various extenuating circumstances. Simpler tax laws might well aim at limiting the range of circumstances bearing on tax obligations. If discriminations were made less complicated, then demands for personal information would drop commensurately. Planners for tax reform could make an enormous contribution to privacy protection by cutting back the range of personal data that bears on tax liability.

A relatively easy avenue for seeking less information-intensive forms of bureaucratic action lies in those areas where the use of personal information is least cost-effective. One of the most intrusive bureaucratic demands now widespread in America is that associated with security clearances. Millions of people must routinely undergo such investigations as conditions of their employment. Yet to our knowledge, compelling statistical associations between the results of these investigations and, let us say, unauthorized leaks of security-related information have never been demonstrated. We suspect that the infomation needs attributed to our security apparatus in these respects simply would not withstand close examination. Such an examination would more likely show that whatever benefits such procedures yield do not nearly warrant the costs in loss of privacy and the chilling effects of dissent and diversity in American life.

Attacking demands on personal privacy that do not really pay off in terms of organizational gain, however, is easy. Indeed, nearly all writers on the subject have exploited this argument. The difficult cases concern organizational use of personal information that is both useful by the standards presently prevailing in organizations and destructive of privacy and autonomy.

Here we feel that serious consideration of the arguments put forward above demands foreswearing bureaucratically attractive uses of personal data. This would mean setting policies in which organizations would relax or abandon the single-minded pursuit of efficient discrimination among persons in favor of other considerations.

No doubt the easiest settings in which to begin applying this thinking are in the planning for bureaucratic systems that do not yet exist. The prospect of national health insurance, for example, is receiving increasingly serious discussion at the time of this writing. The degree of discrimination built into a system of this kind is obviously full of implications for personal privacy. Systems that embody complicated eligibility requirements and other forms of discrimination governing access to treatment are driven to make very intensive demands on personal data. The most appealing alternative is a system that offers its services to all, as in Britain's National Health Service. Since every Briton is eligible, the system need not develop the detailed inquiries into the backgrounds of its clients which would otherwise be the case. Thus, the system actually entails relatively loose central record-keeping. What there is serves mainly to keep track of the numbers of patients for whom individual physicians are responsible. Case histories and other personal background information are stored locally, much as they are in countries where medicine is private.

One can also envisage ways to enhance privacy by restricting surveillance where it is already well established, although resistance would be greater here. Consider the case of consumer credit. The first consumer-credit reporting operations were basically simple listings of bad debts held in common among several firms, to enable each to avoid giving credit to persons who had defaulted elsewhere. Today, by contrast, credit surveillance entails use of a very wide variety of information pooled among many different sources. The sophistication of modern credit systems depends on the use of these rich informational resources to predict which credit applicants should be trusted, and to what extent. The interests of privacy would be well served by deliberately blunting some of these discriminations.

This possibility has not gone altogether unnoticed among writers on privacy. Kent Greenawalt (1975), in his thoughtful study of the status of privacy in American law, has commented,

> If information about credit standing is easily available on a national basis, it is virtually impossible to avoid one's low credit rating. This information allows credit-granting agencies to make more intelligent decisions about risk, but is it socially desirable that persons who admittedly pose a high risk be unable to get credit? Perhaps it would be socially preferable if credit were more freely available, even if good credit risks ended up paying the tab (e.g., in increased prices) so that poor credit risks could get credit [p. 92].

Nonetheless, Greenawalt's remarks here are exceptional; most writers have taken the sacredness of organizational efficiency for granted in these matters. We share Greenawalt's view. The effectiveness of discriminations between good and poor credit risks is hardly the only social value which ought to be considered in this important relationship. Competing values here are those of a looser social world, one with less potential for serving the needs of oppressive centralized powers and more capacity for extending opportunities to those who, in light of "all the facts," may appear to be poor risks. We favor a commitment of resources to pursuit of these latter values over and against those of pure efficiency in discriminating as to who will be the most profitable credit customers.

Any number of concrete measures, more or less sweeping, might serve to put this principle into effect. One might restrict the retention of derogatory credit information to, let us say, 2 years. This would have the effect of wiping the slate clean after a relatively short period for those who have unwilling or unable to pay in the past. Or one might do away with centralized credit reporting altogether, so that every firm extending credit would have to develop its own bases for deciding whether to open an account with a given applicant.* This would surely countervail against the thoroughgoing and intrusive character of modern credit investigations. Our point is not to argue for any particular measure, but rather to emphasize alternatives to the single-minded pursuit of efficient discrimination which characterizes current credit policy. Whether the resulting policies are sweeping or cautious matters less than recognizing that protection of privacy requires compromises in bureaucratic efficiency.

Similar less information-intensive alternatives can be envisaged for many other social settings now marked by growing reliance on surveillance. In all of these cases, gains for privacy and autonomy can be purchased at incremental costs in the relinquishment of fine discriminations among persons in the application of bureaucratic resources. Whether such costs are warranted in any particular instance is not a question to be answered a priori for all settings at all times. Indeed, it is misleading to suggest that such questions have objective solutions, independent of the values of any particular thinker. We scarcely mean to insist, then, on anything so heavy-handed as curtailment of surveillance in all cases as a matter of principle; but we do insist that values of bureaucratic efficiency are not the only ones which ought to inform policy in personal data systems.

Conclusion

One might view very modern, "advanced" societies as characterized by reliance on especially powerful technologies. These include not only technologies in the usual sense, but also what one might term social

---

*To the consternation of the credit-reporting industry, certain large credit grantors, mostly petroleum companies, are developing systems to evaluate applicant credit worthiness without recourse to centralized credit files. Moreover, they are refusing to disclose information about existing accounts to credit bureaus.

technologies—techniques for mobilizing the actions of large numbers of people. These techniques afford relative handfuls of decision makers the means, for example, to activate party faithful in politics; or to direct the movement of investment captial; or to orchestrate the movement of armies in military campaigns; or to determine what people will read or hear or see via mass communications. Surveillance systems, of course, represent simply another refinement in social technologies. They enable elites to monitor the individual behavior of very many people at a time, and to use the data so acquired to shape people's behavior in return.

The growth of such powerful technologies—surveillance very much included here—raises the *stakes* of social planning. When the technologies of small-scale, simple social systems go wrong, the numbers of persons to be affected will at least not be too great. But when the powerful technologies of large-scale modern societies meet with destructive uses, the results may take the form of nuclear warfare or totalitarianism. Individually, there may not be a great deal to choose between victimization in a witch hunt in a small seventeenth-century New England town and persecution in a modern totalitarian regime. Collectively, the scope of human tragedy in the second case must surely be counted far greater.

The dawning realization of the potential evils of powerful technologies gone wrong has injected into contemporary culture a remarkable ambivalence about science and its status in society. Throughout most of the nineteenth century, the idea grew that enhanced scientific understanding of both the natural and social worlds would lead to a richer, more materially bountiful and less socially conflict-ridden existence for everyone. "Know, in order to foretell; foretell, in order to control," thus one might translate Comte's optimistic dictum on the spirit of science. Certainly the growth both of scientific understanding and of the resulting scope of human control have, if anything, overfulfilled Comte's predictions. The expanding sphere of human control has not been an unmixed blessing, however. For members of advanced, affluent societies, life has become more comfortable in countless ways. Yet the unintended effects of the technologies which afford such affluence give rise to the possibility of all sorts of man-made disasters on a scale never before possible. The use in warfare of sophisticated technologies for mobilizing energy for the first time raises the possibility of the extinction of the species. The applications of other sophisticated natural science technologies raises serious possibilities of environmental disaster. And the growth of social technologies, including but by no means limited to surveillance, raises the possibility of totalitarianism. The growth of human control, it would seem, offers the drawbacks of its successes.

These realizations cast an ironic light on the original, almost unbounded optimism concerning the social effects of science, an optimism which social science has until very recently helped to promote.* In many of the earlier evolutionary interpretations of social development, the enhancement of human control was seen as a virtually unambiguous gain in the *security* of social life. After all, the growth of more powerful technologies promised to preserve human life from the uncertainties of disease, scarcity, superstition and the like. These uncertainty-reducing features of social organization thus seemed to offer a more secure role of humankind on the planet. A number of social scientists have contended, even very recently, that growing understanding of social processes will make social systems more rational. Now we must face the fact that modern natural technologies have created highly *un*steady states (Granovetter, 1979). Though we may live in many ways a more bountiful material life, say, than the indigenous North American peoples, we know that present patterns of technology and energy use, drawing as they do on zero-sum resources and pushing against limited environments, cannot continue indefinitely. Thus our relations with our natural environments are *less* stable over the longer run than those of less-developed peoples. Similarly, the development of surveillance and the countless other sophisticated social arrangements of bureaucratic civilization offer all sorts of enriching comforts and conveniences. No one, however, can be certain when we may come to regret the longer-term effects of the application of such powerful systems.

In 1969, we suspect, these arguments would have struck nearly everyone as hopelessly utopian. Today, perhaps, this slightly less the case. We have lately been witnessing, in America and other highly developed societies, a remarkable disenchantment with powerful technologies, at least as they relate to the nonhuman world. These attitudes are perhaps most evident with regard to environmental and energy policy. As everyone knows who has been attentive to public debates on these matters, antagonism toward powerful, centralized approaches to these issues goes very deep among many people. These are of course the same people who prefer soft energy technologies such as wind and water power, technologies which disperse both social and natural power into as many relatively autonomous elements as possible.

In our view, some elements of radical environmentalism have their own irrational tinge, but many of the concerns of the technological skeptics, as we have called them, seem to us to embody certain unassailably valid principles. Very powerful technologies, both social and natural, entail the risks of putting all of one's eggs in a single basket; any disaster is apt to be a very large-scale disaster indeed. By contrast, the failures of soft, dispersed technologies at least limit the scope of the resulting damage. No one who thinks carefully about it

---

*The durability of such reflexive optimism in the face of all sorts of danger signs is truly remarkable. See, for example, Pool *et al.* (1971).

can really like the idea of a world in which man-made concentrations of power grow larger endlessly. Yet only self-conscious efforts to enlarge the array of alternatives considered in planning for these things can reverse the trend in this direction.

If we are right, the current erosion in the once seemingly boundless faith in the prospects of growing human control represents a trend of major significance. At a gut level, people are growing skeptical of more and more powerful technologies as solutions to the problems of highly developed societies. These changes in public attitudes cry out for a redefinition of rationality in these respects. Thoughtful, scientifically reputable people must be prepared to affirm that preference for smaller, more modest forms of control need not be superstitious or irrational. On the contrary, people need to hear it said that limitations on the scope of human intervention need not be antiscientific, but may simply reflect the humility due to planning for situations where the stakes may grow very great indeed. Such humility, it seems to us, is particularly fitting where the damage inflicted by misapplied human powers affects far more people than the planners themselves. In short, we need a program for rational limits to the extension of rational human control.

Happily, a number of thoughtful commentators have begun to play this role. Regarding the risks of nuclear power production, for example, Amitai Etzioni (1974) has written,

> To say that reactors have a 1 out of 10,000 chance to blow each year (or 1 out of 1,000,000 per community), which makes them about as safe as flying, does not take into account the number of persons to be killed in a nuclear disaster. . . . Most persons who would accept a $10.00 bet at odds of 99 to 1 in their favor, would hesitate if the bet was $1000 at the *same* odds, and refuse a $100,000 bet at *identical* odds. Why? Only because the disutility changed.

Moreover, as Etzioni would undoubtedly also emphasize, calculations regarding nuclear power must be calculations of *cumulative* probability. That is, one's concern must be with the probability of such systems' *ever* going seriously wrong; these probabilities of course rise steadily over the time span under consideration. And we hold that planning for powerful technologies in general, either natural or social, must rely on this form of thinking. One wishes to be as certain as possible that a surveillance system *never* becomes a vehicle for repressive control. Given the uncertainty which seems to mark the changing political and social climates in which such systems exist, such assurances are difficult to come by.

In another context, Kenneth Boulding (1977) has written,

> One of the major principles of the universe as a general system is that over a long enough period of time very improbable events will have happened. It is easy to show that an event with a probability of $1/n$ in a year has a probability of happening equal to .9995 at some time in a period

of 10n years. Thus, a 100-year flood is virtually certain to happen sometime within 1000 years. Within the ten-billion-year history of the universe it is virtually certain that some event with a probability of one billionth per annum will have come off [p. 301].

Of course, it is comforting to assume that events which we regard as unlikely are really such remote possibilities as to be discountable. However, Boulding's observation should remind us of the cumulative increase of unwanted risks over time. In developing social and technological powers that have the potential to shape both our world and that of succeeding generations, prudence in dealing with risks of very serious occurrences is surely warranted.

References

Boulding, K. The universe as a general system. Fourth annual Ludwig von Bertalanffy Memorial Lecture, *Behavioral Science* 1977, 22.

Etzioni, A. Letter to the editor, *New York Times Magazine*, March 24, 1974

Fried, C. Privacy, *Yale Law Journal*, 1968, 77.

Granovetter, M. The idea of "advancement" in theories of social evolution and development, *American Journal of Sociol.*, 1979, 85.

Greenawalt, K. *Legal protections of privacy.* Washington, D.C.: Office of Telecommunications Policy, 1975.

House Committee on Government Operations,90th Congress, 2nd Session. Testimony of May 16, 1968. Washington, D.C.: U.S. Government Printing Office, 1968.

Lowi, T. *The politics of disorder.* New York: Basic Books, 1971.

Miller, A. *Assault on privacy.* Ann Arbor: University of Michigan Press, 1971.

Perrow, C. *Complex organizations: A critical essay.* Glenview, Ill.: Scott Foresman and Co., 1972.

Pool, I., McIntosh, S., and Griffel, D. Information systems and social knowledge. In A. Westin (Ed.), *Information technology in a democracy.* Cambridge, Mass.: Harvard University Press, 1971.

Privacy Protection Study Committee. *Personal privacy in an information society.* Washington, D.C.: U.S. Government Printing Office, 1977.

Rule, J., *Private lives and public surveillance.* New York: Schocken Books, 1974.

Rule, J., McAdam, D., Stearns, L., and Uglow, D. *The politics of privacy: Planning for personal data systems as powerful technologies.* New York: Elsevier, 1980.

Seipp, D.J. *The right to privacy in American history.* Cambridge, Mass.: Harvard University Program on Information Resources Policy, 1978.

Shils, E. Privacy and power. In E. Shils (Ed.), *Center and periphery: Essays in macrosociology.* Chicago: University of Chicago Press, 1975.

Thompson, J. *Organizations in action.* New York: McGraw-Hill, 1967.

Wessel, M. *Freedom's edge: The computer threat to Society.* Reading, Mass: Addison-Wesley, 1974.

Westin, A. *Privacy and freedom.* New York: Atheneum, 1967.

Comment on "Preserving Individual Autonomy in an Information-Oriented Society"

Kenneth C. Laudon

I was very pleased when Lance Hoffman asked me to comment on James Rule's paper, and when I received the draft I was not disappointed. Rule's paper is provocative because it questions some of the fundamental values upon which modern American society is based. The paper forces us to evaluate some of the value choices we have made with respect to personal information systems.

To avoid creating a straw man to argue with, let me review some of the arguments in Rule's paper. The place to start is in the conclusion, for here one finds some of the judgments which inform much of the paper. Rule points out that human control—the effort in Western societies to employ science and technology to shape the world according to human designs—has some drawbacks. Systems of human control can fail, and they do fail; big systems of human control informed by big science and big technology can fail in big ways, create disasters, and create unsteady states of human existence.

These observations are important for understanding Rule's treatment of large, personal data banks, which are a kind of social technology. As Rule points out, formal organizations play an increasing role in the life of citizens, as these organizations respond to public demands that citizens be treated as individuals, in accordance with the uniqueness of their circumstances. In response to these public demands for new organizational relationships and greater individual consideration, organizations develop personal information systems in order to make the "fine-grained" decisions demanded, and this marks the growth of uniquely modern forms of social control, or what Rule chooses to call surveillance systems.

Rule claims that the growth of bureaucratic surveillance has resulted in (although he does not say over what time period) more and more personal information in record systems, a long-term decline in privacy and autonomy, centralization of social control, a concomitant weakening of other forms of

89

COMPUTERS AND PRIVACY
IN THE NEXT DECADE

social control such as families, communities, and the like. So long as the value of efficiency is supreme, there is no natural limit on this degradation of the human condition, and the logical endpoint, Rule believes, is a centralized monitoring agency where no area of personal life would exist beyond bureaucratic scrutiny.

Rule dismisses the privacy debate and legislation of the 1970s for having failed to attack established power positions in society (presumably, large organizations), as having been preoccupied with making large personal information systems simply more hygienic, and as having allowed these systems to accrue more information and power.

We should resist these developments, Rule argues, on aesthetic grounds, in order to preserve "looseness" (treating people irrespective of their uniqueness), and because the same tools which bring us efficiency in housing programs, welfare, and social security, could just as well lead to totalitarian regimes.

The alternative, Rule suggests, is not to go back to an organizational "Stone Age," but to become less discriminating, less information intensive, and if necessary, to eliminate especially obnoxious national, personal information systems and replace them with local systems, even if the costs to all are higher.

If I have correctly characterized the arguments, then I raise the following issues. An oft-repeated word in this paper is "surveillance," and it calls up some very nasty literary and historical images. Those who survived Sociology 101 in a conscious state will remember that surveillance—the collection of information for the purposes of social control—is a fundamental requirement of any form of social life whatsoever, from the family, community, city, to the state. Only at Walden Pond is there no surveillance. Those familiar with the revisionist history of the family and community, will probably agree that for those of us who live in families and communities, there is nothing particularly benign about this "local" surveillance. It is incredibly intrusive. Within a few months of moving to a new community or suburb, it is pretty easy to invade the privacy of your neighbors, and vice versa, to the point where you know the state of their marriages, their occupations, religions, shopping habits, travel, indeed endless details of their personal lives, including how they avoid paying taxes; likewise with family life.

I think bureaucracies would give a year's budget to develop this kind of surveillance capacity. The implication of Rule's paper at various points—that bureaucratic surveillance is particularly onerous, intrusive, and threatening to human freedom, dignity, and autonomy, and therefore ought to be replaced by local systems of control—is, I think, wrong.

I believe, too, that Rule's opposition to the notion of fine-grained decision making is wrong. I think organizations would all like to make fine-grained decisions, and some may be able to when compared to other bureaucracies. Yet when compared to small, local surveillance systems, a great deal of bureaucratic decision making can only be compared to a meat cleaver in the hands of an amateur. The redlining of entire zip-code areas by mortgage banks, the withdrawing of insurance coverage from teenagers, the seeking of real human pluralism in universities and businesses (by adding a black, a Jew, a Midwesterner, a female), is not the sophisticated use of statistical techniques to attain fine-grained decision making. The differences between groups on almost any important characteristic are far smaller than the differences between individuals within a group. Briefly, not taking into account the characteristics of individuals, instead deciding about individuals on the basis of their group membership, leads to all sorts of absurdities but clearly not to fine-grained decision making.

The place to find fine-grained decision making is, of course, in the small, local systems of social control. The banker in a small community who lets a resident know that the bank still owns the car he or she bought on their credit, and therefore it had better be kept clean; the grocer who grants credit because he "knows" a person; the cop who detains someone because he does not "know" him or her; the judge who gives someone the stiff sentence because he "knows" that person's family: These are the fine-grained decision makers, and they often are not benign, fair, or even analyzable.

Now, in theory, it may be that organizations are necessarily driven to collect more and more information to achieve fine-grained decision making, but in reality, Rule's statements about more and more information in personal data banks is a knotty issue to untangle.

If we restrict our vision to the period 1960–1980, we find some contradictory empirical evidence. As Westin and I looked at local and state public systems in the mid 1960s, we found some organizations converting from manual to automated systems and, in the process, throwing out a lot of information items in individual records, and throwing out a lot of entire records that had been lying around in manual files for no good reason, for example, criminal record systems. In some instances we found personal record systems being created which had not existed in manual form (for example, centralized social service systems). Then, Westin and Baker looked at private and public systems in the early 1970s and found the amount of information in individual records actually declining with automation (in part because of economic constraints such as memory cost). For the last two years I have worked with the Office of Technology Assessment (U.S. Congress) and other groups looking at three system-development projects in which third-generation designs are being replaced with fourth-generation designs suitable for operation in the 1980s. In looking at truly mammoth systems, such as the FBI Criminal History Message Switching proposal, the IRS Tax Administration System, and the proposed Social Security Future Process System, it would seem that with a few minor exceptions, it is *not the case* that more and more information is being collected on individual records.

On the other hand, from a total system of information perspective, while individual records may be more streamlined and actually smaller, telecommunications advances combined with distributed fourth-generation architecture result in more information being available to more decision makers on more individuals than ever before. Current distributed designs considerably enlarge the security and trust perimeters, strain existing control and accountability mechanisms, and vitiate the force of privacy legislation adopted in the 1970s.

Briefly, the "more and more information" thesis of Rule is rather complicated as an empirical matter. Much would seem to depend on the historical period under consideration, the theoretical perspective (a record versus system perspective), and the cost of computer memory, which is declining rapidly.

Yet another image that Rule invokes is that of totalitarianism, and the notion that development of personal information systems has no logical limit. Rule argues that developing large information systems will, or at least, may result in centralized monitoring agencies. Well, many things have no logical endpoint, like love, but there are empirical constraints. In any event, the image of totalitarianism invoked by Rule is largely literary in origin: the notion that a political decision maker one day will throw a switch, and in an orderly yet rapid transition, democracy ends and totalitarianism begins.

When we look at the history of real totalitarian regimes, we see that they did not originate through an orderly transition from bureaucratic efficiency to bureaucratic despotism. Rather, they seem to originate in the collapse of bureaucratic efficiency, social, and civic order. Totalitarian regimes, in fact, did not require (as necessary or sufficient conditions of coming to power) the existence of large personal data banks of any sort. And totalitarian regimes did not, and today do not, require large personal data banks in order to stay in power. The truly frightening aspect of totalitarian regimes is not their rational bureaucratic character, their reliance on huge personal record files, but just the opposite; that is, reliance on small local systems of social control.

Totalitarian regimes are not so incompetent as to think they can really control people using the frail, gross, and soft decision making powers of bureaucracies. Until recently, in China it was the small, local study group, *hsüeh-hsi*, at the block or factory level, or the use of forced biographies recorded by a neighborhood party team, in which, people were forced to give complete accounts of themselves and their neighbors. The records were analyzed on a local level, and candidates were selected for "reform" by local leaders (Whyte, 1974; Price, 1976). Likewise with the Soviet purges of the 1930s: It was the local party cell operating in neighborhoods and the Army who carried out the orders of Stalin to supply victims (Fainsod, 1965). As in most totalitarian regimes, the selection process is not bureaucratically "rational" in character but just the opposite: merciless settling of local scores combined often with random selection to fulfill quotas.

The key personnel of totalitarian regimes are not bureaucrats. They are the Gauleiter; the block worker; the party member, who is the mechanic or high school teacher; or the secret police goon, who may be a neighbor. When you have these kinds of people in a society—devoted members of the party willing to inform and murder for whatever reason—who needs a cumbersome bureaucracy? Perhaps because totalitarian regimes have far more effective means of social control, namely local systems, we find that computerized personal data banks, say in the Soviet Union, the Eastern Bloc, China, Argentina, and Brazil, are not very well developed at all. It may be that large, bureaucratic personal data banks are a sufficient, adequate means of social control only in relatively free, voluntaristic, consensual societies because they rely so much upon individual compliance.

A good argument could be made that totalitarian regimes are inherently antibureaucratic, and vice versa. It is probably no accident that the totalitarian leaders of the past all distrusted their bureaucracies. Note, for example, the appearance with totalitarian leaders of Black Shirts to circumvent the regular police, the Red Guards to discipline the bureaucrats, the cadre worker to watch the colonels. It is no accident that former President Nixon profoundly distrusted his bureaucracy and found it necessary to create a White House group personally loyal to him. True, Nixon did abuse some large personal record systems, but he did encounter resistance in this effort, he was usually dissatisfied with the results, and I believe it was not his main threat to American democracy.

It may be that the literary image of totalitarianism called forth by Rule will one day be history; but, based on past experience, the best defense against the insanity of local totalitarian control may be centralized, efficient, rule-governed, and humane bureaucracies relying on personal record systems. From the point of view of accountability and oversight, from the view of public surveillance over public decision making, I would much rather oversee a few mammoth centralized systems than thousands of local systems.

Now let me reverse directions for a moment and try to escape Dr. Pangloss's corner, into which some may wish to paint me. I support most of Rule's concerns, which he raised so forcefully and clearly in his paper, even though I disagree with some of the conclusions. Rule seems to me absolutely correct when he suggests that the growth and redevelopment of large personal record systems is moving us toward a "tighter" society, one I would call a "dossier society." Here, most all of the important and not so important events in the lives of individuals are recorded and increasingly influence public and private decision making about one's future. I believe the pursuit of total efficiency in, say, criminal history record-keeping, probably does and will conflict with the pursuit of other critical values such as the integration of urban blacks into a complex economy, or for that matter, any former offender. I believe the technical capability presented by computerized record systems for, say, tracking politically unpopular groups, really does influence the political process which has in fact come to authorize such tracking, for example, the Parent Locator System of Department of Health, Education and Welfare, and numerous "matching" programs. At the same time, the technical capability of large systems can dull the blade of positive reform and social change as, for instance, it becomes possible to efficiently operate antiquated tax, welfare, and criminal justice programs designed generations ago. As it turns out, large personal record systems quite naturally reflect the extant social and political forces of their time. In some instances they do indeed magnify underlying inequities, and mask over irrationality.

At a broader level, I believe Rule, along with others, only some of whom are present at the workshop, are members of a younger generation of scholars, policy analysts, and commentators who take a more critical view of the social impact of personal data banks than previous writers. This "second generation" of writers in the field of social impact of computing and personal data banks is just now starting to coalesce and to have some impact on public and private policy regarding personal data banks. Although I cannot speak for all of this generation, I can speak for myself and a few others whose views I know well.

Many of us believe that we are operating large personal data banks today at both local and national levels whose broad social consequences and whose impact on decision making we do not understand. For instance, I think it is a little ridiculous that a major State Criminal Justice Informaion System is operating a criminal history file used by police, district attorneys, judges, and God knows who else, and in which only 27% of the underlying records were found to be complete and accurate. The Department of Justice wants to link such state files so that by 1985 we will have a National Criminal History File influencing about 19 million criminal justice decisions per annum. My curiosity and fear is heightened by knowledge of the fact that in a system like Social Security, which distributes $7 billion to 37 million individuals every month, there are errors in a minimum of 20% of case files. There are more examples about which I have written (Laudon, 1974, 1979a, b), but at a minimum, it is clear to me the implications of large personal data banks for privacy—in the broadest sense of that word—due process, equity, and the balance of power between citizen and state, are not fully understood and have not been extensively investigated. It may be that we have systems designed by geniuses and run by idiots, but then we should plan for that eventuality. Or, it may be that we are operating systems designed by idiots and run by geniuses, the ordinary human cop or caseworker, who interprets system output before it has a negative impact on citizens. I wonder what happens then as the pursuit of efficiency causes us to eliminate these lower level decision makers and replace many of them with on-line, realtime, decision-making designs.

I believe, second, that we are operating large personal data bank systems whose full complexity is not understood, and which, therefore, are difficult to control and to hold accountable. If programming is an art, then imagine what descriptions of programs are like. As it turns out, we have no really good methodology to explain or describe programs. The first words out of a programmer's mouth when explaining his artful creation is liable to be, "Well, it's kind of complicated but it works this way." Pretty soon, the conference table starts to look like an arterial road map of the United States.

The implications of these remarks are as follows. If we start building systems like the proposed Social Security Future Process system involving 30,000 terminals in a partially distributed design, then what kinds of additional oversight and control mechanisms are required to assure its proper operation? Put another way, if the objective complexity of a system increases tenfold, what increase in management oversight and control capacity is required (none, 1%, 10%)? In the past, we have tended to find out the answers through a seat-of-the-pants, trial-and-error method. I do not think that its good enough anymore. I think Congress, in the appropriations and oversight process, is starting to address the practical side of these questions which is: Are the existing institutional mechanisms sufficient to provide adequate control and oversight for some of these mammoth public systems?

This takes us to the area of future and past legislation, an area of which Rule was especially critical. If you look at the kinds of requests that the Office of Technology Assessment (U.S. Congress) receives from congressional committees, if you talk with certain congressmen and their staffs, there is a growing belief that, whereas existing privacy legislation may provide important legal remedies to individuals to correct failures of personal data systems, the laws do not provide positive institutional mechanisms to monitor, oversee, and gauge the full social, legal, political, and economic impacts of these systems. Many congressmen felt this way in 1974—the year the Privacy Act was passed—but in disagreement with Rule, I do not believe there was sufficient political horsepower to support stronger legislation. I do not believe there was a chance in the early 1970s that privacy could be used as the issue to attack fundamental positions of power in the United States.

Nevertheless, I do believe stronger legislation is on the way, reflecting a growing congressional uneasiness. The political momentum in Congress for such legislation is in part provided by Executive agencies who come to Congress with very complex and mammoth system-development projects whose social impact and whose privacy impact they really had not even considered in the design process. The haughty attitude of IRS—which came to

Congress with its proposed Tax Administration System saying, in essence, we really do not know and have not studied the potential social impact questions, but it should be approved because we say it is more efficient—just will not work anymore. The FBI and Social Security system-development projects have taken this experience into account, and I think are more mindful of social-impact questions as a result. However, as more sophisticated projects keep coming to Congress, there is a feeling that some institutional vehicle is needed to provide coherent knowledge, information, and judgments about the social impact of operating and proposed systems. No doubt, as with other technologies, it may take a few disasters and some near misses before we actually establish such institutions.

All of these remarks put me in the postion of calling for better system design, more critical knowledge and thinking about the relation between systems and society, and stronger oversight mechanisms to assure accountability as we move into the 1980s. The challenge is to envision efficient and humane systems operating within constitutional limits and under strong statutory control. These systems will require a broader base of public participation; they will be more expensive to build, more difficult to manage well, and will be of somewhat reduced efficiency than technologically feasible. The alternative appears to be fewer services delivered in a manner neither efficient or humane. Frankly, I do not believe this last alternative has much political support.

References

Fainsod, M. *How Russia is ruled.* Cambridge, Mass.: Harvard University Press, 1965.

Laudon, K. C. *Computers and bureaucratic reform.* New York: Wiley, 1974.

Laudon, K. C. Complexity in large federal databanks. *Society/Transaction,* May, 1979 (a)

Laudon, K. C. Problems of accountability in federal databanks, *Proceedings of the American Association for the Advancement of Science,* January, 1979 (b)

Price, J. L. *Cadres, commanders, and commissars.* Boulder, Col.: Westview Press, 1976.

Whyte, M. K. *Small groups and political rituals in China.* Berkeley: University of California Press, 1974.

Comment on "Preserving Individual Autonomy in an Information-Oriented Society"

Abbe Mowshowitz

Introduction

Rule's analysis of privacy, autonomy, and personal data systems is in harmony with my own views on the subject (Mowshowitz, 1976, 1977). My only criticism is that the implications of the analysis are not fully grasped in his discussion of alternatives to extensions of bureaucratic surveillance. Before elaborating on this observation, I should like to review the points of agreement.

The foundation of Rule's argument is an insight that should, I believe, be taken to heart by all serious students of the social impact of computing. He views "the most profound changes in relations between personal information and individual autonomy as effects of changes in social relationships, rather than as those of technological change." It follows that no amount of tinkering with personal data management systems can resolve the problems of privacy and autonomy that haunt such systems.

The threat to privacy and autonomy posed by personal data management systems derives from the role of such systems in bureaucratic surveillance. Information technology has been appropriated as an instrument of social control by the organizations that dominate contemporary life. As Rule explains, this crucial fact has been effectively sidestepped by the domestication of the computers and privacy controversy. Instead of coming to grips with the intrinsic nature of bureaucratic surveillance, discussion has focused on the palatability or correctness of its instrumentalities. Thus, privacy protection has come to be defined relative to the "efficiency criterion" of review and amendment, due process, and appropriateness associated with the collection, processing, and dissemination of personal data. Through its failure to question the assumptions concerning organizations' needs for information, the

97

procedural approach to privacy serves to legitimate extensions of bureaucratic surveillance. The rationale for bureaucratic surveillance rests on the belief that the well-being of our complex society depends on the benignly efficient processing of ever more personal data.* Rule rejects this rationale on the grounds that privacy and autonomy are valuable features of our social life, which are undermined by extensions of bureaucratic surveillance.

Organizations, according to Rule, would not cease to function effectively if they were to curtail their appetites for personal data by "lessening discriminations among people in the application of organizational resources." Two avenues for "lessening discriminations" are explored. One focuses on organizational uses of personal information which are not decidedly cost effective. The other poses a direct challenge to organizations whose self-interests appear to dictate policies which are inimical to privacy and autonomy. Because of this inescapable conflict between bureaucratic surveillance and autonomy, Rule urges resistance to the temptations of bureaucratically attractive uses of personal information. I agree completely with his call for restraint, but I do not believe that mere appeals to better judgment will do much to check bureaucratic surveillance.

The Politics of Privacy

The procedural approach to privacy protection, so ably dissected by Rule, is based on a view of privacy that might be termed "organizational voyeurism." Reduced to essentials, this view posits a world consisting of individuals and the organizations that serve them. To provide efficient service to their numerous individual clients, organizations must of necessity gather, process, and use ever-increasing volumes of personal data. Now even in the clearest of skies clouds do sometimes appear. The clouds in this case take the form of over-zealous or criminal Peeping Toms who occasionally sabotage someone's credit rating or insurance application, or harass individuals simply because of their group affiliations. This last-mentioned nastiness is the closest the organizational voyeurism theory comes to attributing sociological significance to the privacy issue. Unfortunately, the significance of this quasi-political observation is lost because of the failure to trace its systemic implications.

The nature of this failure is revealed in the rhetoric of domesticated privacy studies. Big Brother is a standard feature of reports on computers and privacy, but the role played by this specter is analogous to that of the bogey man in children's fairy tales. Reference to Big Brother does not indicate an awareness

---

*I have dubbed this rationale the "argument from complexity." (See Chapter 12 of Mowshowitz, 1976.)

of the impact of bureaucratic surveillance, nor is it meant to convey a sense of imminent political dangers. The invocation of Big Brother (or some more sophisticated equivalent) is a rhetorical device used to dramatize a fantastic possibility, which is believed to be discontinuous with current political reality. In this way one presumes to do one's intellectual duty and then buckles down to the "important" business of procedural reform.

As a byword of totalitarianism, Big Brother conjures up images of concentration camps, armed bullies, brutal repression, and arbitrary violence. But the essence of totalitarianism is not brutality; it is, as observed by Jacques Ellul (1974), the tendency of a social system to absorb the individual's life completely. De Tocqueville (1945) observed this tendency in American society a century and a half ago.

> I think, then, that the species of oppression by which democratic nations are menaced is unlike anything that ever before existed in the world. . . . The first thing that strikes the observation is an innumerable multitude of men, all equal and alike, incessantly endeavoring to procure the petty and paltry pleasures with which they glut their lives. . . . Above this race of men stands an immense and tutelary power, which takes upon itself alone to secure their gratifications and to watch over their fate. That power is absolute, minute, regular, provident, and mild. . . . It every day renders the exercise of the free agency of man less useful and less frequent; it circumscribes the will within a narrower range and gradually robs a man of all the uses of himself [pp. 336–337].

The organizational voyeurism approach to privacy is constitutionally incapable of assimilating this insight. Rule's analysis of bureaucratic surveillance does not spring from a theory of technological determinism, but it does lead to conclusions quite similar to those drawn by Ellul (1964; Winner, 1977). Modern bureaucracies are actuated by imperatives that serve their own internal wants, and these wants are at variance with the needs for privacy and autonomy in a democratic society. This reveals a genuine conflict, which cannot be resolved by applying the efficiency criterion of privacy protection.

The preservation of privacy and autonomy in the face of the mechanisms of social control afforded by bureaucratic surveillance requires countervailing power. Individuals equipped with nothing more than constitutional guarantees of their inalienable rights are no match for the armed police power of the state or the extensive capital resources of large organizations. Rule clearly recognizes the imbalance between center and peripheries, but fails to provide a convincing method for redressing it.

Social Change by Hortatory Moral Appeal?

Although I agree with Rule's rejection of programmatic remedies, I doubt that his call for resistance to bureaucratic surveillance can provide adequate protection against the erosion of privacy and autonomy. Hortatory moral appeals are notoriously ineffective, especially when they run counter to established social trends and the interests of powerful organizations. Imagine the predicament of industrial workers in the absence of unions to represent their interests. To what extent would the entrepreneur's appetite for profit have been curbed by appeals to conscience, from whatever quarter, on behalf of society's need to raise the living standard of the working class? Or, to take a different analogy, how much crime would be prevented by admonishing criminals to mend their ways for the good of all?

Rule states that "organizational monitoring of people is of a piece with broad ranges of other bureaucratic activity." This clearly implies that the bureaucratic appetite for personal information is not a sometime thing. Organizations are not likely to alter their mode of operation so as to lessen discriminations among people in the application of their resources simply by virtue of moral appeals from intellectuals and scientists. Like the industrialist of the nineteenth century, the manager of today is not particularly troubled by bad conscience. On the contrary, he prides himself on the rectitude of his commitment to bureaucratic surveillance which he believes to be a boon to society, and this commitment is reinforced by ready public acceptance of monitoring in exchange for services.

Cost-effectiveness arguments might carry weight in some instances, but it is highly doubtful that organizations could be persuaded by moral arguments to compromise their own concrete interests, as Rule suggests they might, in favor of abstract principles. Something with more teeth than an appeal to conscience is required.

Devolution

I do not presume to have a programmatic solution to the problem of bureaucratic surveillance. My criticism, admittedly unfair, of Rule's paper is that it stops short of examining the root causes of bureaucratic surveillance and thus does not furnish a basis for a critique which might lead to concrete proposals for social change. The arguments that Rule develops to expose the weaknesses of the procedural approach to privacy reform apply to his own suggestions to resist further bureaucratic intrusions on privacy and autonomy. Just as the efficiency criterion advanced by the procedural reformers leaves the data collection authority intact, Rule's appeal for restraint fails to challenge the legitimacy of a social system which relies increasingly on bureaucratic surveillance as a means of social control.

Rule observes that "a fundamental trend in modern, highly developed societies is the progressive centralization of social control in large bureaucracies." A concomitant of centralization is the diminution of local forms of control. Otto von Gierke, in his monumental study of the law of associations in Western culture, revealed the full significance of this diminution. According to Gierke (1938) modern history records a combat in which "the Sovereign State and the Sovereign Individual contended over the delimitation of the provinces assigned to them by Natual Law, and in the course of that struggle all intermediate groups were first degraded into the more or less arbitrarily fashioned creatures of mere Positive Law, and in the end were obliterated [p. 100]."

With the triumph of individualism, which destroyed the oppressive bonds of status and membership characteristic of life in the Middle Ages, new forms of social control came into existence. These new forms, fashioned by the interplay of economic and religious individualism under the growing shadow of the nation state, are still very much with us (Nisbet, 1953). Privacy and autonomy are at issue today precisely because the locus of social control has shifted to the large organizations which have emerged from this upheaval.

We have exchanged the personal solicitude of medieval corporate control for the impersonal solicitude of bureaucratic surveillance. Both the medieval and the modern applications of social control attest to a fine line between solicitude and oppression—a fact that should not be ignored in contemplating new arrangements. Nevertheless, the germ of a solution to the problem of preserving privacy and autonomy lies, I believe, in the idea of devolution. This idea did not originate with our generation, but has recently gained popularity through the writings of Illich, Schumacher, Roszak, and others. Whether one speaks of conviviality, smallness, or community, the plea is for decentralization of control and the revitalization of local centers of authority.

A variety of concrete initiatives aimed at devolution could be coupled with Rule's call for resistance to bureaucratic surveillance. The principle is to return social functions to local associations wherever feasible. If, for example, each level of government were to provide only those services requiring its jurisdictional spread, many services now administered by large bureaucracies could be provided locally. Treatment of questions of cost and efficiency in the public sector could set an example by attempting to deal seriously with externalities and with the relative social costs of large scale versus small scale operations. Higher levels of government could ensure equity through the exercise of fiscal controls rather than through direct bureaucratic intervention. Local producer and consumer cooperatives could be encouraged by means of tax incentives and subsidies.

My aim here is not to elaborate a detailed program of social reform, but to provoke debate on the fundamental issues of privacy and autonomy. A necessary condition, it seems to me, for preserving privacy and autonomy is that we cease to be clients and become members of the organizations that serve us.

References

de Tocqueville, A. *Democracy in America*, Vol. 2. New York: Knopf, 1945. (Reprint.)

Ellul, J. *The technological society*. New York: Vintage Books, 1964.

Gierke, O. V. *Political theories of the Middle Age*. Cambridge: Cambridge Univeristy Press, 1938.

Mowshowitz, A. *The conquest of will*. Reading, Mass.: Addison-Wesley, 1976.

Mowshowitz. A. Computing power and political opportunism. Technical report, Department of Computer Science, Cornell University, Ithaca, New York, 1977.

Nisbet, R. *The quest for community*. Oxford: Oxford Univeristy Press, 1953.

Winner, L. *Autonomous technology*. Cambridge, Mass.: MIT Press, 1977.

Stressing Design Rather Than Performance Standards to Ensure Protection of Information: Comments

T. D. Sterling

An increasing amount of legislation is addressed to preservation of privacy and security of system files.* It is motivated by concerns that information in the files of large public and private organizations and especially of government agencies may be misused; that it may be utilized for unlawful surveillance of individuals; that it may be combined with other information and form a potentially revealing pointer to an individual's whereabouts and activities.

Much of the thinking and attitudes underlying present legislation seeks to establish standards of *performance*. By performance standard we mean that the burden is on the government, on some watchdog agency, or on individuals to show violations.

Take the case of the Privacy Act of 1975, signed into law December, 1974. This is a significant piece of legislation which requires federal agencies to permit the individual to determine what records pertaining to him or her are collected, maintained, used, or disseminated, and to gain access to that information, to have a copy made, and to amend or emend such records. Without distracting from the value of this act, it is clear that individual initiative is required to search for records and implement whatever changes might be required. It is also clear that that type of legislation will work as long as only a relatively small number of individuals take advantage of their rights. A similar argument can be made of the Fair Credit Reporting Act. The act specifies that a report on a consumer may not contain certain information, such as bankruptcies older than 14 years, or judgments, paid tax liens, accounts placed for collection, records of arrest, indictment or conviction of crime, and other adverse items of information that are older than 7 years. How does one

---

*The 95th Congress alone passed more than 80 pieces of legislation addressed to deal with privacy and data security problems. (From comment of R. L. Chartrand, pp. 125–131.)

COMPUTERS AND PRIVACY
IN THE NEXT DECADE

ensure that individual records do not contain such information? It requires not only the initiative of individuals to check their own records on files to which they do not have complete access, but also places a burden on credit organizations to review their own files, a review which they may not have the means to conduct even if they had the intentions of doing so. State and municipal legislation now being written may give citizens sweeping rights including the right to sue the state in case of damage, but the proposed legislation still requires the individual to initiate monitoring and supervisory procedures.

While, on paper, organizations may be required to update and evaluate records in their files (and sometimes such requirements are implied rather than specifically stated), performance actions need to be initiated with special grants and infusions of monies. If funds are lacking, then incorrect information may be permitted to remain on file with potential harm to the affected individuals. Typical is a case encountered by the Computer Ombudsman of Vancouver. An individual discovered that his name was on file as a possible criminal with the Royal Canadian Mounted Police (RCMP) because his name and identification had been used as an alias by an armed robber. In the end, he was unable to remove that potentially damaging record because removing it hinged upon the decision to reevaluate all records in Canada's Crime Information System, which was not done because of lack of adequate funding (Sterling, 1980). Such an example may be typical for U.S. agencies as well. Being swamped with data, they might correct a particular record in case of direct inquiry, but the necessary means may be lacking to constantly update and evaluate information on files unless the funds, the work force, the time and, for that matter, the intentions are there. Thus legislation requiring agencies to update and evaluate their records may be unenforceable from the very beginning.

Using performance standards to monitor manipulations of individual files not only is difficult to enforce but seeks to correct possible abuses after they have occurred. One of the major difficulties faced in monitoring uses of individual records is the facility with which records may be combined and screened through administrative fiat. Decisions to process combined records may be made on some administrative level that is far removed from the locus of record control. In the end, neither duly elected legislators nor stockholders may have much say in the use of individual records. Lest this situation be viewed as a future threat, I draw attention to the increasing use of MATCH type programs by government agencies. Project MATCH first compared a list of 6000 persons of the Washington payroll of the Department of Health, Education and Welfare (DHEW) with welfare rolls of the District of Columbia. It was successful in ferreting out individuals on welfare who simultaneously were employed by the District of Columbia, who were ineligible for welfare or, for other reasons, were overpaid. MATCH was expanded in 1978 and now screens federal and military employees. Here are other current examples of MATCH type actions. Social Security numbers of former students are matched to files of federal workers to detect those who had not paid back student loans. Dishonest physicians and pharmacists are detected by checking Medicaid records for patients that have been treated often or repeatedly for the same diseases. The Treasury Department runs an enforcement communications systems (TECS) for the U.S. Customs service with thousands of names of suspected smugglers, in cooperation with the Drug Enforcement Administration, the Bureau of Alcohol, Tobacco and Fire Arms, the Internal Revenue Service, the Department of State, the Immigration and Naturalization Service and, of course, with various national and international police agencies.

Not to be misunderstood, let me stress that there is nothing objectionable in locating welfare swindlers. There is nothing objectionable in locating any sort of swindler, smuggler, or criminal. Questions ought to be raised, however, about the extent to which a search through linked files may be carried out before it meets constitutional restraints. No less important is the question of who may decide what sort of search is to be carried out. Who is to be monitored and by which department? There are dangers here to the security of individuals and their private lives. There are opportunities here for large-scale abuses and, above all, there are dangers here to democratic institutions.

John Shattuck (1978), Director of the Washington office of the American Civil Liberties Union pointed out to the secretary of HEW that project MATCH exemplified "precisely the kind of manipulation of personal data that people most fear when they contemplate the vulnerability of their privacy in a computer age. We cannot think of any better example of a constitutionally prescribed general search than a random rummaging through the contents of massive record systems on the chance that 'something will turn up'." Can we rely exclusively for control over arbitrary surveillance on watchdog agencies? It may even be questionable to what extent alarms raised by such agencies are heeded or effective.

Thus, performance standards may not be adequate to deal with the multiple threats to the individual's security in our democratic haven.

In fact, performance standards have proven to be inadequate safeguards in the one situation which they have been specifically intended to control—to safeguard workers from excessive exposure to toxic and hazardous substances in the workplace. In order to force industrial establishments and employers to provide reasonably safe working conditions, the Occupational Safety and Health Administration (OSHA) has relied almost exclusively on performance standards. The result has been a bewildering number of often bizarre regulations mixed with many very much needed rules. At the same time, OSHA cannot really monitor more than a small fraction of possible violations. It is open to question if, in a modern industrial economy, compliance with the multitude of rules even can be monitored. Even with monitoring, violations are almost impossible to detect.*

Yet, if employers were forced to use design standards, control measures often could be introduced that would prevent contamination beyond some set criterion. For instance, levels of fumes or gases are controlled by prescribed threshold levels that require the employer, the union, or the government to monitor the air in the workplace. Very often, such rules are bolstered by making available personal protection equipment. Yet a desired standard may be met simply by requiring the employer to establish proper and adequate ventilation. Evaluation of performance may not be eliminated completely, it never is, but the need for review of performance may decrease to the point where it becomes practically feasible.

Gaining Control over What Is Done with Information as a Major Design Criterion

We may start with a conclusion shared by many, that there may not be a way to keep information private, safe, or secret (Gottlieb and Brodin, 1973; Miller, 1971; DHEW, 1973; Westin, 1971). Of course, one could simply not collect a particular class of information. However, that would not be desirable in many instances. If collecting information and putting it on a computer is both unavoidable and creates a hazard for data subjects, the way out may be to prescribe very carefully what may be done with the information. Thus, one design standard to safeguard the security of information may be to control the instances for which it may be used. This is what we mean by designing *use control.*

In essence, design for use control means that the only programs permitted to be used for a set of data may be those wich have passed public muster. The underlying software, the system that permits access to the computer, can be made to trigger an alarm any time a program is loaded into the machine that is not properly identified, recognized, and authorized. Enforcement of such a design rule would make it less important to consider how secure a particular file is or how to monitor its security. What counts is what may be done with the information on file. Any affected agency would be entitled to run only previously cleared programs, approved analysis, producing a set of approved printouts. Nothing else should be permitted. If and when a public or semipublic organization (and perhaps even a large corporation) wishes to add another analysis to its lists of programs it should have to clear that program and

---

*See for instance the tedious process with which number of asbestos fibers per cubic centimeter of air are determined, still with appreciable error of estimate (DHEW, 1976).

analysis first with a supervisory body. Perhaps, in addition an *impact statement* ought to be submitted with any proposed new program. (The same rules could cover such semipublic services as banking, and especially electronic funds transfer.)

References

Gotlieb C. C., and Borodin, A. *Social issues in computing.* New York: Academic Press, 1973.

Miller, A. R. *The assault on privacy.* Ann Arbor, Mich.: University of Michigan Press, 1971.

Sterling, T. D. The computer ombudsman: A possible model for accountability. *Transactions of Society,* 1980, 17.

U. S. Department of Health, Education, and Welfare. *Revised recommended asbestos standards.* Washington, D. C.: U.S. Government Printing Office, 1976.

U. S. Department of Health, Education and Welfare. *Records, computers, and the rights of citizens.* Cambridge, Mass.: MIT Press, 1973.

Shattuck, J. quoted in *U.S. News and World Report,* April 10, 1978.

Westin, A. F. *Information technology in a democracy.* Cambridge, Mass.: Harvard University Press, 1971.

Privacy Implications of Transborder Data Flows: Outlook for the 1980s

H.P. Gassmann

Introduction

The 1970s have seen a spectacular increase of computers in Western democracies. As automatically processed information systems have grown, legal, organizational, and technical safeguards for their access, handling, dissemination, and storage have been introduced in many countries. With a growing number of countries having their own privacy or data legislation, and the emergence of international data transmission, the international regulatory aspects of these transborder data flows have become important today with respect to national privacy protection legislation.

While the general principles of privacy protection in the United States, Canada, and the European countries are largely similar, there were, at the beginning of 1979, significant differences in their implementation. This obviously creates some problems so far as the transnational regulatory aspects are concerned. Differences among countries are already evident in the raising of the computer privacy issue. These concerns have been expressed in various terms: "the need to protect people's privacy" is a favorite term in English-speaking countries, whereas the Scandinavian and German-speaking countries in Europe prefer the notion of "data protection." The French think about this problem in terms of "data processing and individual freedom" (*informatique et libertés individuelles*).

These implementation differences can be briefly sketched as follows:

1. In the United States, there are partial privacy laws, by sector, whereas in European countries a comprehensive, "omnibus" approach is taken, with one single privacy law covering the private and the public sector.

*The opinions expressed in this paper are those of the author alone and do not necessarily represent the views of the OECD.

109

COMPUTERS AND PRIVACY
IN THE NEXT DECADE

2. In many European countries, privacy laws apply only to automatically processed personal data, whereas in the United States, privacy protection legislation does not specifically mention the form of processing; hence, manually processed data are also included. However, the German Federal Data Protection Law covers both manual and automatically processed data.

3. No special machinery in the form of specialized agencies or commissions exists in the United States to monitor and supervise the application of privacy legislation. Enforcement of the law is carried out by the judiciary. In Europe, on the other hand, many countries have special data-protection boards or commissions with special staff, which have a watchdog and regulatory function to supervise the application of privacy legislation.

4. During 1978, Norway, Denmark, and Austria passed privacy protection laws, whose scope also extends to legal persons; no such legislation exists or is contemplated in the United States, at least not at the federal level.

The implications of these differences in privacy legislation among countries and especially between the two sides of the Atlantic are rather far-reaching, particularly concerning the treatment of transborder movements of personal data.

In trying to explore what these implications could be in the 1980s, several trends and factors need to be addressed:

1. What kind of new international information infrastructures are evolving?
2. What trends of privacy legislation, and its implementation can be seen, especially in its international dimension?
3. How might transborder data flow (TBDF) develop?
4. What kind of agreements are needed, and what cooperation mechanisms might become necessary?

The period of the 1980s is treated in two parts. First, the period from 1979–1984, on which reasonable assumptions can be made, mainly from the extrapolation of present trends; and the second period from 1985–1989, where nothing more than intelligent speculations can be put forward.

The Period 1979–1984

It is probable that in this period the use of all kinds of information machines will grow. On the one hand, we will see national and international data networks taking up operation in a substantive way. On the other hand, we will witness microprocessors making possible inexpensive personal computing. It is likely that these two trends may be linked in the form of personal computers having data transmission capabilities; that is, they will be linked to substantive data bases or host computers via the ordinary telephone system.

National and international data networks will become operational during 1979–1981. Examples are Euronet (scheduled to start service in July, 1979), Venus for Japanese international data transmission (1979), Nordic Data Network for the Scandinavian countries (1980), and the ATT proposal for Advanced Communications Service (ACS) (1980?).

Since multinational firms are increasingly demanding *one* provider for all their various communication needs, and technology makes this feasible, plans for satellite business systems are laid, and Satellite Business Systems (SBS) expects to start service of an integrated voice, data, facsimile communication and teleconferencing service in 1981.

Speaking more generally, future business communications will take place largely through electronic means, so that electronic mail, electronic funds transfer (EFT), and viewdata facilities for business information will develop greatly and will constitute strong growth markets.

In Europe, Japan, and Canada, it is expected that home information services, such as videotex services, will develop rapidly. These services consist of linking a suitably modified television set equipped with a touch-tone pad to remote data bases using normal telephone lines.

The central question concerning privacy protection is how much personal data will be handled, stored, and transmitted by these systems? Will the existing first-generation laws on privacy protection curb the rapid growth and dissemination of personal information in electronic form, or will the market forces be so strong that collection and dissemination of such data will continue to increase at the same pace as they have done so far, but adhering to the new provisions and safeguards as enunciated in privacy protection legislation?

It is probable that by 1982–1983, we might see a generalization of second-generation privacy laws—those covering not only physical persons (private lives), but also extending to legal persons (business lives). At present, at least in Europe, there exists a clear trend toward such legislation, since all new European privacy protection legislation passed in 1978 (Norway, Denmark, Austria) and 1979 (Luxembourg) contains provisions on legal persons. It should be noticed, however, that so far the extension of privacy legislation to legal persons has occurred only in smaller countries, where a relatively large number of small- and medium-sized firms exist, and where the legislator has found it necessary to treat legal persons in a similar way to physical persons. The main argument to do that is the belief that for small businesses, say shopowners or insurance agents, it is often difficult to distinguish the quality of information on the owner of the business: information on him or her as a physical person (his or her private life) or as a legal person (his or her firm).

Another feature of privacy protection legislation, which might be achieved during 1980–1984, is the general acceptance of the notion that manual data and automated data should be treated in the same way. We will probably see a rapid generalization of the notion of privacy protection of personal data regardless of how they are handled or processed.

The international division of labor, which is still growing and is impacting more and more information activities, calls for further proliferation of information streams. We will probably see a greater focus on information in ever-narrowing segments of professional activity. This is simply an expression of structural change. Already today we are witnessing important shifts of white-collar information activities of the industrial sector toward activities in the private service sector. This means that activities that were once carried out by industrial firms themselves (such as market research, tax advice, legal advice, executive talent research, and computer and software services), are increasingly carried out by specialized consultant or service firms, which typically constitute activities of the service sector.

For these reasons it is reasonable to expect that the data streams between corporate clients and their "information activities subcontractors" may considerably increase. A good example in the personal data field are the executive talent search firms, called "headhunters" for short.* Once, one of the important functions of top management and the head of personnel was the search for good executives. Today, the performance of this function has become a very profitable business carried out by specialized consultant firms that operate at the international level. The correspondence between the consultant firm and the client deals mostly with personal data and has become very specialized. In most cases, it is not transmitted by automatic means because there is a need for confidentiality and prestige best answered by hand-typed letters and hand-transmitted elegant canvas folders. However, the background material for prospective candidates (curriculum vitae, interview results, etc.) is in many cases already kept by the executive talent search firm in a computerized data base, or will be in the near future. This data base is accessed remotely via terminals often located in another country by the consultant firm's various branches. The example shows how personal data streams can grow rapidly due to specialization of functions. In the past, this very confidential information was handled inside a firm in manual form and never left it.

It is safe to assume that these developments of specialization from industrial firms to private service companies will continue in the future; they might create a critical data mass for which it is economical to automate the personal data handling and make access by terminals very easy; and this increases transborder flows of personal data.

Another trend toward increasing data flows comes from information

*See "The Headhunters Come upon Golden Days," *Fortune*, October 1978, page 102.

technology itself. Although during the 1960s and early 1970s computer technology favored a concentration of information streams in private business, banking, or public administration into large computer centers, present and future computer and communications technology will favor decentralization. More precisely, centralization of storage and of access occurred in the past, whereas the present trend is toward a centralization of storage in large data bases with a decentralized input or access, and even decentralization of storage in small computer units. The implications of these developments are clear: Electronic mail, EFT, and videotex applications will grow dramatically, and with them the flow of all kinds of data, including personal data.

The year 1984 will be Orwell year. As things look today, at least for Western democratic countries, the Orwellian prophecy might not come true. From a technological point of view, although Orwell did not know the present computer and communications technologies in detail, he described rather correctly the functions made possible by these technologies. In the wake of World War II his fiction predicted an all-powerful state and complete control of the individual by this state using modern technology. However, during the 1970s, there was great preoccupation in Western democracies with privacy protection as the most modern form of human rights, in some cases triggered off by widespread fears of the public and some scandals. This has caused a tendency in these countries to create a tight societal control mechanism on the utilization of computer power. Today, these controls are effected either through the judiciary system (such as in the United States) or through some independent commissions or boards (the situation in many European countries), with some representation of the various segments of society in the data protection commissions.

It may be that in the general line of increased public preoccupation with science and technology developments, the citizens at large might ask for more and more participation in the control of computer systems. If this trend persists, it is possible that citizens may request continuous control and monitoring of public data policies through "citizen data control boards." This might be the case for the utilization of sensitive data held by public or semipublic institutions, such as in the fields of law enforcement, health, education, and, in the private sector, banking and insurance.

Technology will lead to increased data flows, as already discussed. Whether or not TBDF of personal data will increase drastically will depend on the degree of political integration or closer cooperation among countries. It is possible that the various privacy protection laws may severely limit the amount of personal data transmitted abroad, unless an international convention can do away with specific controls for those countries which adhere to such a convention. This is the aim of the guidelines on transborder data flows presently being developed by the Organization for Economic Cooperation and Development

(OECD) in Paris for its 24 member countries, and by the Convention of the Council of Europe, which covers the 21 European member states and will also be open to other countries.

The OECD guidelines are expected to be ready by the end of 1979 and to apply as of 1980. They might well develop into an international convention, if enough consensus on a need for such an OECD-wide convention can be found. The Council of Europe Convention is expected to be ready by the end of 1979, and will be sent to countries with the invitation to have it ratified by their respective parliaments. This will take time, and recommendations stemming from the convention will probably not become effective before 1982–1983.

While up to now the notion of "data havens" has been an intellectually attractive nonreality, it may be that increasing data regulation could indeed influence the motivation to construct such data havens in some remote, paradisaic, and cheap-labor locations, especially since satellite technology with rooftop antennas will greatly facilitate global communications in the next few years. It is therefore necessary that national privacy safeguards be continuously checked to make sure that continuing technological progress and its practical utilization does not infringe on the individual's privacy.

During the early 1980s, we will witness the emergence of many national and international data networks. This situation can be compared to the one existing when international civil aviation emerged on a mass scale after World War II. Most national airlines had their statutes and regulatory and controlling mechanisms at a national level, but there was a need for international standards, rules, and recommendations for tariffs, so that the various national airlines could offer a service that was comparable in quality, price, safety, and, in the case of disaster, liabilities. This is why the International Civil Aviation Organization (ICAO) was founded in 1947.

International data networks will soon face a similar need for more uniform rules for the provision of information or data services that are comparable in quality, price, access rules, and security, and that offer a certain degree of liability. In a way, networks need to be certified or perhaps even licensed to guarantee compliance with certain minimum international standards, including privacy protection standards. A relevant example already exists: In 1977 the Swedish Data Inspection Board visited the Brussels headquarters of SWIFT (the international finance transaction network to which more than 600 banks adhere now) and inquired about its privacy and security conditions before granting Swedish banks the license to connect to this network.

The aforementioned increasing centralization of data streams will, however, probably increase the so-called vulnerability of computerized societies. It will be necessary to make sure that in the design of new data systems, both organizational and technical vulnerability aspects are taken into account much more explicitly than in the past. This, in turn, might have an impact on the economic viability of such systems. It might slow down the trend toward inexpensive data processing and might also slow down the substitution of information capital (automatic computerized data systems) for information labor. A parallel is to be seen here with the effects of environmental regulations, which today are resulting in marked cost increases of the provision of basic public utilities such as water and electricity.

We have already seen that in 1979 there are marked differences between Europe and the United States in privacy protection machinery—specialized commissions or agencies in European countries, no machinery in the United States. What are we to do and where are we to go if TBDF regulation problems arise? A bilateral approach might be the fastest, simplest, and most efficient—and certainly will be used in many cases. But what if there were several countries involved? Only a multilateral approach will help if an international system of privacy protection needs adaptation or firming up. In this case the best solution might be a consultative mechanism, as already proposed in the OECD guidelines: a commission or committee that meets regularly two or three times a year and can consider trouble areas, improve bilateral communications, and regularly review privacy protection implementation, with special regard to TBDF of personal information.

This would enable the U.S. federal or state administrations to see their OECD partners regularly, and to resolve potential TBDF problems which in the absence of a privacy protection focus would be otherwise difficult to tackle.

The Period 1985–1989

For this time period, it can be anticipated that TBDF will have increased enormously, owing to the general utilization of international data networks. Since on-line situations will be very frequent and inexpensive, there might be a natural temptation to overuse data-communication facilities. International business, international banking, international providers of all kinds of information services, and, of course, international tourism, might have increased to proportions unknown today. The driving force behind this is the continuing international division of labor and a general trend toward more leisure.

Since energy might have become very expensive, there will be strong motivation to substitute some forms of physical business travel with teleconferencing and all sorts of data and voice transmission. This again forms a strong positive growth element for increased TBDF.

It can also be anticipated that by 1985 the Western industrialized countries will have become "mature" in the privacy protection movement. There is a likelihood that they will have evolved more toward real information societies.

While the Western democracies will continue to rely strongly on the balance of powers within their governments to the classical three government powers—the legislative, the executive, and the judiciary—a fourth will have been associated. Already in the 1970s, the press and the mass media were called the "fourth power"—a strong power if we consider, for example, the role played by the American press in the Watergate scandal. During the 1960s and 1970s this information power existed, but it was not institutionalized.

The emergence of data or privacy protection commissions during the 1970s paved the way toward a more institutionalized control of certain aspects of this information power. After 1985, these bodies may have evolved toward "data policy commissions," completely independent of the other three powers. In their policymaking they will follow criteria not only of a social, economic, and political nature, but also of a cultural and behavioral nature. Because they are able, through regulation, to influence the quality, direction, and nature of information streams, they will have a very important safety-valve function for the whole social system. They might become essential to avoid or dampen destabilization attempts of the political system, while at the same time effectively ensuring the high standards of human rights of the individual in the limits imposed by values and economy.

On a world scale, many nations that today are still counted in the developing countries cohort will have developed to such an extent that they, in turn, will have built up impressive computer and communication facilities, with a consequent need for more privacy protection. The degree of such protection will obviously depend on the political system of such countries, but to a certain extent it is safe to assume that regardless of the political system there will emerge a general need for the protection of particular data about individuals not to be accessed freely. Transborder data flow which at present is taking place primarily across the Atlantic, and to a lesser extent across the Pacific, might increasingly take place in a north–south dimension. It is possible that privacy protection laws of such newcomers might be rather different from the Western type of privacy laws, because they might protect information that is worthwhile protecting in a different value system. This could also have the consequence that data protection mechanisms at national level might be very different. While in Western countries these mechanisms will probably evolve toward increasingly citizen-oriented participatory control, it may be that in other countries a more government-controlled situation might prevail. While developed countries will become ever more decentralized in the use of computer systems, many of the developing countries might prefer, for economic and political reasons, more centralized systems.

This might pose some new problems of international cooperation in the privacy protection field, and it is an entirely open question as to what kinds of international cooperation mechanisms will evolve.

Conclusion

During the 1980s, because of the ease and cheapness of treating and processing information, we might face a severe information overload. People might become increasingly allergic to an information pollution. In a mass society, privacy might well constitute a precious value, which to protect and defend becomes *the* most modern form of human rights.

This will be the case not only at national, but also at international level. Care must be taken that modern information technology, which is welcome because of its innovation and revitalizing potential, does not alienate the citizen and does not provoke rejection effects which can already be observed in some other technologies, such as nuclear reactors.

Therefore, preventive action for privacy protection is essential. The public at large needs to be widely informed about these developments. Both public and private policymakers should attach great value to these measures, and in the implementation of new data systems, they should seek a large consensus on their use from the people directly or indirectly affected.

The 1980s might well be a decisive decade for the emergence of a world government. In the struggle for influence, two systems face each other; the pluralistic, individual-oriented Western democracies, and the monolithic, state-oriented Eastern countries. The Western values of human rights and self-determination are among the most important cards in this game. Privacy protection should enhance both values. This is a challenge which should be taken very seriously, even if we have to pay a price for it.

It is to be hoped that the opinion often heard today, that privacy protection may become too expensive and should therefore be kept to a minimum, will disappear. The costs of privacy protection are negligible if compared to the sums spent on car safety (and accidents), alcohol, tobacco, and other drugs. Even if the price were high, it would be worthwhile paying it for the goal of preserving the privacy of the individual.

/

Comment on "Privacy Implications of Transborder Data Flows"

Rein Turn

Gassmann's paper summarizes very well the concerns of numerous OECD countries regarding privacy rights of individuals vis-à-vis organizations that maintain personal information records about them, and the similarities and differences of the national privacy protection laws that about eight of these countries have enacted to date in response to these concerns. It appears that each new law has broadened the scope of coverage beyond what earlier laws in other countries have provided, and explicit privacy protection requirements regarding transborder data flows are being included. Thus, the so-called second-generation privacy protection laws are emerging.

Privacy Protection in Transborder Data Flows

Concerns about privacy protection in transborder data flows (TBDF) arise from the recent growth in internationally operated computer communication systems and the attendant increases in the amount of data transmitted over these systems. Some of the data involved are personal information about individuals, and it is considered necessary in countries where such data flows originate to be able to extend any available privacy rights to any country where the personal information in question may be sent. Some countries have taken the view that data protected by their national privacy protection laws should not be sent to countries where privacy protection laws are weaker or do not cover personal data about nonresidents. Hence, there is the possibility that so-called "nontariff barriers" may be set up to restrict data flows across national boundaries and stifle what is referred to as the "free flow of information."

I would like to make a few observations about this situation from the broader context that has been brought up in the media and at conferences on data

119

regulation. In rather general terms, transnational computer communication systems could be classified as (1) internationally operated data processing service bureaus, (2) private systems operated by or subscribed to by multinational business firms, (3) systems operated by international business or industry associations, and (4) international public data networks. It is well known that most of these systems are headquartered in the United States and, thus, data flows are rather unidirectional.

From this perspective, countries could be classified as "data importing-information products exporting" and "data exporting-information products importing." The United States is a prominent member of the first class. Nearly all European countries that have enacted privacy protection legislation could be regarded as members of the second class, the data exporting countries (even though with respect to Third World countries the European countries, too, may be data importing and information products exporting—there is a hierarchial structure here). It is interesting to observe that differences in privacy laws correlate very well with this classification of countries; those of data exporting countries tend to have stronger provisions and a broader scope of coverage (e.g., the most recent national privacy protection laws have extended protection to legal persons in addition to physical persons, and both the public and the private sectors tend to be covered in an omnibus manner by essentially the same set of provisions.

Data exporting countries have expressed other concerns that, as maintained by various parties in data importing countries, are part of the rationale for strong privacy protection–data protection laws: (1) vulnerability to disruption of industrial operations or government functions when the required data are processed or stored abroad, (2) desire to achieve self-sufficiency in data processing despite the higher costs this may entail (as illustrated by Brazil), and (3) inability of domestic data processing industry to compete with services provided by internationally operated systems. From the viewpoint of these concerns, data exporting countries would like to reduce the use of data processing services from abroad; perhaps by restricting the types of data that may be sent abroad. Data importing countries certainly would like to continue benefiting from their strong business position abroad in marketing data processing services and, thus, are strongly in favor of a status quo (i.e., no constraints on free flow of information).

It is maintained by some that privacy protection (data protection) laws could be used as vehicles by data exporting countries to achieve the foregoing goals of reduced vulnerability, self-sufficiency in data processing, and increased business for domestic data processing services and industry, using the principle that protected data should not be exported to countries where protection is weaker. Indeed, the greater the mismatch, the stronger is the justification for applying this principle and the more effective the result (from the exporting countries' viewpoint). Against the application of this principle, data importing countries want to play down any discrepancies and show that they can satisfy the data protection requirements in the data exporter's laws (e.g., by voluntary compliance with those requirements). The scope of protection of all but the most recent data protection laws is too narrow to be useful for the above purposes—only physical persons are covered. Only a small fraction of TBDF deals with physical persons (mostly information about employees of trans-national organizations and information associated with tourism and travel). However, if data protection is extended to cover legal persons as well, then nearly all types of data would be subject to protection requirements in privacy laws, and they would be effective in regulating TBDF so long as data-importing countries could not sufficiently match the privacy protection requirements of the data exporting countries. However, any country broadening the scope of its privacy protection laws to provide for itself more options for regulating TBDF must also bear in mind the domestic implications of broader protection requirements: political, economic, and even technical. Excessive regulation of domestic organizations may negate any gains that could be expected from uses of these laws for regulating transborder data flows.

Minimal Privacy Protection Requirements

As discussed by Gassmann, there are now two international efforts un-derway to define minimal privacy protection requirements to be adopted by communities of nations to harmonize their privacy protection laws and, thus, satisfy at least in part privacy requirements for transborder data flows. The Council of Europe member-countries, all in Europe and all data exporters according to the classification system I am using, are expected to adopt a mandatory Data Protection Convention. The OECD member countries (data exporters as well as data importers) are developing a set of voluntary Data Protection Guidelines. As a result of resolutions adopted at the SPIN Con-ference, the Third World nations are likely to launch an effort on transborder data flows, self-sufficiency in informatics, and erosion of national sovereignty due to foreign dominance in informatics.

Both the Council of Europe and the OECD at the present time are debating the scope of coverage and the types of privacy protection requirements to be included in the Convention and the Guidelines, respectively. As can be expected, representatives of data exporting countries are urging broader scope of coverage and stronger requirements. Representatives of data importing countries strive for the opposite, except for one particular item: They insist on the inclusion of manually maintained (not-directly-computer-readable data) records, too. This is one area where the privacy laws in data importing countries (e.g., the United States) tend to be stronger than those in most of the data exporting countries. The outcome of these debates will certainly have strong effects on the future of TBDF and privacy protection laws that other countries will adopt. It is also likely to have a strong effect on the approach that will be taken toward transborder data flows by the Third World countries and Intergovernmental Bureau of Informatics.

If the OECD guidelines debate is resolved by excluding legal persons and including manually processed data, the guidelines will, indeed, be strongly focused on protecting individual privacy, rather than giving the appearance of protecting the data processing interests of data exporting countries. However, inclusion of manually processed personal information makes implementation and enforcement more difficult.

Independently of the details of the scope of coverage of the guidelines or other international agreements,certain procedural and technical means must be developed for making it easy for the individuals concerned to exercise their privacy rights in TBDF situations. Hence it seems clear that those organizations in the individuals' home countries that send personal data abroad should be responsible for serving as interfaces between the individuals and the data processing organizatons abroad. While the latter should be required to assure (e.g., through contractual agreements) that confidentiality and security of the data are maintained and that their quality is not degraded, these organizations cannot be held responsible for the uses made of these data by their international customers that may be in violation of privacy protection laws or for the original quality of the data for the purposes they are used (e.g., relevance, completeness, timeliness, original accuracy). It would be quite preposterous to require a foreign data processing bureau to seek more personal information on individuals in other countries in order to improve the completeness of personal information records kept in the system by their customers. The situation is different, of course, when the organization abroad is also a first-hand collector of personal information on individuals in other countries, as might be the case in international consumer credit reporting or mailing list organizations.

It is quite important that the procedural and technical aspects of implementing privacy protection requirements in national as well as transborder privacy protection laws, conventions, or guidelines be considered while these requirements are still being formulated and drafted for inclusion in such instruments. Otherwise there is a definite possibility that the adopted requirements cannot be implemented effectively and the protection they are to provide will remain largely illusory.

Some of these observations may appear to be overly cynical or unfair to those who are striving to strengthen human rights in the TBDF area. However, the existence of ulterior motives has been suggested many times and the suggested scenarios appear too plausible to be left unexplored. Indeed, there appears to exist sufficient circumstantial evidence to suggest that the use of privacy protection laws to achieve other ends is contemplated by some. Meanwhile, as Gassmann points out, the technological imperative is at work—new computer communication systems are emerging and new applications will require increased transborder traffic in personal information. It would be irresponsible not to be concerned about protecting individual privacy vis-à-vis global record-keeping systems.

Comment on "Privacy Implications of Transborder Data Flow"*

Robert L. Chartrand

Introduction

Within the lifetime of contemporary human beings, there has been a spectacular revolution in communications and the ability to collect, process, and disseminate information. As recently as the 1930s, the man-on-the-street reveled vicariously in the adventures of Richard Halliburton and Lowell Thomas; or, if one sought a slightly more vintage treatment of those faraway places with the strange sounding names, there were always the writings of Sir Richard Burton and Sir Henry Stanley.

Today, with the advent of transoceanic cables, radio technology, and communications satellites, modern man can reach out and maintain contact with other individuals and institutions around the globe. In the decades since World War II the means of spanning great distances have diversified, with as many new names to be learned and understood as the dozens of appellations which now identify fledgling nations. Those who deal with such matters, either within a policymaking context or as program overseers, having mastered such terms as computers, telecommunications, facsimile, microforms, and the like must now cope with packet switching, bubble memories, fiber optics, holography, and various laser applications.

For those with specific concern about the transfer of data across national boundaries—a matter justifying an increasingly intensive focus around the world—there must be developed, with a sense of urgency, an accurate perception of this prismatic problem in the sharing of information resources:

---

*The views expressed in this paper are those of the author and are not necessarily those of the Congressional Research Service or the Library of Congress.

COMPUTERS AND PRIVACY
IN THE NEXT DECADE

1. What information is *wanted* by the various components of a given user community?
2. What information is *really needed* by them?
3. Which mechanisms can best collect, store, process, and deliver these essential elements of information?
4. What impediments (cost, accessibility, form in which data are kept) to distribution must be identified that require ameliorative action by government or corrective initiatives by corporations or individuals?

Related to these considerations is the recognition that must be given to those classes of data which require protection (to what degree and through which security mechanisms) at the beginning; that is, before a "system" is created and set in motion.

Privacy Protection in the United States

The U.S. attitude toward the protection of privacy is, in many ways, indicative of our pluralistic society, the "many axes to grind" syndrome, and this has led to a quandary yet unresolved because of congressional actions that presented the nation with both a Privacy Act and a Freedom of Information Act. The confidentiality standards have not been sufficient, in all instances, nor have all of the relevant factors in disclosure determination been identified. The result: The courts have had to assume the responsibility for the government's disclosure policy regarding personal information. Further legislative action can, of course, help diminish the existing dilemma. During the 95th Congress, 26 public laws were passed which dealt with information disclosure, confidentiality, and the right to privacy. Illustrative of those dealing with personal privacy are

1. P.L. 95-115, "Juvenile Justice Amendments"
2. P.L. 95-216, "Social Security Amendments";
3. P.L. 95-540, "Privacy Protection for Rape Victims Act"; and
4. P.L. 95-622, "Extending the Assistance Programs for Community Health Centers and for Biomedical Research."

Just as the Congress has had to become involved in this knotty problem area, so must other institutions which fulfill key roles in the acquisition and provision of information: federal, state, and local governments, libraries, information-analysis centers, private-sector services, and foundations. Some of these entities concentrate on handling information that is primarily of internal value, but all have certain responsibilites for external clientele.

Within the recent past there has been a spate of governmental interest and action as the awareness of a need to address the question of international information exchange has emerged. Studies, seminars, workshops, and conferences have sought to sort out the critical ingredients, pose alternative approaches, and suggest the assignment of oversight responsibilities.

One initiative of unusual significance was undertaken by the Domestic Council Committee on the Right of Privacy (1976) through its staff report entitled *National Information Policy*. In the section, "International Implications of Information Policies and Developments," the problems and opportunities ensuing from "the growing reality of instant world-wide communications" are acknowledged. And in noting that information technology is becoming extensively internationalized, the report avers that this development "will blur the effectiveness of territorially bounded regulatory authorities." Another key point stresses that "international organizations are well behind in meeting their responsibilities to fix standards and develop necessary levels of harmonization for maximum transnational utilization." Inhibiting the "full utility" of computer communications, as noted by then Assistant Secretary of Commerce for Science and Technology, Dr. Betsy Ancker Johnson, are such factors as the slowness of institutional response, inadequate data transfer safeguards, and the "massive financial commitments required."

While this major study purposely leaves many questions unanswered, it does focus (in "Issue 11") on the pressing requirement to "establish necessary rules and data protection mechanisms to allow continued free flow of information across national boundaries." Among the milestone actions which deserve fresh scrutiny are the assertions of the International Communications Convention held in Montreux (1965). The guidelines now being developed by the Organization for Economic Cooperation and Development (OECD) and the Convention of the Council of Europe undoubtedly will address several aspects of the concerns spelled out in the *National Information Policy* report.

The crux of uncertainty, as expressed both officially and unofficially, can and must be resolved in time. A present overview of significant activities which are treating selected aspects of information policy formulation in general and the transborder data flow (TBDF) cum protection of privacy conundrum looks like this

1. Department of State Interagency Task Force study designed to develop a policy for the United States, with special attention to the diverse viewpoints of domestic and multinational private sector groups.

2. National Telecommunications and Information Administration (NTIA) "Information Policy Program," which includes identifying the seven aspects of information policy; these address in part the problems of privacy and international concerns, and in the latter context the report states that "As international information exchanges and trade in information technologies are increasing, the United States must take account of the views of many other countries about information and must recognize they frequently do not share the same information policy assumptions as the United States."

3. White House Conference on Library and Information Services (autumn, 1979), while emphasizing domestic foci, nonetheless will have an influence on the formulation of national information policy.

4. Office of Technology Assessment study of such information policy areas as electronic mail systems, electronic funds transfer (EFT), and law enforcement information systems, all of which carry international implications.

5. Congressional Research Service study on "Scientific and Technical Information (STI) Activities: Issues and Opportunities," prepared for the House of Representatives' Subcommittee on Science, Research and Technology.

6. Office of Science and Technology Policy (OSTP) staff effort addressing those provisions of P.L. 94-282 (National Science and Technology Policy, Organization and Priorities Act of 1975) concerned with science and technology information.

7. National Academy of Sciences' fulfillment, for NSF and OSTP, of the P.L. 94-282 requirement for a 5-year projection treating scientific and technical activities.

8. Congressional Clearinghouse on the Future "Chautauqua for Congress" series featuring workshops and seminars about "Information and Communications."

In some instances, the result of this activity will be limited to an enhanced awareness of the role of information, policy options, and the diverse benefits and limitations of technology. More than this will result, in other cases, as specific action alternatives are identified and institutional response roles assigned. The "actors" will become more familiar with their roles and hopefully gain more insight regarding the scenarios which can be scripted. To repeat, although some of the endeavors listed previously are not concerned primarily with TBDF and the protection of privacy, the broader orientation and education of many public officials and private participants in the kaleidoscopic ramifications of information policies, programs, and technology cannot fail to have a beneficial effect in the long run. Experience has shown that *understanding* leads to *involvement*, with subsequent *commitment* that can in turn bring about assertive *action*.

United States Privacy Protection versus International Standards

In commenting about Gassmann's excellent paper, most of my observations necessarily amplify his core statements. When he accurately notes that "partial privacy laws, by sector" are the norm in the United States, I might add in a spirit of optimism that an approach to a more sweeping set of standards and controls has been put forth in the Omnibus Right to Privacy Act of 1977 and subsequent new legislation. And yet, the thrust of that bill, like the 654-page report of the

Privacy Protection Study Commission in 1977, deals with conditions on the domestic front. Once again, those responsible for planning for the equitable protection of privacy simply have not focused on the international aspects of that imbroglio. The legislative elements found in many European laws, as enumerated by Dr. Leó Packer, former counsellor for science and technology, U.S. Mission to OECD, include:

1. a national inventory of data collections;
2. governmental bodies to register, license, and regulate compilation, storage, and transmission of data;
3. control of transmissions in and out of the country; and
4. coverage of all categories of personal data systems.

As mentioned earlier, no specially created agencies exist in the United States to monitor and to supervise the application of privacy legislation. The resolution of different interpretations occurs as a result of litigation, with the courts fulfilling the key judgmental role. Sometimes interagency agreements limit the transfer of data from one govermental entity to another (e.g., IRS and SSA have had such an arrangement). It should be noted that many observers are far more concerned with the private-sector collection and use of personal information than they are of federal, state, or local government efforts of that sort. In the late 1960s and early 1970s, there was an often bitter debate over the possible establishment of a Federal Data Center. Although that idea was never consummated, the scope and volume of federal activities resulting in the acquisition and storage of data have grown apace. Robert Belair, former Acting General Counsel of the Domestic Council Committee on the Right of Privacy, reported that "there are perhaps 8000 separate federal record systems that are accessed by personal identifiers."

It is true that within the United States no legislation yet has tried to cope with legal persons, but as the sophistication of those on the field of action grows, I anticipate that this will be addressed. Some of the conferences and studies now underway or planned may well include such items as part of their agendas or research. Gassmann's four "trends and factors" are particularly trenchant as he phrases each as a question. As regards "new international information infrastructures," he identifies several; to those I would add the proposed SPINES pilot program, a UNESCO germinal concept to gather in and make available information related to science policy activities. The range of technological support systems that might be brought to bear here is wide. In my opinion, there should be a study that evaluates existing and proposed information transfer systems, matching those resources against identifiable needs. This could be undertaken either by a private group (such as a foundation) or with support from several countries. And it is also true that some TBDF will simply just happen as a result of marketplace machinations or certain governmental initiatives. Often, these will not be calculated, but appear as a by-product of another related action.

A movement appears to be underway (sometimes overt, perhaps more often subliminal) in the United States to commence molding the kind of cohesive mechanism that can help articulate a national policy and follow-through capability that will be on hand to deal with TBDF matters. The private sector, on its own initiative, can only do just so much! In the long run, official sanction becomes a sine qua non, and the combined authority and responsibility will be vested in a suitable governmental institution.

Privacy and the Period 1979–1984

Gassmann's prognostications concerning the period 1979–1984 are well taken. His opening observation about the divergent trends, networks vis-à-vis microprocessors, rings true, and is already being borne out in the U.S. Congress where the annual expenditure of funds on information technology and its applications has risen more than 900% in 8 years! Even the use of commercial satellites has been experimented with successfully in support of congressional teleconferencing; I recall a forecast which says that 30 communications satellites will be in orbit in 1984.

Integrated voice–data–facsimile services most assuredly should be in use by 1981. On Capitol Hill, all buildings are being wired to allow the transmission of audio, video, and computerized data. The use of a Viewdata type of modified TV set is being looked at, and portable terminals already are being tested for use as "electronic mailboxes." Gassmann notes that manual data and automatic data "should be treated in the same way." The management of certain transactions or proceedings will become vital; for example, the floor proceedings of the U.S. House of Representatives is now placed on videotape and archived. The question is being asked: "Is the gavel-to-gavel, unexpurgated record of that chamber in action more accurate–hence one day more "official"–than the edited version which has traditionally appeared in the *Congressional Record?"* Such a consideration is *not* far afield from certain aspects of data capture and availability across national boundaries.

The discussion of corporate "data streams" and the role of consultant firms are among the most important topics cited by Gassmann for here one can see a shift in conventional handling of personal and corporate data alike. The human being's role, whether as a generalist who can synthesize, a highly specialized analyst, or a "broker" who can point to previously unknown resources, may well be affected as electronic means, regulated or unrestricted, are employed to move selected data from country to country. Government intrusion in information collection, storage, and processing activities already is a problem. I predict that the role of consultants who can advise on the complexities and legal niceties of such matters will expand significantly by 1984.

Conclusion

Perhaps the most useful comment which I can make in closing is to dwell for a moment on some of the key characteristics of the technology-supported environment as it is possible to penetrate the future:

1. U. S. ability to reciprocate in information exchange, especially through the adoption of international guidelines, becomes a vital prerequisite.
2. Faced with a four- to sevenfold increase in the volume of information flow (by 1985), improved controls and the use of data handling systems to keep such transfers within bounds are essential.
3. Anticipatory information handling systems which allow policymakers and program operators to "stay on top" of high priority problems must be refined. The best possible 24-hour "watch center" must be developed, and be capable of dealing with threats to the public welfare (e.g., man-caused terrorism, natural disasters).
4. New techniques for handling media-reported events that seem to require instant or short-term official reactions must be developed; the leisure to consider such intrusive happenings seldom is available.
5. Through the conceptualization and implementation of various information policies, decisionmakers in government and private establishments will understand in advance their options for action and hopefully be able to render more socially responsive solutions.

Nearly 200 years ago, Thomas Jefferson observed that

> Laws and institutions must go hand in hand with the progress of the human mind. As that becomes more developed, more enlightened, as new discoveries are made, new truths disclosed, and manners and opinions change with the change of circumstances, institutions must advance also and keep pace with the times.

References

Belair, Robert. Agency Implications . . . The Impact of the Government Collection of Information. *John Marshall Journal of Practice & Procedures,* 1977, p. 466.

Chartrand, Robert L. *The Legislator as User of Information Technology.* Oct. 9, 1976. 22p. Revised Oct. 9, 1977. 34p. Congressional Research Service Multilith 77–217 sp. Supercedes Multilith 76–199sp.

Chartrand, Robert L., and Morentz, James M. (Eds.). *Information Technology Serving Society.* New York: Pergamon Press, 1979.

Domestic Council Committee on the Right of Privacy. *National information policy.* Washington, D.C.: U.S. Government Printing Office, 1976.

Packer, Leo S. Privacy Protection and Transborder Data Flow. Appendix 5 in *Scientific and Technical Information Activities (STI): Issues and Opportunities.* Report to the Subcommittee on Science, Research, and Technology of the Committee on Science and Technology. Washington: U.S. Government Printing Office, 1979. Pp. 100–102.

Personal Privacy in an Information Society. The Report of the Privacy Protection Study Committee. Washington: U.S. Government Printing Office, 1977.

Science and Technology: A Five Year Outlook. National Science Foundation. San Francisco: Freeman, 1979.

U.S. Congress. House. Committee on House Administration. Policy Group on Information and Computers. *Information Policy: Public Laws From the 95th Congress.* Washington: U.S. Government Printing Office, 1979.

U.S. Department of State. Bureau of Oceans and International Environmental and Scientific Affairs. *Selected Papers: International Policy Implications of Computers and Advanced Telecommunications in Information Systems.* Washington, D.C. 1979

U.S. Library of Congress. Congressional Research Service. Science Policy Research Division. *The Congress and Information Technology.* Staff Report; prepared for the use of the Select Committee on Committees, U.S. House of Representatives. Washington: U.S. Government Printing Office, 1974.

U.S. Library of Congress. Science Policy Research Division. *Scientific and Technical Information Activities (STI): Issues and Opportunities.* Report to the Subcommittee on Science and Technology of the Committee on Science and Technology. Washington: U.S. Government Printing Office, 1979.

U.S. Library of Congress. Congressional Research Service. Science Policy Research Division. *The Role of the United States in Scientific and Technical Information Assistance for the Developing Countries.* Washington: CRS, 1979.

Wood, Fred B., Coates, Vary T., Chartrand, Robert L., and Ericson, Richard F. *Videoconferencing via Satellite: Opening Congress to the People.* Final Report. Washington: George Washington University, 1979.

Comment on "Privacy Implications of Transborder Data Flows"

Oswald H. Ganley

Introduction

Let me begin by saying that I believe the one thing we have not sufficiently emphasized in our discussions of transborder data flow (TBDF) is "border." I am not really in favor of reducing TBDF to TDF. The essence of the debate, as I understand it, is that data are crossing national frontiers. Let us not forget that these national borders are not the frontiers between state and state in a federal system or, in Canada for instance, between province and federal system. The borders we are concerned with are those of sovereign entities, each with their own characteristics and their own concepts, concerns, and interests in terms of cultural, security, economic, and commercial aspirations. I think we cannot keep this too much in mind, since it colors the approach to the question of free flow of data, and it sometimes leads to acrimonious debates on the subject.

Even in 1979, borders are still felt to be totally necessary to guide and control national sovereign interests. But electronics are making those borders increasingly porous, and, to a certain extent, less real. Hertzian waves and digital data cannot be picked up by a customs inspector at a border station, but have either already reached the interior, or are completely outside the country before the national guardians are aware of it. One reason why nations are frightened of what is happening is that this concept of having a border where things can be somehow contained and controlled is being threatened. This is especially true now, or will be in the near future, when all data transmitted will be just so many digits. Those who guard these porous borders will not be able to know whether they are dealing with news, or entertainment programs, or facsimile, or any type of information. It is a scary thing for a nation not to be able to choose what will enter or what will leave its borders.

As concerns privacy, the United States is a leader in this area. This is an issue

133

about which we ought to give thought and ought to strengthen our knowledge. However, I am convinced that if privacy were the only international issue we faced in TBDF, our problem would be much like those in a lot of other areas where we have conflicts of law and questions of choice of law. With guidelines and other techniques familiar to practitioners of transnational and public international law and to businessmen and diplomats, I am convinced remedies could be found with relative ease.

I do not believe that privacy is the only, or even the main issue. I believe the main issues of international concern in TBDF have to do with commerce, economics, and national sovereignty. I have always though this to be the case, and the work I have been doing for the past few months has given me even greater conviction.

Since last summer, I have been examining U.S.–Canadian information and communications relationships, not just in TBDF, but across the board. The Canadians have a vital interest in all phases of communications technology as it affects them socially, economically, and politically. They have given a lot of thought to this and have written about these problems at great length.

Privacy Protection in Canada

In the specific area of TBDF, the Canadians have been very frank in saying that privacy is not the problem. They say that the problem is rather one of jobs, of balance of payments, of the capability of Canadian management to function competitively in the modern world. That is, it is a problem of the maintenance of their research and development capability and of the continued growth generally in Canada of this important new industry. It is a problem, they say, of not wanting their most vital economic data, their banking data for instance, analyzed in a foreign country.

At the present time, Canada does not have laws that deal directly with TBDF. They do have a Human Rights Act, and Part IV of that act is concerned with the protection of personal information. This applies only to federal government data banks, and so far, the Canadian government has interpreted this law as not affecting TBDF per se. Canada also has 23 federal and 92 provincial laws which are said to have some bearing on interprovincial and international TBDF, but these laws have had no perceptible affect on the international flow of data.

The Canadian government, at least within the Department of Communications, is very much interested in this subject. As it is put in one of their reports, they would like to be "positive competitive and follow stimulative approaches as these would best serve the needs for advancing the development of computer communications services in Canada." How long this "positive competitive and stimulative" approach will be followed is a big question.

Last year, an amendment to the Bank Act, which does not deal with personal data, was introduced in Parliament. Its pertinent point, so far as we are concerned, reads: "A bank shall not process, store, or otherwise maintain any of its corporate or clients records at a location outside of Canada, or transmit data relating to any such records to a point outside Canada, with the object of having that data processed, stored, or maintained outside of Canada." The penalty for violation was set at $5000 or 6 months in jail. There has been considerable discussion about this law internally, and it is unlikely to pass in its present form.

Another proposed law with equally little to do with personal data is the so-called Combines Investigation Act, or the Competition Act. It is essentially a law dealing with how the Canadian government can obtain certain types of records that are processed or stored outside the country for purposes of criminal or certain civil investigations. This law deals with search and seizure of data and information, and, according to some observers, it is of a questionable nature. The Canadian Association for Data Processing (CADAPSO) has opposed many features of this law.

While these specific laws may well not pass, since the Canadian government must face the electorate this summer,* I would predict that sometime soon, Canada will enact some restrictive legislation. Various Canadian officials have made it clear to me that they feel this issue is just too important to Canada to be allowed to go totally unregulated. Furthermore, they have stressed that their concerns are of an economic and sovereignty nature, and not primarily ones of privacy.

Implications of Transborder Data Flow Regulation

On a more general level, I would like to say that there is no doubt in my mind anymore that we are dealing with a real issue, and an issue that is going to become more and more vital in diplomatic relations in the future. Those of us who have been involved in the TBDF issue for several years had some doubts at first whether or not the issue was real. I think there are many factors that make it a very real issue, but I do not think privacy is at, or near, the head of the list.

I do not think that attempts at restrictions on TBDF are anti-United States inspired, either. The United States may well suffer the most because it is the most advanced in and has the greatest market penetration in the countries that count. I think that foreign multinational corporations suffer and will suffer at

*The final act of Parliament before the elections was to extend the Bank Act without the passage in question.

least as much if not more than U.S. corporations from the imposition of restrictions.

Among my main concerns is that for the technology itself. Several speakers at this conference have expressed confidence that information and communications technology will move ahead, inevitably and unhindered. As a practitioner and policymaker in the area of innovation for almost two decades, I cannot share their optimism. There are hundreds of ways to kill a technology before it can prove its true worth. And fear of the unknown by peoples and governments is often the impetus behind this. I regard the full development of computer and related communications technologies in the international area as vital to the United States and to international trade generally. I cannot, in fact, see how close to a trillion dollars worth of annual international trade can take place without a free flow of information.

There are many unsettled questions to be considered in the area of TBDF. We may very well have to have new international institutions to deal with new concepts. Indeed, we may have to create new concepts in international law. We are going to have to think about the implications of large data banks outside national jurisdiction for criminal or civil investigations. Data extradition treaties may have to be considered. We need to look at questions of what rights, if any, a government has to data in transit within its borders. We must look at the restrictions there should be on access, and how these can be safeguarded. The question of legal person is a very bothersome one, and so on.

Imaginative guidelines are being drawn up for handling these problems in the Organization for Economic Cooperation and Development (OECD), but their implementation is voluntary. In the United States it has not yet been decided how to implement such guidelines. Will this be by private contract law? What will be the attitude of the U.S. government? Will it take a *laissez faire* stand or will the U.S. government exert pressure for enforcement? If so, how?

Like all changes, those occurring as a result of information and communications technology will not establish themselves without disrupting some things we are used to. Our problem is to recognize the true nature of these changes, and to make appropriate plans for what ought to be done about them.

Comment on "Privacy Implications of Transborder Data Flows"

Lucy A. Hummer*

Dr. Gassmann is far more an expert in computer communications and computer and information technology than I, so I defer to most of his projections as to what is in store for us in the future in the way of privacy protections in transborder data flow (TBDF). I agree that we will see a growth in national and international data networks. I am inclined to agree that future computer and communications technology will favor decentralization. I agree that both individuals and governments may manifest increasing concerns with the uses to which computers can be put, and that this concern may be expressed through regulatory or legal controls that do not now exist.

I think, though, that in the future the concern of government with computer technology and computer communications will be motivated in only miniscule part by concerns over protection of personal privacy. Without detracting from the importance of the privacy issues that are being addressed now by the Organization for Economic Cooperation and Development (OECD) and the Council of Europe, and our own domestic efforts to legislate further privacy protections in the private sector, I think there will be increasing recognition that there are other fundamental issues of legitimate business and governmental concern which will, in short time, be seen as more important than the privacy concerns.

As is probably known, there was intense speculation a few years ago about the motivation of European countries in passing their data protection legislation, since it so clearly appeared to regulate the data processing industry. The legislation was viewed by some commentators as a privacy charade, a smoke screen behind which a country could impede the growth of the American data

*The comments expressed are the personal opinion of the commentator, and do not represent official U.S. Government policy.

COMPUTERS AND PRIVACY
IN THE NEXT DECADE

processing industry and encourage its own industry. Some referred to the European data protection legislation as nontariff trade barriers.

Over the years the world's trading nations have sought to erect extensive and sometimes ingenious nontariff barriers to trade in order to protect domestic industries from foreign competition. This is nothing new. Major ways to accomplish this have included government subsidies; government procurement policies; safeguards, that is, devices to impose limits on imports that are threatening domestic industry, product standards and licensing standards; and customs valuations.

Trade in services, including data processing services, is a rapidly growing sector of national economies. Dr. Peter Robinson of the Canadian Department of Communications has estimated that Canada, in 1978, imported some $300–350 million worth of computing services. He has estimated that by 1985, Canada will import about $1.5 billion worth of computing services and that, as a result, there will be a loss of some 23,000 directly related jobs from the Canadian economy. Canadians are concerned about those implications, and rightfully so.

In the United States, U.S. Department of Commerce data show that U.S. data processing and transmission corporations earn $1.1 billion in foreign exchange per year, and that this amount grows annually at the rate of 15–25%. This figure does not include the exchange of information within corporations in their normal course of operations. In addition, the closely related $60-billion-a-year U.S. computer industry earns $5 billion annually from exports.

Regulations and laws which impact on the data processing and computer communications industry are therefore of importance to a national economy.

We in the United States, through the work of the Inter-Agency Task Force chaired by the State Department and through the work of our Advisory Committee, have, as one of our tasks, been attempting to assess the European data protection laws in light of the suspicions that they are really designed as nontariff trade barriers. My own feeling is that the European laws are what, on their face, they purport to be, that is, attempts, through regulatory controls aimed primarily at personal information in data processing systems, to protect privacy and individual rights and liberties.

Have the European laws on data protection impacted on American business? There might be one case. The French refused to permit an American data processing company to do business in France; the French would not give it the necessary license. The French have never been entirely clear as to the reason for their refusal. However, at a November meeting of OECD's Invisibles Committee, the French stated that the primary reason was because the company's "data-treatment center" was not in France and that this, in turn, created a problem of "business confidentiality," and that the French authorities were afraid that, if the license were granted, it would not be possible to impose French laws on data processing.

Do we have any indications that forces other than privacy concerns have created TBDF problems for American business? Yes, we do.

Sweden is considering restrictions on foreign storage of economic data because such data could be incorporated in an air force targetting system.

Japanese regulations do not permit Japanese data to enter the United States at one point for transmittal to a second point.

In Germany, an American financial corporation has been informed that the German banking laws require it to process financial data, formerly processed at its U.S. headquarters, in Germany.

A Canadian banking bill would prohibit processing of banking transactions other than on Canadian facilities.

Some governments are considering rate structures for data transmission that would be detrimental to private data networks and to U.S. companies.

With regard to the German example I just cited, Dr. Peter Robinson of Canada has also noted that there are Canadian statutes that have been on the books for some time which contain provisions for maintenance of books of account and other records in Canada. He has stated that it is not clear whether computer printouts received from foreign locations, where the records are stored and processed, are sufficient to comply with the statutes.

It is clear that vital concerns over sovereignty, security, and the national economy are increasingly emerging as important factors in assessing issues of TBDF.

Because of the growth in the service sector of national economies, the United States proposed to the OECD Trade Committee in December 1978 that the OECD undertake an analysis of the service sector in international trade. We mentioned specifically data banks and data transfer, computer services, and government controls and licensing regulations on the service sector. It is my understanding that the OECD is presently canvassing its various directorates to determine what kinds of work are already being undertaken in this area.

Now that I have expressed my feeling that personal privacy will be of decreasing concern in transborder data flow issues in the future, I would like to comment on some statements in Gassmann's paper.

On page 110, Item 3 of his paper, he characterizes the difference between the American and European approaches toward enforcement of privacy protections. Besides stating that in the U.S. enforcement is carried out by the judiciary, I think it important to note that the U.S. approach toward privacy protection is designed to put the individual in the center of the action, to let him have a large voice in decisions as to what information will be collected, used, and disseminated about him. The Europeans take a paternalistic approach choosing to vest enforcement in bureaucracy, that is, the state looking out for the individual.

Gassman also refers in more than one place to recent European legislation extending privacy protection laws to legal persons. I can see the rationale for this in terms of a small shopkeeper trading by himself. My problem with these laws is in how the term "legal person" is defined. For example, the translation into English supplied by our Embassy in Vienna of the term "person concerned" in the Austrian data protection law is "physical or legal persons, *or* individually owned commercial enterprises, whose data are collected, processed, or transferred" (emphasis supplied). If legal person, under the law, is not synonymous with an individually owned commercial enterprise, then what is it, and what are its limits? A small club or assocation? A medium-sized partnership? A corporation of undetermined size? It is no wonder the uncertainty surrounding the protections given to legal persons in European laws has raised suspicions in the American business community about the reasons for them. For example, at our last Advisory Committee meeting, a representative of a major multinational stated that the Europeans really were addressing themselves to "mom and pop cartels."

The fuzziness surrounding where European laws are going when they legislate concerning legal persons, with the obvious impacts such laws can have on a national economy, lead me back to my opinion that what is in store for us in the future in transborder data flow goes far beyond questions of protection of personal privacy.

Nonuniform Privacy Laws:
Implications and Attempts at Uniformity

Gordon C. Everest

This paper begins with some introductory comments relating to data privacy, then briefly explores the reasons for and the impact of nonuniform state laws, and finally provides an overview of the current suggested Uniform Freedom of Information and Privacy Acts from the National Conference of Commissioners on Uniform State Laws.

Data Privacy Issues and Legislative Approaches

Before addressing the question of nonuniform state laws, one must have a common understanding of what is meant by data privacy, the legislative approaches in various sectors, jurisdictional questions, and constitutional limits.

The term "privacy" relates to the right of an individual to be left alone, and to determine what information about oneself to share with others. In addition, as currently used in "privacy" legislation, the term also encompasses the right of an individual to have access to his or her own data. Privacy is an issue at the interface between individuals and organizations that hold or use data on those individuals. Whether they are public-sector government organizations or private-sector business organizations, the rights and responsibilities are similar from the standpoint of the individual.

Whereas privacy relates to the individual, data privacy relates to the personal data pertaining to an individual. The privacy rights of an individual can be violated when data pertaining to that individual are misused. With modern computers providing the ability for organizations to amass and quickly search through large volumes of personal data, there comes a need to establish an open, honest, and fair relationship between organizations and the

141

persons about whom they collect and store data. This is the central thrust of all privacy legislation.

Three Basic Rights

Privacy as it relates to personal data involves three fundamental rights:

1. *Personal privacy.* The right of an individual to determine what information about oneself to share with others, and to control disclosure of personal data.
2. *Personal access.* The right of an individual to know if data, what data, and where data are collected, stored, or disclosed when such data pertain to that individual; the right to dispute incomplete or inaccurate data.
3. *Public access.* The right of people (having a need to know) to access data in order to maintain the health and safety of society, and to monitor and evaluate the activities of government.

The right of personal access to one's own data held by a federal or state government is rooted in the Fifth and Fourteenth Amendments to the Constitution. There are no constitutional roots for personal access to data held in the private sector.

The right of public access, that is, the right of an individual or an organization to have access to someone else's personal data, is rooted in

1. the recent public records laws or freedom of information laws allowing private access to government held data,
2. certain acts such as the National Labor Relations Act which provide for private access to data held in the private sector, and
3. certain other acts such as the Bank Secrecy Act and criminal justice laws which provide for public access or government access to data held in the private sector.

Until 1974, support for the second and third rights outweighed any constitutional or legislative support to the first right, that of personal privacy. At best, the Constitution only weakly supports a right to privacy. The First Amendment "right of the people peaceably to assemble" seems only peripherally related to data privacy. The Fourth Amendment "right of the people to be secure in their persons, houses, papers, and effects, against unreasonable searches and seizures" protects one's body from assault ("persons"), private places from trespass ("houses"), and personal property from theft ("effects"). It is interesting that there is no legal term for "papers" equivalent to assault, trespass, and theft. By separating papers from effects, the original framers of the Constitution had more in mind than just the physical papers—perhaps the information on the papers! These rights coupled with those in the Ninth

Amendment leaving all other rights "retained by the people" have led some to infer a "penumbra" right to personal privacy surrounding and permeating the Bill of Rights.

To correct the imbalance among these three basic rights, the state of Minnesota passed the first omnibus, public sector privacy legislation in April 1974. Then in December 1974, the U.S. government passed similar legislation. Since then, eight other states have passed some form of public sector, privacy legislation. In addition to a federal commission, state commissions have been established in Minnesota, Indiana, Illinois, and New Jersey.

Personal Data and Secondary Disclosures

For personal data held in the public sector there is clearly a conflict between the right of personal privacy and the right of public access. It is first important to distinguish between personal and nonpersonal data. For nonpersonal data there is no personal right of privacy at issue and therefore, the right of public access, embodied in public records laws or freedom of information laws, should dominate. It is also important to distinguish between primary disclosures and secondary disclosures of data. A primary disclosure occurs when an individual first releases personal data to some organization in order to obtain some benefit or to meet some requirement. Secondary disclosures occur later when the first recipient gives or shares the personal data with a third party. It is here that most abuses occur. Furthermore, it is with secondary disclosures that the Bill of Rights is even less applicable.

Figure 1 lists the three sectors in which personal data may be held, namely federal government, state and local government, and the private sector and lists down the left-hand side the three basic rights listed above. Entries within the chart indicate constitutional and legislative coverage. This chart is intended to highlight some of the jurisdictional questions which arise when personal data are held by different organizations.

Basic Rights in the Public and Private Sectors

Several observations stem from Figure 1. Most public sector legislation (federal government and state and local government) has taken an omnibus approach to privacy legislation. Omnibus legislation attempts to take a set of rules and apply those rules uniformly across different types of personal data, across different types of agencies holding those data, and across individuals or organizations using those data. Perhaps this reflects the fact that government has jurisdiction over the activities of government!

The situation in the private sector is a different matter. Very little legislation has been passed at the state level, and some specific pieces of legislation have

	PERSONAL DATA HELD BY AN ORGANIZATION IN		
	Public Sector		Private Sector
Basic right	Federal government	State and local government	Organizations
Personal privacy	Limited right expressed in PL 93-579 [Omnibus] "Privacy Act of 1974"	Limited right expressed in Omnibus legislation in 9 states	Limited Federal legislation in selected areas, e.g., PL 95-630, "Right to Financial Privacy Act of 1978"
Personal access	Due process rights of Fifth Amendment reflected in PL 93-579	Due process rights of Fourteenth Amendment reflected in state privacy laws	Limited Federal legislation in selected areas, e.g., PL 91-508, "Fair Credit Reporting Act," FERPA
Public access by government (federal or state)	Yes, for law enforcement, public health and safety, and national security		
			Otherwise, in specific areas such as PL 91-508, "Bank Secrecy Act"
by private sector (includes the media)	US Freedom of Information Act (552, USC)	Similar FOI or Public Records Laws in most states	Some Federal laws in specific areas, e.g., National Labor Relations Act grants access to unions if there is a grievance

Figure 1

been passed at the federal level covering selected areas of the private sector such as credit reporting agencies, depository institutions, educational institutions, labor unions, and the need for data in law enforcement, public health and safety, and national security. At the time of enactment of the U.S. Privacy Act of 1974, Congress also established the Federal Privacy Protection Study Commission. The commission essentially studied the private sector on a sector by sector basis. It made recommendations within each separate area of the private sector. Furthermore, it appears that the current tone in the U.S. Congress is not to entertain omnibus privacy legislation in the private sector. The 95th Congress passed the first piece of legislation stemming from the Privacy Protection Study Commission in the Right to Financial Privacy Act of 1978 which only covers depository institutions. The 96th Congress will consider legislation in other areas.

Nonuniform State "Privacy" Laws

Why do we have nonuniform state laws? Any time states act independently to enact legislation in any particular area, there are bound to be differences. In the area of privacy legislation the differences are more pronounced because the issues are so complex. In some areas the federal government has jurisdiction such as with law enforcement, public health and safety, national security, or interstate commerce regulation (which can be put forth for almost any legislation). Sometimes there is a legitimate issue of jurisdiction since federal government action is limited in intrastate and private sector activities.

The problem of nonuniform state laws is similar to the problem of transborder data flow at the international level, except that in the latter, no one has global jurisdiction; regulation must depend on mutual (bilateral or multilateral) agreements. At least within the United States, there is a federal government that can pass laws and regulate activities in all federal government agencies, some state and local government activities, and some private sector activities.

The Need for Uniform Privacy Laws

Uniform privacy laws are desirable from the standpoint of several different constituencies:

1. Organizations maintaining collections of personal data
2. Organizations providing equipment and services to organizations maintaining collections of personal data
3. Individuals seeking to exercise their basic rights of personal privacy and personal access
4. Organizations and individuals seeking access to personal data pertaining to other individuals.

For companies whose activities carry them across state boundaries, the problems of nonuniform state laws can place a real burden on their activities. This is even more pronounced if they have a nationwide communications network to transmit data across political jurisdictions.

Privacy legislation may lay down requirements such as

1. Maintaining an audit trail of past disclosures of data, perhaps distinguishing routine from nonroutine uses
2. Maintaining a record of sources of all data
3. Maintaining an up-to-date record of the location of an individual on whom data pertain in order to meet notice requirements
4. Storing statements of dispute when an individual disagrees with the accuracy of data on file
5. Mechanisms for limiting data access to authorized users.

If different laws provide for different ways of meeting these types of requirements, a multistate organization could be faced with real problems in developing systems to store, maintain, and retrieve personal data.

Organizations providing equipment, software development, or consulting services, or educational institutions training people to operate data processing functions would also have to be aware of any differences in laws. Laws may be nonuniform between the public and the private sector and may be nonuniform depending on the type of data being stored; they may be nonuniform depending on who uses the data or why. Legislative differences can occur geographically, across data types, and across areas in the private or public sector.

Faced with nonuniform laws, individuals would also have difficulty exercising their basic rights. They may have to follow one procedure when dealing with state and local government, another procedure when dealing with federal government agencies, and still many more when dealing with financial institutions, educational institutions, medical institutions, or any other institution. The current multiplicity of laws and the anticipated further fractionation will present some real problems for individuals wishing to exercise their basic rights of personal privacy, personal access, and public access.

Obtaining Uniform Privacy Laws

Several different approaches are necessary to obtain uniformity in privacy laws. Any number of these could be followed, but complete uniformity can probably never be attained.

Striving for omnibus privacy legislation wherever possible can have real advantages, particularly for individuals seeking to exercise their rights with respect to their own personal data. Legislative attempts to have similar provisions in laws covering public and private sectors are desirable. Wherever the government has jurisdiction, preemptive federal legislation may be desirable both over states and over areas in the private sector. Uniform state laws are desirable when the federal government does not have jurisdiction or does not exercise its prerogative in passing privacy legislation.

All legislation should follow a fair code approach rather than attempting a constitutional amendment, enabling legislation, or detailed legislation. A constitutional amendment is always too general; therefore it provides little guidance to individuals and organizations concerning their rights and responsibilities, and it defers to future judicial interpretation in court cases.

A detailed law is very difficult to pass, and very slow to change if it does get passed. On the other hand, a detailed law does provide specific guidelines for organizations and individuals. The problem is in developing all of the minute details so that all organizations and all individuals know exactly what their rights and responsibilities are in all cases. This is wishful thinking in such a complex area as privacy legislation.

Enabling legislation sets up a regulatory agency to make and enforce rules, perhaps licensing, auditing, and probing into the organizations under their jurisdiction. In theory, enabling legislation tends to be more responsive to the needs of the society, but in practice such legislation soon serves the controlled.

The approach of a fair code of information practice seeks to spell out rights and responsibilities of data subjects and "dealers" in personal data with reasonably general statements that can provide guidance today. With such legislation it is possible to encourage desirable behavior by making undesirable behavior costly on the part of organizations maintaining personal data. Fortunately, this last choice represents the approach taken in most privacy laws in the United States, particularly in the public sector. This is not so with similar legislation in some other countries.

The National Conference of Commissioners on Uniform State Laws

During 1978 the National Conference of Commissioners on Uniform State Laws established a committee to develop a Uniform State Fair Information Practices Act including both a Freedom of Information Act and a Uniform Privacy Act. The following comments reflect the drafts as of December 1978. A word of caution: Revisions are bound to be made and the commissioners have not yet endorsed a proposed statute.

Draft Uniform State Freedom of Information Act

The purpose of the Uniform State Freedom of Information Act is to guarantee access to the public records—information about the policies, functions, and operations of state and local governmental agencies. This is fundamental to the democratic process and is the right of every person (individual or organization) in the state.

The draft act provides a broad definition of public record: any writing in any form relating to the conduct of the public's business. The draft covers all agencies of the executive branch and the commission considered whether the law should be extended to cover the legislative and judicial branches, noting that few existing state freedom of information laws do so. The stated default for all data held by a state or local government agency is that it be available to any person or organization to inspect and copy unless specifically exempted by statute. The draft goes on to mention some specific duties of the custodian of public records.

There is no explicit recognition of the distinction between personal data and nonpersonal data held by a state agency. Also, the draft legislation is silent on the relationship between the Freedom of Information Act and the Privacy Act. In fact, there is no distinction between "public records" and "records" because there is no definition of any other class of records. No suggested, acceptable exemptions to the right of public access are stated in the draft legislation. The commission totally avoided the difficult question of the apparent incompatibility with the Privacy Act.

Draft Uniform State Privacy Act

While recognizing the need for public access to government-held data as fundamental to a democracy, the draft also recognizes the need for limiting access to government-held data to ensure the right of individual privacy. Access should be limited to data subjects or their authorized agents and to others who need the information to meet substantial public purposes. The draft legislation only covers the executive branch of state and local governments and the commission is debating the inclusion of the legislative and judicial branches.

The protections of the privacy legislation relate only to individuals and personal data, not to organizations. It grants individuals or their agents the right to access data pertaining to them, to know the purpose for which data are maintained, to have an accounting of previous recipients of the data (outside the agency, since 1975—name, address, date, and purpose of disclosure), and it provides for charging the cost of copying but not searching to an individual requesting access to their own personal data. So-called "public records" are exempted from the above requirements. Access to personal data by the individual to whom they pertain is exempted for investigative information, if there is a specific statute to withhold, or if disclosure would constitute a clearly unwarranted invasion of another individual's privacy (the phrasing of the federal Freedom of Information Act).

The draft legislation spells out the right of an individual to amend their data record. The procedure to be followed is

1. The individual first requests a change.
2. The agency acknowledges receipt of the request.
3. The agency changes the data and advises past recipients, who should, but would not ordinarily know, of the change, or report back to the individual why the change is not made, in which case the individual may file a statement of dispute, which the agency must furnish to all recipients of the personal data being disputed.

The draft legislation would make it illegal to *disclose* government-held personal data (in sharp contrast to the Freedom of Information Act) unless

1. There is prior written consent of the individual to whom the record pertains
2. Such disclosure is required by the Freedom of Information Act (this covers

all public records which is all records held by the state government—obviously a conflict)

3. It is a "public record" (same as above?)
4. It is for some other routine use, for a purpose (*a*) authorized by law (*b*) for
   which the data were originally collected, or (*c*) for which there were
   representations, conditions, or reasonable expectations for use, given or
   implied when the data were originally provided
5. Disclosure is required by state or federal law
6. Delivery is to state archives
7. It is for purposes of law enforcement
8. It is to protect the health and safety of *any* individual
9. Under subpeona or court order (The above two must be accompanied by
   a notice to the individual that such disclosure has taken place.)
10. For research or statistical purposes (subject to certain limitations and
    procedures).

Duties of the agency in the collection and maintenance of personal data are
as follows:

1. Collect only data that are needed.
2. Collect data directly from the individual if possible.
3. Do not collect data under coercion.
4. When data are collected, state the authority under which such collection is
   made, the purpose(s) for which the data are to be used, whether the
   disclosure is mandatory, the consequences of not providing the data,
   whether the information will be available to the individual to whom the
   information pertains (if it is another individual), any expected interagency
   use, and the name and address of the responsible authority.
5. Maintain the records in an accurate, timely, complete, relevant, secure, and
   confidential manner.
6. Give advance notice of material changes to a system or the development of
   a new system of records.
7. Issue guidelines and educate employees regarding compliance to the
   privacy laws.
8. Ensure that recipients of "private data" understand the requirements under
   this act.

The draft legislation provides for an annual report to be prepared by each
agency. For each "system of records" the agency would provide the following:

1. Name and location of the system and the responsible agency official
2. The legal authority to maintain the collection of data
3. The categories of individuals on whom the data are collected
4. The categories of data maintained
5. The categories of use, purpose, and disclosure

6. The policies and practices of the agency regarding storage, access control, retention, and disposal of personal data

The draft legislation calls for the establishment of an administrative agency:

1. To receive annual reports
2. To assess the impact on personal privacy of new or modified systems of records
3. To assist agencies in compliance
4. To issue interpretive rulings under this act for an agency
5. To monitor, review, and recommend changes to compliance procedures for any agency
6. To investigate problems of possible violations under the act
7. To solicit public comment and offer help to individuals seeking to exercise their rights under the act.

Advice to Organizations

I will close with comments in the nature of advice to organizations that maintain collections of personal data, whether in the public sector or the private sector, and to organizations that provide equipment and services to such organizations. As a general comment, greater danger of nonuniformity lies in the private sector. At least most public-sector laws at the federal government and state level are of an omnibus nature. Nothing of the same nature is anticipated in the private sector at the state level or at the federal level.

Organizations seeking answers to what they should do in response to the principles in privacy legislation are ill-advised to rely solely upon or to get hung up on the specifics of state and federal legislation. They are even further ill-advised to look for the loopholes and to do the minimum that is required. In most cases, some interpretation or judgment must be applied; operating at a minimum level of compliance places the organization at a greater risk of noncompliance.

At a different level I do not have a problem with nonuniform privacy laws. The principles of personal privacy and personal access are relatively well known and accepted by now. Organizations are advised to comply with the spirit of these principles which are or may become embodied in specific law.

At the same time I would hasten to add that legislation should not be imposed so that organizations are forced to retrofit current computer-based systems to meet some of the more difficult provisions of privacy legislation. However, every effort should be made to encourage organizations to infuse the principles of privacy and due process in any redesign or any new computer-based system involving storage and dissemination of personal data.

Comment on "Nonuniform Privacy Laws: Implications and Attempts at Uniformity"

Elmer R. Oettinger

Man versus machine is not an unfamiliar theme. In the years following World War I, economist, sociologists, psychologists, and politicians sang the new dirge, and artists, novelists, and playwrights sounded the warning tocsin. Mr. Zero, the bookkeeper in Elmer Rice's (1956) *The Adding Machine*, epitomized the fate of the drudge who had become slave to the adding machine. Rossom's Universal Robots, in Karel Capek's (1923) play *R.U.R.*, symbolized the mechanical lockstep of workers in the industrial society. Long before George Orwell, early-twentieth-century Cassandras warned us of impending doom. The genius of our inventive minds had created a monster which belched destructive flames of routine, boredom, unemployment, neuroses, and ultimate self-destruction. If only they could have been prescient enough to foresee the advent of the computer and its challenge to personal privacy, to the right of the individual to be left alone! Alas! Our early warnings came from later soothsayers!

Over the years, we have learned that humans can control machines. Most recent warnings have related to more fantastical menaces: invasion from space, or by giant bugs, or birds, or simply natural calamities. Yet, with or without science-fiction adaptations for the stage or media, we are faced now with the fact and implications of computerization of information by the government and private sector. The apparition is almost *deja vu*: a new version of machine versus the individual—a new threat to personal rights even as it stores and spreads personalized records.

Although neither Arthur Miller nor Neil Simon may yet have seized on the challenge of the computer as a foreboding theme in drama or literature, the tocsins have been sounded on other fronts. "It is a rare American who does not live in the shadow of his dossier," wrote Ralph Nader (1971), one of the new breed of Cassandras. "What misuse of computers is doing and can do to

151

individual's freedom [constitutes] a warning of a new form of human slavery [Nader, 1971]." "As such, the computer is capable of immense social good or monumental harm, depending upon how human beings decide to use it," said Arthur Miller (1971, p. 273), who adds: "There will be no one to blame except ourselves if we then discover that the mantle of policy-making is being worn by those especially trained technicians who have found the time to master the machine and have put it to use for their own purposes [p. 274]." Miller and others foresaw "the need for a rational and comprehensive plan . . . once the computer's ever-widening impact on our society and its permeation of our daily affairs is appreciated [p. 273]."

Since that prescient prediction, the blueprint for a comprehensive federal plan has been formulated. A plan for states is only a gleam in a few eyes.

It is essential that we understand not only that privacy concerns have led to extensive action by the executive, legislative, and judicial branches of federal and state government, but that we also analyze directions, needs, and significances. It is important that we recognize the evaluative quality of the report and the five appendices of the Privacy Protection Study Commission (PPSC) (1977) with regard to the federal and state legislation and the mesh of related problems. Against a backdrop of principles and practices—in the light of the Code of Fair Information Practices, based on five principles first enunciated by the Advisory Committee of the Secretary of Health, Education and Welfare in 1973 and later expanded to eight principles by the Congress, in the perspective of the Fair Credit Reporting Act and the Privacy Act, among others—the PPSC proposed a foundation for further federal and state action on privacy. The proposals clearly are designed to balance the need of government and the public, including the press, to be informed and the individual right to privacy for certain personal information. The practices of public and private organizations in accumulating, maintaining, disseminating, and sometimes withholding, or sealing, or destroying information of people were analyzed and placed in some perspective. If the period of innovation and ferment is still with us, the challenge, the trends, and the stakes now are clearer; so is the importance of sensitive, practical, philosophically sound decision-making and action to our laws and our lives.

The breadth of Everest's presentation suggests the scope and complexity of the area that has come to be known as privacy and the huge challenge of drafting any uniform state legislation. Acutally, his comments on the initial draft of our (PPSC) proposed act derive in critical part from the fact that he had access only to an earlier draft. Since then we have decided to draft Privacy and Freedom of Information Acts. Nor can I tell you the full scope of our endeavor because that has not been finally determined. It is conceivable that, before we are through, we shall have drafted a privacy–access code for states. There may even be a "government in the sunshine" segment although at this point that cannot be stated with assurance.

My point is, of course, that privacy and access to information are inextricably bound to one another, not necessarily as opposites, but often as facets of an intricate labyrinth of situations, facts, law, dangers, opportunities, fears, and hopes. We are talking about threads that weave together the fabric of human freedom or tear it apart, that can compose something whole cloth, or a Joseph's coat of many colors, or a pauper's rags.

Perhaps I should, in passing, respond to Johnston's comment to the effect that "one problem with uniform laws is deciding which uniform laws to use." The National Conference of Commissions on Uniform State Laws (NCCUSL) believes that it is the *only* conference producing *uniform* state laws. A number of organizations produce so-called *model acts*. The NCCUSL does sometimes decide that a certain act is better introduced as a model act, but there is a distinction. The PPSC is working on *uniform* legislation.

How important is uniformity in state privacy law? Let me start by quoting from a recent letter that I received from Stuart Eizenstat, Assistant to the President for Domestic Affairs and Policy, who writes: "I wish you the best of luck on your project. Development of uniform state law is an *essential* piece of a complete privacy policy." The Carter administration is about to make significant legislative proposals to Congress. Those proposals will have implications for the states. Not the least of those implications should be the essentiality of developing uniformity in state law.

Even before the PPSC report, other studies had confirmed the Nader thesis that "information about virtually every aspect of an individual's life is now compiled and maintained as a matter of course by numerous government and private agencies," but that "in many cases . . . safeguards against privacy invasion have lagged behind the mushrooming technological development" (Larsen, 1975).

The PPSC report (1977a) also bore witness that, despite the federal efforts to address the privacy challenge, "the role of State government in protecting personal privacy is . . . still enormously important. The records a State government keeps about individuals under its jurisdiction are often as extensive as those kept on the same individuals by the Federal government and, in some respects, even more so."

Let us consider closely the opening paragraph of the preface to Appendix I of the PPSC report (1977b) titled *Privacy Law in the States*:

Through constitutional, statutory, and common law protections, and through independent studies, the fifty states have taken steps to protect the privacy interest of individuals in many types of records that others maintain about them. More often than not, actions taken by State

Legislatures and by State Courts, have been more innovative and far-reaching than similar actions at the Federal level. For example, constitutional protections for personal privacy have traditionally been safeguards against governmental rather than private intrusion. That distinction, however, has disappeared in several states whose constitutions protect against both. Ordinarily, the states have also shown an acute appreciation of the need to balance privacy interests against other societal values.

However, those innovative and far-reaching state efforts to protect individual privacy are patchy, inconsistent, and sometimes ill-conceived. Although "a large number of state statutes . . . affect government maintenance of personal data records and provide some protection to disclosural privacy [National Association of Attorneys General, 1979, p.6]," they "do not add up to a comprehensive and consistent body of law. They reflect no coherent or conceptually unified approach to balancing the interest of society, and [that of] the organizations that compile and unified approach to balancing the interest of society, and [that of] the organizations that compile and use records against the interest of individuals who are the subject of record [Government Information . . . ,1975, p. 34]." That is the salient fact confronting us. State statutes do not add up to a comprehensive and consistent body of law. They reflect no coherent or conceptually unified approach to balancing the interest of society and the organizations that compile and use records against the individuals who are the subject of record.

We must face certain facts:

1. Thousands of pieces of information can be stored on the head of a pin.
2. The miniscule computer is the single most significant technological development looming ahead.
3. "The computer is the ubiguitous instrument of managerial, technological progress [Management Information Report, 1978]."
4. Sensitive personal confidential data can be collected and stored, cheaply, as never before and retrieved in seconds.
5. If computers are one modern phenomenon, society's ever-increasing expectations, high expectations of government and the private sector, is another.
6. The three major objectives stated by the PPSC need to be kept ever before us. These are (a) minimize intrusiveness, (b) maximize fairness, and (c) legitimize the expectations of confidentiality.
7. Too much information is being given and recieved.
8. Information should be used only for the purposes collected.
9. Organizations should not transfer information without the knowledge and consent of the subject.
10. Information subjects should have a right to see and copy personal records and have them corrected.

As the PPSC (1977c) puts it in its Appendix volume on *Technology and Privacy*:

> The most significant implication of transaction data captured in machine-readable form stems from the fact that they can be readily utilized for multiple purposes, some of which may be unrelated to the transactions or events that generated them. . . . A major problem created by the widespread application of computer and telecommunication technology to personal-data record-keeping is the inability to anticipate and control future uses of information. Systems evolve on the basis of immediate need, often with little or no explicit consideration of their long-term consequences for individuals of society as a whole. . . . It is clear that there are inherent dangers, and while it may sometimes be difficult to visualize them in their full array, it is essential to understand the kinds of choices they may present and, broadly, the kinds of public-policy initiatives that will tend to keep them from being realized.

Only recently, in the expanding capacity of government and the private sector to handle and spread information have state legislators recognized a threat to privacy that requires comprehensive and consistent state legislation. "To meet both constitutional standards and the needs of government, such privacy legislation should take into account the interests affected by government records-keeping: the individual's need for privacy, the government's need for information, and the public's need for access to government records [National Association of Attorneys General, 1976, p. 6]." In addition, privacy legislation must take into account the effects on the individual and on society of records keeping in the private sector.

This can be an extremely important workshop, but it is only one of the numerous meetings, workshops, and conferences on privacy held during the 1970s. Indeed, I participated in a fascinating international workshop on privacy and confidentiality in England last fall. Computerization of records has been instrumental in bringing about a conjunction of legal, social, and political ferment and events in the privacy field that has led inevitably to emotional and intellectual interest and profound inquiry into its significance in terms of our innermost values. It should not be surprising that the NCCUSL appointed a committee to determine the feasibility and desirability of drafting a Uniform Law Act and, on receiving that committee's affirmative response, instructed it to draft a Uniform Act for States.

The State Information Practices Act is but a beginning of the committee's endeavor to prepare and propose appropriate uniform state privacy legislation. The final act will encompass public and private sectors. Among the governmental areas being studied for possible inclusion are criminal justice, hospital and medical records, social services, financial and tax records, and in the private sector, insurance and possibly, credit and bank records. Actually, the committee has been advised to "punt" in certain areas on the theory that those areas have either been fairly well preempted by federal law or simply do not lend themselves to uniformity in state law. Such areas include educational records, personnel records and, to some degree, credit and bank records. We have made no final determination as yet.

So, the Fair Informations Practice draft is only the first paling in a fence that ultimately should constitute a Comprehensive Privacy Act for states.

The committee recognizes a central concern in the record-keeping practices of government and private agencies regarding personal information. That concern extends to what information is recorded, who has access to it, and what use is made of it. Clearly, vast stores of personal information are maintained by government and private agencies and organizations through computerized and manual records, often without knowledge of the subject who, if he knew, may not have the power to see or correct the record. State legislation currently is at best a leaky umbrella. It needs not merely patching but a new carefully wrought statute embracing a creative, coherent, and practical approach. We are aware of the various principles which have been agreed on at federal level: openness, individual access, individual participation, collection limitation, use limitation, disclosure limitation, information management, and account-ability. We know that we must identify and require compliance with appropriate information principles and practices designed to guard against potential harmful consequences from personal data systems by protecting privacy, accuracy and fairness. Our provisions relate, in various ways, to subject access to personal records, power to challenge the accuracy of records and to correct erroneous records, confidential status for certain records, effective sanctions to ensure compliance with prescribed information practices, and appropriate recourse to civil and criminal remedies for actual violation. The final statute will have application to records kept by both government and the private sector.

A guiding principle is avoidance of secrecy for its own sake. There should always be an excellent reason for confidentiality. Nor are privacy and access always opposites. For example, the access of a subject to records relating to self is an inherent part of privacy legislation. Although the committee deals with disclosural privacy, it will consider other types, including electronic surveillance.

Let me stress our awareness of the tradition of access and openness. Let us always remember that the First Amendment guarantee of freedom of speech, press, and worship preceded the recognition of any constitutional guarantee of privacy. It is no chance occurrence that the Congress enacted Freedom of Information and "Government in the Sunshine" Acts in the same time span as the Privacy Act. Access is vital in a democracy, for people must be informed to make intelligent decisions about themselves and their government. President James Madison said it early and well: "Knowledge will forever govern ignorance and the people who need to be their own governors must arm themselves with the power knowledge gives. A popular government without popular information or the means of acquiring it is but the prologue to a farce or tragedy or perhaps both." Accordingly, the PPSC has decided that our product should encompass both privacy and open access (or freedom of information) as both sides of the same coin. In other words, we are seeking an integrated product that will embrace the principle of open access, except as it is and should be limited by appropriate privacy considerations. Thus, ours will become a Uniform Privacy and Freedom of Information Act, composed of a number of parts or sections and ultimately constituting, it is hoped, a Privacy Code for States. Our immediate goal is to have privacy in government records, that is, a State Information Practices segment, ready for adoption by the conference this summer, to have an initial draft of the Freedom of Information Act up for first reading, and to give a priority to later segments relating specifically to criminal justice and hospital and medical records. The entire project will be promulgated over a period of years.

This will be a complex process. The problems of concept, drafting, and administration are immense. For example, in my own state of North Carolina, the Police Information Network (PIN), Corrections computer, Motor Vehicles computer, and the Administrative Office of the Courts computer will all circulate information which often is related and tempts the use of interface. Some information on those criminal justice computers could be interfaced with that on Social Services and Mental Health computers. Should this be? How should the uniform law affect this kind of decision? The contract existing between the PIN and the FBI computer assures national distribution of information gathered in state, but it also may violate the state's public records laws. Can uniform state law resolve the myriad conflicts and confusion of current law and practice? Certainly much needs to be done in this area, and we expect to move with courage and determination in our drafting process. With the advent of a new computer vocabulary and a remarkable catalog of computer capabilities, with universal identifiers and human curiosity, how do we assure that those parts of our lives and of the record of our lives that are strictly personal (no one else's business) do not become an open book to be thumbed, read, and used by intruders with no rational or justifiable interest?

The PPSC will need the advice of interested and concerned individuals and groups. We are striving to collate and interpret the experience of states which have fair information practices acts, privacy acts, freedom of information acts, and other laws affecting privacy and access. We seek the broadest spectrum of ideas and opinions. We are blessed with an able, tough review board and distinguished advisors. We will need both—and more. Our subject is complex and sensitive, involving divergent principles, needs, and directions. If a free flow of information is fundamental in our society, and if liberty and freedom are dependent on public awareness of fact and truth, then the right of individuals to maintain personal privacy is equally fundamental and essential.

As one legal scholar puts it: "Invasion of the sanctity of a person's privacy will be as destructive to a society's freedom and liberty as will the foreclosure of information about the acts of government in such a society [Government Information . . . , 1975]."

If privacy is as Justice Harlan put it, "implicit in the concept of ordered liberty" *(Griswold* v. *Connecticut,* 1975), is a right of personal privacy, or a guarantee of certain areas or zones of privacy does exist under the Constitution *(Roe* v. *Wade,* 1973) and under state statutes, then it is important that the states have a harmonious and consistent approach to the law of privacy. "At a time when government and private sectors are acquiring and retaining more information about individuals and their files than ever was possible or conceivable in the past, there is special need for concern about 'personal autonomy' and the ability of any human being to pick and choose for himself the time and circumstances, and most importantly, the extent to which his attitudes, beliefs, behavior, and opinions are to be shared with or withheld from others [Ruebhausen and O'Brien, 1965]."

As we pursue our quest for a fair, effective Uniform State Information Practices Act, embracing privacy and access in appropriate balance, we welcome counsel. The plethora of legitimate questions facing us can only be indicated here. Does an open record become any less a public record under law because it is placed in a computer containing confidential matter? How should the presence of divergent kinds of information in a computer affect public and private access? Is the real problem that of determining what goes into a computer?

If I could not bring a draft of our Uniform Privacy Act to the workshop today, it is because we are still drafting. Only last weekend, in Arlington, Virginia, the PPSC moved to implement decisions reached in New Orleans in December. We defined more specifically the scope and purpose of the Uniform Privacy Act. We sought guidelines to give meaning to the standard "clearly unwarranted invasion of personal privacy."

What categories of records, we asked again and again, should be protected in terms of privacy or freedom of information? What records should be open? Which should be closed? When? How? Why? Are we creating a set of new rights, we asked ourselves, and, if so, how do we identify and define them?

Clearly, one person's privacy can be another person's freedom of information, and vice versa. At this point the PPSC majority voted to set up classifications or categories of information requiring records to be protected for the reason that access would represent an unwarranted invasion of privacy. We debated whether the list should be merely illustrative or presumptive, or a legally binding, nondisclosable, definitive list. The PPSC majority decided that the list should be presumptive.

That decision may or may not stick. New drafting is underway. More questions still exist: What triggers disclosure? How are exceptions applied—exceptions such as health, safety, imminent peril, statutory exemption? What other specifics or categories of information not on the laundry list may be covered under the catch-all "unwarranted invasion of privacy" standard?

The laundry list approach may be desirable from the standpoint of making the Uniform Information Act application more explicit, but it may also result in overbroad, simplistic, and generally undesirable applications of the privacy concept. I think it is safe to say we are at a waystop, but not at our final destination in the drafting of the Uniform Information Act. Once the new version is distributed and comment received, circulated and considered, more soul-searching, perspiring, thinking, and changes will be in order.

The PPSC did agree on a statement of scope and purpose. It reads:

> This Act recognizes and enforces the individual's right of privacy as to records in the possession of government. The Act does not affect the availability of records otherwise open to the public except to the extent that access to the records is restricted or prohibited under this Act.

The PPSC also received the first draft of a Freedom of Information Act. In the months ahead a strong effort will be made to make the acts consonant so that concepts, processes, and procedures will be consistent, integrated, and workable.

Obviously much work lies ahead, but, lest the degree of challenge be mistaken for pause, I can assure you that the PPSC *unanimously* believes that our task is worthwhile, needed, and possible and has no doubt that we will reach our goals. To say more than that at this time or even to attempt to give you a timetable would be unwise.

It is sufficient to state that our Uniform State Information Practices Act will be presented to the conference in San Diego in August for second reading. Our Freedom of Information Act should be ready for a first reading. Whether a "laundry list" or categories are included in that act, work on new, separate sections relating to criminal justice, health and medical records, and other areas will begin in the fall. By the summer of 1979, we hope we shall have the *entire* act, embracing Privacy and Freedom of Information, ready for adoption by the Uniform Laws Conference and submission to the states.

The subject predictably is proving so complex that any notion that simple solutions are either possible or desirable should be dispelled at once. I have before me a letter from one who has been intimately involved with the revision of the Ohio Fair Information Practices Act. In one sentence he writes

> . . . it is analytically clear that disclosure of the same record might be required in the public interest in one set of circumstances and required to be kept quiet under another set of

circumstances. It is also analytically clear that legitimate reasons may be given for permitting a rather widespread disclosure of personal information to persons charged by law with the duty to keep it confidential. When you add these and other analytical concepts to the volume of people and personal information about them, the rights of the public and the individual not only collide—they become commingled and confused.

Our task is to untangle the comingling, clear up the confusion, and come up with a cogent Uniform Law Act founded on such proven virtues as balance and integrity. We expect to do just that.

There are questions to be answered regarding the propagation of amendments and corrections, oversight or review by a state agency or direct access to the courts, the nature and extent of controls, including those over research of statistical records, and, indeed, the existence, type, and authority of an agency charged with control of state record-keeping policy and practices, and so practices, and so many more.

Our Information Practices Act is in its fifth draft. We call for an Information Practices Agency with powers in a person, not necessarily in a separate agency grafted upon an existent agency. We recognize that this may be a sticky point. So may be our decision to exact civil and criminal penalties, and our concept of personal records having privacy applications. The road ahead is long and dangerous.

Yet, the benefits of having uniform laws are many. For example, the certainty of concept as to those particular personal, individually identifiable records to which privacy law applies could bring greater efficiency and economy nationwide to the handling of government records and encourage official and citizen awareness of rights through standardizing law, practices, and working relationships between state and local officials and public personnel, press and public in the various states. Consistency would be encouraged in the practices and laws governing the collection, use, release, sealing, and destruction of records. The assurance that individuals be made aware of the existence and content of records can be given on a uniform basis. The responsibility for providing access, for supervision, and for review can be clarified and put in more serviceable context through the uniform pattern. More specifically, the existence of similar civil and criminal penalties would be useful in the prosecution of offenders and the accumulation of precedent. The uniform approach to the research and statistical records has obvious advantages to the faculties of colleges and universities and other research people throughout the land. Overall, there are clear advantages in dropping the barriers of state lines working with and through uniform law, principles, and goals.

To permit the chaotic state of state law to continue without an effort to harmonize statutes would be in itself a disservice to the cause of good government. Who can question that "the basis for collecting and manipulating data is increasing at a far greater rate than our skill in examining the mechanics of how decisions are made and how those can be improved (Wedin, 1978)? Who can deny the vision of a time when data is perceived in the interest of humankind?

We have come a long way since George Bernard Shaw said Americans have no sense of privacy. We have come a longer way since Oscar Wilde wrote that all advice is bad and some is worse, Yet, in our odyssey, we still taste the lotus flower and view too much through the single eye of Cyclops. The Elizabethan poet said of himself on his deathbed: "John Donne, Undone." The computer is a wonderful tool for more, quick, and essential access to information almost unlimited. The human challenge is to make the utmost appropriate use and application of computer technology, yet to resist its siren song to expose everything. We must, through law, preserve and enhance *both* the guarantees of freedom of information *and* privacy. So long as laws are patchy, inconsistent, and inadequate, the records of our lives will remain patchy, inconsistent, and inadequate. The very existence of computerized files will continue to pose threats to individual well-being.

The first song that Ginger Rogers ever sang in a motion picture began: *I'm a little lonesome babe in the woods—uh-huh! I've got it, but it don't do me no good.* We've got it, but it may do us limited good, unless we achieve a balance and enhancement of personal and group freedoms in privacy and access legislation at state as well as federal level.

Sometimes there may be a temptation to resort to lyrics of another song sung by Groucho Marx: *Whatever it is, I'm against it, and ever since I first commenced it, I'm against it.* However, if we cannot eliminate the negative, we can accentuate the positive. There's irony and paradox in all this. We need *much* more access to assure that we reach our goals in *privacy:* Access to facts as a basis for comparison, evaluation and legal drafting; access to minds and hearts that the problem may be better understood and decisions made wisely and well.

In sum, people must continue to be master of the machine. The computer must be understood—in all its potential, actuality, and implications—and harnessed to the philosophical, social, economic, political, and personal needs of a free people. The need of the individual to be protected in his personal affairs must be fully preserved. The right and need of the public to be informed in a way to protect both the development of information and talents in a participatory democracy must be fully preserved. The balance to be struck must in no way diminish the two rights. To achieve these goals, a consistent, coherent, Uniform State Privacy and Freedom of Information Act is essential. To do less is to tarnish all our shining new computer vocabulary and process, hardware and software, and to endanger the realization of the American dream.

References

Capek, K. *R. U. R.* New York: Doubleday, 1923.

Government information and the rights of citizens. *Michigan Law Review*, 1975, *73*, 34.

Kent, L. (Ed.). *Privacy, a public concern: A resource document.* The Domestic Council of State Governors. Washington, D.C.: U.S. Government Printing Office, 1975.

Management Information Report, 1978, *10*, 1–3.

Nader, R. The dossier invades the home. *Saturday Review*, April 17, 1971.

National Association of Attorneys' General. *Privacy: Personal data and the law.* 1976.

Privacy Protection Study Commission. *Personal Privacy in information society.* Washington, D.C.: U.S. Government Printing Office, 1977. (a)

Privacy Protection Study Commission. *Privacy law in the states.* Washington, D.C.: U.S. Government Printing Office, 1977 (b)

Privacy Protection Study Commission. *Technology and privacy.* Washington D.C.: U.S. Government Printing Office, 1977. (c)

Rice, E. *The adding machine.* New York: Samuel French, 1956.

Roe v. *Wade*, 410 U.S. 113, 1973.

Ruebhausen, O., and O'Brien, O., Jr. Privacy and behavioral research. *Columbia Law Review*, 1965, 1184.

Wedin, W.D. Technology and the future of local government. *Public Management*, 1978, *60*, 5.

Comment on "Nonuniform Privacy Laws: Implications and Attempts at Uniformity"

David Johnston

Dr. Everest's presentation covers a considerable area and suggests a number of possibilities for further comment. A legislative researcher might well like to explore the relationships between privacy laws, freedom of information laws, and the data used in legislative research. He or she might be deeply concerned with interrelationships of privacy and freedom of information laws; certainly, we in Ohio have been confronted with real problems concerning where one law leaves off and the other takes over. The drafter–researcher should also be concerned with the unintended effect the legislation has on those it affects. One unintended effect arises when one person or firm is required to conform to two or more state privacy laws which differ in content.

Everest has indicated well the nature of problems which might occur under nonuniform state privacy laws and has defined those persons who might be expected to benefit from uniform privacy laws. He correctly points out that the greater problems of nonuniformity lie in laws which affect the private sector. If Illinois and Minnesota have different requirements for their handling of state data, their requirements only affect Illinois and Minnesota, respectively, as collectors and maintainers of data. Illinois does not conduct state operations in Minnesota so it can ignore Minnesota law. Although there are significant exceptions, for the most part, at the state level the data subjects are mostly residents of the regulating state.

In a private operation things may be different. A single company could have to conform to Illinois, Minnesota, and Ohio law. A system that meets Illinois requirements might not meet those of the other states. And for the firm that wants to do the least possible, this could be a problem in that it would require more programming and more complex programming to have a records system which minimally meets the requirements of three jurisdictions. Even here, the problem is not as great as it seems because the states have not entered into

163

general regulation of private information systems, nor does there seem to be any great demand for them to do so on a broad comprehensive scale. They are, however, considering laws in selected areas such as consumer credit reporting or financial records.

The states are still trying to find answers to the problems of protecting privacy of the individual in an age when all sorts of information about an individual can be assorted and dispensed automatically. They do not have all the answers, but neither does the federal government, nor do those persons who write uniform laws. As the separate states try to find answers they will pass laws. Those laws will be similar in many respects but they will vary as well. It is hoped that out of that variety we will determine the adequacy of each policy. Is Policy X cheaper than Policy Y? Does it work as well or better? What problems were encountered by one as compared with the other? Out of that we will get a better idea of what works well and what does not.

There may be a tradeoff—the special costs and problems of complying with nonuniform state laws versus the improved understanding which comes from taking more than one approach. We have not determined the cost of these as yet. It isn't all that clear that uniform law is necessary.

One problem with uniform law is deciding which uniform law to use. Everest has discussed the one which is being drafted by the National Conference of Commissioners on Uniform State Laws (NCCUSL). The NCCUSL are perhaps the most prestigious group, but they are not the only ones to have a uniform state privacy act. NASIS has put forth a model act. The Council of State Governments has a privacy act among its suggested state legislation. This is modeled after the Ohio act which borrowed from the NASIS model. The National Conference of State Legislatures' Ethics and Elections Committee (NCSL) has also developed a model law which will soon be available to state legislators. Although strictly speaking, only one of these is held forth as a uniform act, each by the nature of its sponsorship, can be viewed as such.

Everest's paper points out a failure on the part of the uniform law to reconcile freedom of information and privacy acts. The NCSL model attempts to reconcile the two by distinguishing between "public records" and "personal information classified as private or confidential." "Private personal information" is not public but is accessible to the data subject. "Confidential personal information" is neither public nor accessible to the data subject. A Government Information Practices Board classifies by rule, personal information maintained by government agencies as public, private, or confidential. The model sets forth some standards for the classification of personal information and for its collection.

The NCSL act would allow an individual, upon request, to know whether he is the subject of personal information collected, whether that information is classified as public, private, or confidential, and to have disclosed to him the public and private information of which he is the subject. It gives him the right to contest the accuracy of the data and requires the agency holding the data to (1) correct the data and notify those who have received the erroneous information of the correction, or (2) notify the individual that the disagreement continues and that the Government Information Practices Board will determine the issue. The contested information could not be disclosed until the Board made its determination. A person asked to supply personal information is to be informed of its purpose and intended use, whether he is legally required to supply the information, how the information will be classified, and the legal consequences arising from supplying or not supplying the information or giving false information.

The NCSL act includes a section on rights to public records and lists records which would not be subject to public disclosure. Private and confidential personal information are exempt by definition.

The act sets forth some limitations on public agencies in collecting, classifying, and permitting access to personal information and requires them to establish procedures to assure confidentiality and accuracy of personal information. The act needs further refinement with respect to use of private and confidential personal information for research and statistical purposes.

The foregoing is not intended to be either the promotion of the NCSL draft or a detailed explanation of it, but rather an illustration of the possibilities of going in different directions even while drafting so-called uniform laws. I like the NCSL model because of what it does to reconcile privacy and freedom of information statutes, but I am certain some new, eclectic model could be generated from a careful review of it, the other model laws, and an analysis of problems the states have faced. This in itself seems to argue that adopting a uniform law has disadvantages which can be revealed through each state reviewing its problem, looking at the experience of others, and coming up with the law which best meets its needs. As we evolve the system which has the fewest bugs, then we can also develop a more adequate uniform law.

Everest's advice to organizations to avoid sole reliance on the specifics of state and federal legislation and to foresake trying to operate at minimum compliance levels is well taken. Organizations that are operating with a program that is sensitive to the rights of individuals should experience little trouble.

Our political system is essentially an open one. Those who are to be affected by legislation should be aware of it, relate it to their operations, provide information on how it affects their operations, and work to have their position taken into account in its development. If they do this well, the absence of state-to-state uniformity should not be too much of a problem.

The Long-Term Implications of Computers for Privacy and the Protection of Public Order

Alan F. Westin

Introduction

My assignment at this conference is to discuss the long-term implications of computers for privacy and the protection of public order. Having suggested this topic originally to Lance Hoffman, I feel comfortable in trying to state the topic with somewhat greater specificity. What I want to discuss is how computers (by which I will always mean in this paper the combination of computers and communication devices) have been used in the criminal justice system during the past two decades in pursuit of public order for a democratic society (that is, in keeping with our traditions of individual rights, of which privacy has become an increasingly important element). On the basis of my analysis of the past two decades, I promised to venture some speculations about the way computers could and should be used in the criminal justice area during the 1980s.

To keep my paper to a reasonable length for its initial presentation, I have used a lot of shorthand (though, I hope, little jargon). I do this because our group is a collection of experts in the privacy and computers field. However, I trust enough specificity has been provided here to offer either a firm target for attack or a persuasive statement for the like-minded.

A Brief Roadmap of My Trip

I propose first to clarify just where computers have been used with any significant effect in the criminal justice process as a whole. Having identified that area for closer inspection, I will analyze how such computer uses have affected both the protection of public order and of personal privacy.

167

As a matter of preliminary definition, let me indicate that when I talk about the criminal justice system or process I am referring to the interconnected operations of six sets of governmental institutions: police, prosecutors, courts, probation, corrections, and parole. Some would add the defense counsel, especially where this is institutionalized into publicly funded defender offices; I can accept such a broadening of the system though it seems to insert a set of actors with different, even adversary relationships to the other players.

Continuing the swift definitions, I will use the term "privacy" to cover three major issues of informational policy involving individual rights. These are (1) questions as to what personal information is legitimate for an institution or organization to collect or record about individuals or groups; (2) questions about how personal information, once collected, is handled inside organizations to protect the confidentiality of the data and when or how it will be released outside the organization; and (3) questions of access by individuals to their own records, in order to question or challenge the accuracy, completeness, and uses being made of such information.

Next, I see both privacy and public order as representing equally compelling social interests in a democratic society that are often unavoidably in tension. The goal of law and public policy is to identify where the interest of each basic value may in fact collide, to narrow as much as possible the area of conflict, and to adopt rules of law and organizational behavior that choose one or another value in a particular context. Despite the rhetoric of ideologues at both extremes, democratic policy at its best, and most effective, is rarely absolute and global when it is adjusting the balances between these two values.

I should also indicate that I subscribe to what is sometimes called the "soft determinist" view of technological change. When a powerful (and expensive) new technology such as computers and communication systems is developed, the questions of who will use this new power, for what ends, and under what constraints becomes (once the potential of the new technology is recognized) more a matter of social policy than of technological determinism. The "social filter" of modern, complex societies is extremely dense, amounting to a web of legal, economic, organizational, and social constraints. Technology rarely if ever bursts through this web. Rather, it makes a gradual passage, and, in the process, both the technology is altered in its forms of application and the strands of the social web are rearranged, sometimes opening to accommodate new forms of action and sometimes holding firm to block or reshape the technology. Following this perspective, as I have written in other places, I believe that the computer did not create our current privacy problems; that we would be deeply engaged in debating the balances between privacy and public order even if no computers were around, but that once the computer did spread through the organizational world, and the *execution* of organizational policies has increasingly been through the assistance of computer systems, our debates over how to balance the values of privacy and other social interests will increasingly be conducted in terms of how computerized data bases and communication networks are to be created, managed, and controlled.

Finally, let me indicate that I approach the problems of crime and criminal justice with a sober sense that there are no easy solutions to be applied here. Having read much of the professional and academic literature in the field, I come away with these beliefs:

1. Nothing that we are practically able to do will be likely to reduce dramatically and quickly the levels and types of crimes that are now prevalent.
2. We know far less about how to understand and apply solutions to the policing function than we like to admit.
3. The structure and procedures of the classic American adjudicative system are seriously failing to provide prompt and efficient justice.
4. Our correctional system is often medieval in its rigors and neither its mainstream nor the hopeful experiments of recent decades show signs of accomplishing large-scale rehabilitation of offenders.
5. The only overall stance that seems realistic and politically viable today is one of controlled *experimentation* with new techniques and structures.
6. The preservation of basic civil liberties and the lessening of race bias in the social system will be critical to the long-term viability of any new solutions or structures that we attempt.

Each of these terse statements could be a chapter in a book, and they obviously raise more issues than they settle. But they more or less define the landscape from which I look at computer use, and that ought to help in judging some of the things I will say.

Computer Use in the Criminal Justice Process

There is no need to dwell at length for this group on the early and widespread adoption of computers by the police at local, state, and federal levels over the past two decades; the heavy expenditures of money by the Law Enforcement Assistance Administration (LEAA) during the past decade to expand such uses; and the more recent spread of computer systems into other areas of criminal justice through so-called "court information systems" and uses in corrections and parole. The presence of computer systems now permeates the conduct of criminal justice administration.

Yet it is striking how *little real effect* computer use has had on the great majority of issues and problems that make up the total criminal justice process. For example:

1. We do not understand the *causes* of crime much better as a result of computer uses.
2. We have not been helped in knowing how to *define* what should be criminal.
3. We are not able to *predict* criminal behavior in individuals more effectively.
4. Computers have not been of importance in the *adjudication* of guilt or innocence in trials.
5. Computers have not helped in the assessment of *punishment*.
6. Computers have not helped in the *correction* of offenders once convicted.
7. Computers have not been able to help us determine more fairly or with better success which offenders to *parole* or to put on *probation*.
8. Computers have not played a role in *rehabilitation* policies for exoffenders.

As I will discuss in more detail shortly, it is only in the area of police *apprehension* of certain types of suspected criminals that computer use has so far had significant impact, for better or for worse.*

The point of my catalogue of nonimpact is not that computers are really Tinkertoys for cops but that it helps to start with the awareness that though computers pervade the criminal justice process daily, their real impact so far has been limited to a very small part of the total criminal justice process. To the extent that efficiencies have been achieved in that small area, police apprehension, without basic improvements in the rest of the criminal justice system, we may well be accentuating the institutional failures of (and, thereby, public concern with) the overall criminal justice system in the nation.

What accounts for the limited role of computers in the larger criminal justice process? I do not believe it has been any basic weakness in the technology itself. Both in terms of hardware capacities and software support, there is no shortage of information-processing power and flexibility, at reasonable costs. The impediments lie in the capacity of our society to apply the kind of power that computers offer to the improvement of our criminal justice system. Why? To remind readers of the obvious, but which so often is left unmentioned in discussions of computers and public order:

1. We do not agree as a society on the "real" causes of crime and how to treat them. Conservative views of criminal culture and the vice of permissiveness are at war with liberal notions of the class, race, and opportunity-structure foundations of much criminal behavior. While most leaders of both camps support the need at present for apprehending, trying, and punishing those guilty of crimes of violence and against property, whatever the deeper social causes of their conduct, the conflict over the sources of our current high crime

---

*As a scheduling and case-management tool, court information systems have proved to be an aid to hard pressed administrators. This has, alas, made only a very small contribution to resolving the larger problems of the adjudicative process.

rates prevents the creation of a social consensus for the use of government power and blocks the kind of institutional reorganizations that would be necessary to apply computer resources as more than big adding machines and telephones.

2. Our system of federalism and our departmentalism within each executive branch has fostered the kind of "every agency gets its own computer" policy that may delight vendors but makes it very difficult to change the compartmentalization of information and the development of new policies derived from it. In addition, competition and conflict between the various agencies of criminal justice is such that it sometimes seems an act of religious faith rather than a description of reality to speak of the "criminal justice system."

3. We are not presently in a time of venturesome reform in American life. Our paralysis in providing systemic solutions to problems such as energy, employment, and race parallels our paralysis in mounting the kind of coordinated institutional and social policies toward crime prevention and treatment that might allow computers to play a larger, significant role.

4. Civil liberties limitations certainly help to explain some important failures of computer resources to improve the criminal justice process. To attempt to predict deviant trends in young children and provide program interventions, to apply probability theory to pretrial detention decisions, or to use computer analyses for matters such as sentencing or parole would require the collection of highly personal data beyond what currently surfaces through the criminal justice process. It also raises issues of due process in the requirement of making individual rather than probability judgments. As a result, some types of computer uses have been blocked because of privacy and due process interests.

5. Even though the great majority of Americans want more law and order, the distrust of authority that marks our post-Watergate era, the tarnished reputations of some law enforcement agencies, and general public apprehension about "computer data banks" and "Big Brother" have created a legislative climate in the late 1970s in which it is politically attractive to oppose large criminal justice information systems. Many state and federal legislators now believe that delaying or denying new computer projects may not only be serving civil liberties values but may also be good for politics, especially if the new systems cost a great deal of money (as they always do) and step on some established institutional or political toes (as they also tend to do).

In one area, police apprehension, I have said that we can observe significant computer impact. The main tools here have been (1) automated warrant-and-wanted information systems as developed by local communities (such as Alameda County, California's PIN system), the states (e.g., the New York State Identification and Intelligence System, NYSIIS), and the federal government (as with the FBI's National Crime Information Center, NCIC); (2) automated criminal history or "rap sheet" files (Project SEARCH, the FBI's Computerized Criminal History project, etc.); and (3) automated police command-and-control systems (such as IBM's system for mapping a community geographically, recording crime incidence in each unit by various factors, and assigning police resources according to the patterns detected). Computers have also been used by police, as we know, for various intelligence purposes, compiling lists of names and data about various classes of people such as member of organized crime, suspected terrorists, members of "radical" political groups, and the like, and either using these within a particular department or exchanging them with police in other jurisdictions.

Since my interest is in suggesting ways to analyze the impact of computer use on privacy and public order, and it is the police more than any other segment of the criminal justice system that has made significant use of computers, let me move on to a discussion of alternative techniques for making such an assessment of police use of electronic data processing (EDP) during the past two decades.

Perspectives on Police Computer Use and Privacy

I want to apply here what may be called a "functional analysis" of computer impact. The focus here is on how the use of computers affects the conduct of a particular function and the observance of privacy in that setting. The methodology consists of specifying what information policies and practices the organization used to carry on this function before it went to computer applications, and what the rules and practices as to privacy were in that precomputer setting. One then traces how computer use has altered the operations of the organization (using measures of efficiency and cost) and may have affected its observance of the privacy rules. There is always the problem of taking into account changes in public or special-group attitudes toward privacy or new legal rules that may have developed along with, but were not directly caused by, the use of automated systems in this area.

This is essentially the technique used in the National Academy of Sciences (NAS) study in 1969–1972 (Westin and Baker, 1972), covering 14 functional areas of record-keeping about individuals in society. It was also applied to the studies of computer use in health care and in personal administration conducted through the U.S. National Bureau of Standards (Westin, 1976, 1979). Without doing its own empirical research, the Department of Health, Education and Welfare (DHEW) report (1973) *Records, Computers, and the Rights of Citizens* adopted a similar concentration on general principles of fair information practices, to be applied whether computers or manual processes might be creating unfairness, or intrusiveness. In its creation of the Privacy Protection Study Commission, the Privacy Act of 1974 called for an inquiry area by area in the private sector to examine just how organizational data practices might be altering traditional rights to privacy.

Applying the functional approach to the past two decades of police computer uses, the judgments reached in the NAS study in 1972 do not seem to me to be dramatically different in 1979. The 1972 conclusions were that police uses of warrant-and-wanted systems, criminal history systems, and intelligence systems were

1. Not yet leading the police to collect more intrusive or sensitive personal information about the subjects of these records than had traditionally been collected and recorded in those systems in manual operation;
2. Not yet exchanging personal information with different types of agencies or institutions than had received such data previously;
3. Not yet limiting or making it less practical for individuals to see and challenge their own records, where such right of inspection had been afforded by law or practice;
4. Improving in some ways on the accuracy and security of personal data used in the precomputer criminal justice process while, at the same time, creating new problems of accuracy and security in the automated systems that would require major attention to control.

The functional analysis also found that the adoption of computer technology by the police was having some important positive effects. It was leading to the creation of centralized networks uniting users at a given level of government, or across levels of government, in police data systems that were creating more uniformity and would lead to a greater central supervision than had previously existed in police data exchanges. It was also found that most of the sensitive privacy issues in police collection and use of personal data were not basically computer-generated as much as broader social policy questions now involved in how either manual or computer record systems should operate. Should police records of arrest or even of conviction be available for non-law-enforcement uses, such as for government licensing and employment? Should any information be recorded about political protest activities protected by the First Amendment, and how was the line to be drawn between such conduct and potentially violent or terrorist activity that society expected the police to monitor through data collection? What kinds of offenses should or should not go into a criminal history system (juvenile offenses, misdemeanors, "political" violations, morals convictions, etc.)? Should notations of arrests without disposition be entered in a criminal history record circulated outside the jurisdicion where the arrest was made?

All of these issues were found by the NAS study to be matters of social policy in which the building of automated police information systems essentially *supplied the occasion* for concentrated attention by interest groups, the media, legislators, government chief executives and other participants in the policymaking process. For them not to press for clear privacy-respecting policies in the new computer systems would have been to ignore the fact that more and more police transactions were being moved into automated forms of storage and communication, and that controlling such conduct would be basic to protecting privacy. But to assume that such problems were something that the computer use as of 1972 had *caused* would be to make a fundamental error of social analysis.

One point might be made in updating the 1972 findings to the present. The NAS report was published prior to the unraveling of the Watergate conspiracy and its associated invasions of privacy; prior to the disclosure of the FBI's COINTELPRO files and their uses and prior to revelations of the CIA's files about American citizens. In *all* of these situations, though computer systems were used as large file drawers, the EDP was *by no means* the essential mechanism of the improper data collection and use. But the revelations that law enforcement and intelligence agencies had usurped powers and violated legal restraints provided the American public with the answer to what had previously been the major skeptical response to warnings about government invasion of privacy: Show us which public officials would abuse their informational resources. Privacy advocates know that they have Richard Nixon and the plumbers to thank for passage of the Privacy Act of 1974, since the misdeeds of executive and law-enforcement officials uncovered in the Ervin and Church Committee hearings provided the clear-cut examples of official misuse of personal files. This, in turn, supplied the justification for enacting privacy legislation that would have substantial costs in money, personnel time, and program convenience.

It can be argued that the functional approach, based as it is on a precomputer baseline and an application-by-application analysis of computer usage, contains a conservative bias. The assumption is that if one focuses so intently on empirical changes in the scope of data collection, patterns of data sharing, individual-access policies, and comparative opportunities for data security, one may miss a leap of cumulation. Organizational operations, it is assumed, may develop into a system with such great reliance on automated data and network communications that key balances of power will be altered—between individual and organization, between state units and federal managers, or between the executive and legislative branches.

This fear might be worth considering *if* the functional approach inevitably counseled doing nothing about installing privacy protections until computer impact reached some level of explosive social proportions. But the functional analysis of the NAS and DHEW reports were linked to proposals for new privacy laws, regulations, and policies to govern the use of computer systems in each specific area of information activity. And, far from being accepting of computer *laissez innover*, the functional approach tries to pinpoint the places where policy interventions can truly affect organizational uses of power.

As proof of this, many managers of large organizations that I know look back rather wistfully to the good old manual-era days when it was largely a matter of organizational policy what they collected, how they verified it (if at all), with whom they exchanged it, and what rights of notice, inspection, and challenge they chose to give to the subjects of records.

Now, they sometimes lament, the damn law doesn't let them run their "internal" affairs in the autonomous ways they used to. In this critical sense, *privacy protections for individuals*—in an irony we should not miss—*are basically sunshine laws for the information practices of organizations.*

This is, I submit, the record of the past decade in the development of both computer use and privacy protections in the police function. When I first became a consultant on privacy to the New York State Identification and Intelligence System, in 1967, right of individual access to rap sheets was the rare exception in any police department. Error rates of 30–40% in such files were the norm, and as many as one-third of the rap sheets lacked disposition data for arrests. Employers enjoyed widespread access to police arrest records, sometimes by law and even more often by payoffs to cooperative police officials. Extensive manual dossiers on alleged subversive political, radical, and social groups were a standard feature of local Red Squads, state police, and federal agencies. The racial bias of arrest records in denying employment opportunities to blacks and other racial minorities had not yet been recognized or held to constitute a violation of the federal Civil Rights Act of 1964. The record systems were full of arrests and/or convictions for civil rights protest, antiwar protest, marijuana use, and other offenses whose character raised serious questions. Though the Warren Court had been at work for over a decade in striking down unlawful police practices involving coerced confessions, illegal detention, delayed arraignments, illegal wiretapping, and other police misconduct, the record systems of our law enforcement system were permanently enshrining and relying on the results of such illegalities in their operations. No widely known or practical system for correcting mistakes of fact or errors of constitutional practice were in operation. In short, the manual-record milieu was horrendous in terms of privacy protection.

When I looked at the FBI's NCIC system for the NAS study in 1970–1972, our society was just in the process of changing the rules of the game as to police information policy, whether in manual or automated systems. Protests by the racial groups, studies of police record uses and their effects, media treatment of these problems, court rulings declaring record practices to be violations of privacy and due process, early state privacy legislation, progressive policy recommendations by projects such as NYSIIS and Project SEARCH, and a host of other actions were greasing the way. Hoover had seen only a little of the light by then, but even under his internal rules, new policies of individual access, rules of data limitation, and requirements of record completion were beginning to be installed in the NCIC. The functional approach informed an often unbelieving community of civil libertarians and media reporters that the NCIC was *not* full of intelligence data, that it did not even have summary criminal history information, and that it represented, at that point, only a faster version of the wanted-person and stolen-property files that the FBI had maintained since the 1920's with access to those data available to the same set of law enforcement agencies and "others" that had long used the mails, teletype, and telephones to share the same type of data. What our analysis warned was that allowing the FBI to run a national automated criminal history system just because it had done a good job of getting the national wanted-and-warrant file into operation would be a serious threat to state management of local law enforcement; would place a policy agency in charge of records needed by courts and other criminal justice agencies; and would ignore the considerable dangers to independent statistical resources as to crime and criminal justice programs in having any one line agency of criminal justice run the nation's basic criminal justice record system. By suggesting what were fantasies and what were real issues, the functional approach helped to set the policy debates on their proper course.

Today, little is left of the "good old days" of the precomputer era, or the early "get the systems up and running" days of the 1960s. Plenty of policy issues of privacy in law enforcement information systems remain, let me emphasize, and there are many social issues other than privacy that now demand our attention in computer system projects. I submit that the functional analysis showed us the right places to focus our concern, identified the kinds of policy interventions that would bring computer uses into visibility, and allowed the public, through the legislative process, to install the first generation of privacy laws for a computer age.

What about the other side of the coin that I am supposed to examine, the impact of computer use on the protection of public order? I have no hesitation in saying that, in addition to its value in general personnel administration, computer use has helped the apprehension function of the police forces using this tool. Clearly, more fugitives have been located more frequently or more quickly with the NCIC system than would have been true without it. Computerized rap sheets have helped police in their preliminary assessment of a suspect's likelihood of involvement in criminal conduct. Tracking what crimes regularly take place at what time in what areas has also helped police officials make somewhat better allocations of personnel and resources. I have more doubts about the value of some police intelligence systems, but even here, what

I know of Justice Department use of computerized intelligence data about organized crime operations or Secret Service files relating to persons who might represent threats to the president and other officials, leads me to believe that there has been improvement in agency operations through these systems.

If one, however, has to weigh these improvements against not just the dollar costs of the computer systems but also what economists call the *opportunity costs* of foregoing other policy actions, I am not sure what my judgment would be. My experiences with law enforcement agencies that have embarked on bold computer projects only to see them wither or misfire because of a variety of organizational, political, and social realities makes me conclude that not much of police computer use between 1965 and 1980 will be assessed by observers in the 1990s or the year 2000 as very effective. In his recent book *Criminal Violence, Criminal Justice,* Charles Silberman (1978) concludes that most of the bright new "high technology" programs in police departments have not accomplished much. He notes that the command and control and rapid response systems based on computers and communication links, as well as the reliance on modus operandi files and rap-sheet analysis, have not significantly aided the way the great majority of criminals are actually apprehended. Most are still caught because a victim identifies them, not through hits on the NCIC or its state and local counterparts.

This raises another point that Silberman makes with eloquence. Our society's racially biased economic and social policies and our unwillingness to spend the moneys necessary to help overcome past discrimination have led to widespread hostility to and noncooperation with the police in minority areas. With police detection and apprehension so heavily dependent on local resident and victim cooperation for its real success, it is our police who suffer the most direct harm from the failure of society at large to use its resources to reduce race and class conflict, and give more of our poorer citizens a meaningful stake in supporting "the system."

In this perspective, the ways in which society has allowed the police to use large amounts of public money for computerization efforts in the 1960s and 1970s brings to mind the classic story of the policeman who came upon a drunk on his hands and knees in the gutter, under a lamppost. "And have you lost something, sir?" the policeman asked. "Yesh, officer," the drunk replied, "I dropped my cufflink when I got out of my car." "But sir," said the policeman, "your car is 20 feet down the block. Why are you looking here?" "Why, because the light is better," came the answer.

I do not entirely fault police officials for trying to use computers where the light seems to be brighter, even though the basic problems lie somewhere else. They know what legislators and the public will pay for, and they also want to have tools that they can use in the here-and-now. The real problem seems to me our society's value system and its unwillingness to commit a larger share of its admittedly scarce resources of money and attention to the root causes of most crime, and the support of a dignified, modern, and humane court and correctional establishment. No sensible observer would expect such policies to *eliminate* crime, but it could begin to reduce it, and that may be as much as our complex, driven society ought reasonably to hope to accomplish. As long as we do *not* commit major new resources in this way, however, I believe computers will be of only marginal help to the police, as were other hopeful new technologies of the past, such as fingerprint identification and two-way radio communication in police cars.

Prospects for Computer Use in Criminal Justice in the 1980s

Starting first with the conduct of the criminal justice system, I expect the following trends to continue more or less as "natural administrative" developments:

1. Expansion of court information systems to more local and state jurisdictions, and application of EDP techniques to improve the administrative efficiency of case-management and "prisoner handling."

2. Creation of a national exchange system of computerized criminal history records, run by a state consortium and not by the FBI. However, there is still a possibility, which I would want to examine closely, of creating an independent federal criminal justice information agency to conduct this function.

3. Expansion of the antifraud and antiabuse programs by which computerized records of government benefit programs are matched against other automated records, both government files (employment, Social Security, income tax, etc.) and files maintained by private employers, agencies receiving government aid (hospitals, schools, etc.). The possibility of banning or foregoing such computer-match programs seems to me politically impossible, and the real-world policy debates will be over just how much to do this, and with what safeguards.

As for what might or should be done beyond these things that I see as likely, I have several suggestions:

1. The great promise of automated data bases for criminal justice—as early pioneers such as NYSIIS hoped to pursue—was to supply heretofore unavailable bodies of data that could be processed and used to expand our knowledge of crime patterns and causes, the effectiveness of various criminal-justice agency policies and programs, and the effect of various kinds of interventions (court rulings on rights of suspects or prisoners, for example). For a combination of reasons—the priority given to getting such data systems

running, providing the services they promised, satisfying powerful agency clients—the research and evaluation function of most criminal justice information systems have been brutally starved for two decades. Yet, if we are entering a period of experimentation with new forms of police programs and utilization, new techniques of adjudication, and new concepts of probation, then we need to commit a substantial portion of criminal justice EDP budgets to carry out that function. After all, this is what the power of computing can do, in the hands of skilled researchers and professionals. We have been wasting this potential for 20 years.

2. We may have reached the point in the use of computers at which the techniques for *predictive assessment* of a major proposed system's impact on a set of key social, economic, legal, and organizational values can be made. An interesting, if young, literature is developing dealing with such technology assessments, both prior to system adoption and after its institution. We have a variety of forums for conducting such assessments. These include government agencies such as the Office of Technology Assessment and Congressional committees; private scientific organizations such as the National Research Council of the National Academy of Sciences; organizations of computer professionals, such as committees of AFIPS; academic centers and programs, such as the Harvard Program on Information Resources Policy; advocacy groups such as the Scientists Institute for Public Information; and many others. It is hoped that if we apply the emerging techniques to criminal justice information systems, we will have not only stronger assessments of what has been done but also predictive assessments that will help legislators and the public to know, in advance, the major implications of computer-systems proposals.

3. It also seems to me a hopeful sign that organizations considering building large computer systems have recognized that public and legislative concerns require serious efforts to plan for and be ready to deal with a broad range of qualitative matters in EDP operations—complying with privacy and freedom of information rules, for example, developing strategies for detecting and dealing with errors and distortions in program operations, and building client-oriented procedures into the design and implementation of new systems. This early trend needs encouragement.

4. It would seem to me a sad event if the creation of some kind of independent privacy-watching institution is not recommended by the Carter Administration or not created by Congress in the next few years. The economy and the antigovernment agency mood being what they are, prospects do not look bright today; but either as a general mechanism, or perhaps an agency of professionals and public members for the national criminal justice information system(s), I think we will need a national institution of research, monitoring, and publication of findings to deal with privacy and computer systems in the 1980s.

On the privacy front, I expect us to face a series of serious pressure points in the coming decade.

1. As more giant administrative systems are built in the 1980s to replace overloaded current systems, such as the Internal Revenue Service's Tax Administration Project, the Social Security Administration's Future Process, and various next-step electronic funds transfer systems, the legal right of law enforcement agencies to have access to such files for particular kinds of investigations and the security of such systems against penetration by law enforcement agents will represent a major arena of debate. We will find ourselves reconsidering the present rules of access (what I have called our "first-generation privacy rules") in light of new opportunities, new problems, and new social attitudes toward privacy. I expect these debates to run throughout the decade.

2. In the body politic, inoculations against bad humor (such as the post-Watergate concern to control intelligence activities) tend to have only limited duration. If we experience substantial domestic terrorism (and it is remarkable that we have been spared this so long, compared to our fellow Western democracies); if we move to develop a substantial domestic nuclear-power supply and this leads (as I believe it will) to widespread protest activities and civil disobedience campaigns; and if urban minority protest quickens in the mid 1980s in response to blocked employment opportunities, then one response we can expect will be the re-creation and use of large-scale intelligence files. Because I think we have a few years before the pressures for such actions become major ones, this makes it all the more important that we complete the unfinished work of enacting strong and clear rules for criminal justice information systems, including the intelligence types.

Conclusion

I am not sure that a concluding sermonette is needed, but I suppose a sense of one's frame of mind is the apt way to close the kind of swift overview I have attempted here. I favor using computer technology imaginatively and widely to help contain crime, improve the adminstration of justice, and enhance observance of due process while we work, as a society, on the deeper causes of crime and reshape our structures and processes of criminal justice. I would hope that computer systems could support more experimentation and evaluation than we have thus far used them for. During these efforts, I expect there to be continuing struggles to prevent computer technology from being adopted for repressive and dangerous purposes, since the technology represents an available instrument tempting all the insensitive and antidemocratic forces that exist in our political system. In short, computer systems represent another instrument that we can use wisely, stupidly, or unthinkingly in the administration of justice, or elsewhere. The praise, or blame, of people at conferences such as this in the 1990s will fall on us.

References

Department of Health, Education and Welfare. *Records, computers, and the rights of citizens.* Washington, D.C.: U.S. Government Printing Office, 1973.

Silberman, C. *Criminal violence, criminal justice.* New York: Random House, 1978.

Westin, A. *Computers, health care, and citizen rights.* Washington, D.C.: U.S. Government Printing Office, 1976.

Westin, A. *Computers, personnel administration, and citizen rights.* Washington, D.C.: U.S. Government Printing Office, 1976.

Westin, A., and Baker, M. *Databanks in a free society.* New York: Atheneum, 1972.

Comment on "The Long-Term Implications of Computers for Privacy and the Protection of Public Order"

Charles W. Joiner

I believe the major implication of computers for privacy and the protection of the public order is now, and will continue to be, not the nuts and bolts of computer use, but the changing moral and ethical standards of human beings brought about by the computer; in other words, computer use will foment a reexamination of what is the essence of being an individual human being.

The computer is a tool permitting persons interested in public order to develop, maintain, recall, and relate information about individuals that was never before possible. In addition, it permits people interested in the public order to use instantaneously, for police purposes, information developed and maintained for other purposes such as, for example, information gathered for credit investigations, as a result of individual travel, as a result of the delivery of health services, or in the insurance or banking industries.

In the past, before the computer, society lived and privacy was protected without many rules. Individuals could move, run away. Memories were short. In an earlier year, communication between places was sporadic, if not spasmodic and slow. Reports were often erratic and inaccurate and not fully relied on. However, the computer remembers, and that memory can be omnipresent and ever useful. This scientific and technological development has been and is forcing us to think, and it is changing and shaping our thinking about what is right and what is wrong and what should be and what should not be.

Individuals could lose their ability to remain individual individuals because of the omnipresence of this memory and recall device. As a result, people have become more conscious of what are the rights and wrongs in knowing things about others, and what are the responsibilities that each of us has in order to see that others are not destroyed by needlessly invading privacy which is a major part of the essence of a human being.

We have chased criminals and people accused of crime all over the world for

183

COMPUTERS AND PRIVACY
IN THE NEXT DECADE

hundreds of years, but we did not catch all of them, and as time went on and good lives were led we did not feel uncomfortable if they were not caught; particularly, if the same individuals did not seem to be committing new crimes. We have relied on the passage of time and our ability to forget and our imperfect ability to follow, to solve the moral problems that we would face only when some escapee was caught who had lived an exemplary life. Now with the computer fully activated and operational in a system utilizing all information in all other computers, there is no escape, and the moral judgments will have to be made. As a result of this, although all persons want criminals caught, there has been for a few years for the first time a facing up to what is or should be right and what is or should be wrong in fully using the tools that are not available.

Let us look at some of the categories related to public order that Westin has so elegantly discussed.

In the predicting of criminal behavior and in the adjudication of guilt or innocence, he asserts, and I agree, that the computer has not helped. I believe, however, that the computer has not helped, not because it cannot, but because we will not let it help, and I assert a major reason for this is that our sense of ethics and morality as it relates to the privacy of the individual is sharpening and developing rapidly.

There is no doubt in my mind that information could be gathered and computer programs written that could, with a significant degree of certainty, predict criminal behavior and determine an individual's guilt. We already rely on such programs to predict behavior in many other areas of activity, as, for example, admission to college. But all of this could be done only at a very great cost—at a cost of becoming a police state and permitting nothing a person does to be private. And so, rules have become necessary. Efforts to make such rules stimulate the discussion and debate on who and what we are.

In the area of the apprehension of criminals, I sense much less resistance based on the mores of privacy; but even here the rightness and wrongness of invading privacy is being discussed. Clearly, the gathering of bits and pieces of information about crime and persons who have committed crimes or those suspected of crime has long been the traditional method of the police. The use of the mathematical programs, which only a computer can solve rapidly, to point fingers and to establish hypotheses should be helpful in identifying and ultimately convicting the criminal in the same way the computer's interrelated network helps to prevent persons from running away.

But even in the use of the computer in the area of search and identification, I sense at least a ripple on the smooth pond. Discussion of the right and the wrong way of gathering information about people that may be used to assist an agent of the police to capture the criminals has been stimulated and accelerated. What I sense is a resistance to great information storage banks containing detailed information on large segments of society , which information is used in sophisticated programs to attempt to find and prevent crime. I have seen a draft ordinance aimed specifically at the right of any law-enforcement person to collect and to hold data about beliefs, opinions, associations, and expressions of individuals. This is the stuff of privacy, except that the ordinance covers not only privately expressed views but also those expressed in public. This is a part of the debate on ethics and morality that is really being brought about by the computer because the computer makes the information accessible when in the past it was not. I know also that when people have been forced to think for the first time about moral and ethical priniciples, as is being done as a result of the computer, the results of that process are likely to become pervasive and cut far beyond the narrow triggering subject.

The bottom line of my comment is that the computer and what it can do in law enforcement have been and are forcing us to face up to and debate, both in meetings like this and in the legislatures, the questions of what a human being is, how private a person must be to be able to function in an open society and to raise a family, be happy, look out for him or herself, and help make rules to provide for the common good. We see the results all around: the Privacy Act of 1974, the recommendation of the Privacy Protection Study Commission (PPSC), the efforts in Congress to implement the PPSC Report, the draft of a uniform law on privacy, the Fair Credit Reporting Act, and Regulation Z of Truth in Lending.

All of us must participate in the debates on establishing rules regarding what information will be gathered, how long it will be maintained, how it can be corrected, and how it can be used. Law enforcement and the ability of society to protect itself against deviant behavior must be protected, but not at the cost of destroying the essence of being human. These are decisions that should be made only after balancing what can be done against possible harm. The debate itself, premised on changing moral and ethical standards, will prove, I believe, to be the major long-term implication of the computer in protecting the public order, and it will reach far beyond the computer and its actual use.

The computer may help law enforcement, but its major impact will be not on how it helps directly but on the discussion it forces on us as a result of options it gives to us. This discussion of ethical and moral values will far transcend the computer and its use; it will extend to areas not directly related to the computer and will challenge accepted law enforcement activities. I believe that, as a result of the computer and how it is forcing us to face all the problems discussed at this workshop, each of us will be better as individuals and, if that is true, we will have a better society.

Comment on "The Long-Term Implications of Computers for Privacy and the Protection of Public Order"

Jerome J. Daunt

From my career background in law enforcement and computer-based systems, I agree with Westin's observation that both privacy and public order represent equally compelling values in a democratic society. I also reject the extremes—namely, an absolute right to individual privacy in a democratic society, on the one hand, and police state to enforce unreasonable public order, on the other. If we accept the fact that history is prologue, then the 1980s will compare better with the 1960s than with the 1970s. There are tensions, domestic and international, which have or will surface demanding greater efficiency and effectiveness of criminal justice, and its technology will be on "stage." The excuses for lack of progress and nonperformance in the 1970s will no longer be accepted, nor should they be since the constraints were solvable and not technical.

With respect to Westin's paper I offer my comments to his major issues in chronological order, and I will add information concerning my own experience in developing computer-based systems for national law enforcement.

Westin refers to the "good old days" of the precomputer era or the early "get the systems up and running" days of the 1960s. For local and regional systems this action continued into the 1970s, but state and national systems fell "victim" to the 1970s "let's study it again." Going back to the 1960s, local, state, and federal law-enforcement agencies recognized and quickly applied the new on-line computer technology to meet operational requirements. It is not surprising that the national system (NCIC) was the first use of the new technology to link together local, state, and federal governments (1967). This did not happen by chance or because of a crime crisis of national proportions. Historically, local, state, and federal law-enforcement agencies have had an established information exchange, cooperative relationships, an association (IACP) within which the necessary setting of national standards had earlier

187

COMPUTERS AND PRIVACY
IN THE NEXT DECADE

success (fingerprint identification, police statistics, etc), as well as respected federal leadership (the FBI and J. Edgar Hoover). It is these elements which fostered and developed interstate police information systems logically and rapidly. Prosecution, courts, and corrections did not have the apparent immediate need nor such other catalysts for interstate information exchange.

It should be understood that the design of NCIC in 1965–1966 placed the responsibility for use of the system on local, state, and federal law-enforcement agencies. A state control-terminal concept was implemented, which called for the decentralization of criminal records based on the relevance of such information at local, regional, state, and national levels. These policy and procedural decisions in a national network were made by NCIC representatives, who were local, state, and federal law-enforcement personnel. Agency management at all levels accepted these recommendations without real comprehension of the nature of the "tool," namely computer-based systems. For example, in January 1966, the Office of Legal Counsel, the Department of Justice and the Attorney General agreed that Public Law 533, dated June 1930, was the authority for the FBI to implement and manage an NCIC system. As Westin points out, these were the "good old days of get them up and running." Yet, sound decisions were made that were compatible both to our way of life and to future demands on national law enforcement telecommunications.

During the same period, computer "czars" at all government levels as well as in private industry reached out for the "big box" and bigger empires without regard to system functions or service needs. This became a problem in the development of local and state criminal justice systems and again pointed out the failure of top-level governmental management to recognize a computer as a "tool" and a system as the only cost-effective program.

The National Crime Information Center defined a system as not merely a computer but rather *users*, staff to operate, hardware, communications, and terminal devices. From the very beginning, NCIC resolved dedication of the system to law enforcement in order to meet immediate information needs, 24 hours a day, 7 days a week. After all, computer-based systems, properly designed and managed, give great support to our traditional way of life, namely, local and state responsibility for crime and public safety. In the past, information and lack of rapid communications especially across state lines made this constitutional goal difficult, particularly in an increasingly mobile society. Local crime problems became *federal violations* because of the information–communication and continuity of investigation problems across political (state) lines.

Westin's concern about the "little real effect" computer use has had on the causes of crime, better definition of criminal behavior, better prediction, correction, and rehabilitation is not solely the fault of computer-based systems. We agree that more deep-seated data elements are necessary to answer many of these difficult questions. Yet, the law enforcement–criminal justice systems which have emerged, while they are targeted at operational day-to-day information, do provide a wealth of harnessed information for research and statistical decision making. There are about 300 local, county, regional, state, and federal computer-based systems (versus manual) in the criminal justice environment with relatively easy retrievable analytical data on criminal incidents and offenders. This information is used to some degree by the criminal justice agencies, especially police, for their administrative needs. Much of this harnessed information however is more properly analyzed outside the criminal justice system and yet little is used in a consistent way by the academic community. For example, National Crime Information Center–Computerized Criminal History (NCIC–CCH) has stored in machine form millions of "bits" of information concerning 10 years of criminal history on federal offenders (50,000 a year) with their known past and subsequent criminal history. This is the most complete and accurate criminal history file in the country, if not the world, and except for selective Federal Bureau of Prisons' analytical programs it has virtually been left untouched. The information is there. Where are the users?

The organizational–functional approach to computer-based national systems is the only real world, as demonstrated by NCIC. It has proven to be cost effective; it has restricted access to criminal records and has improved the accuracy, completeness, and timeliness of police records. In 1969, NCIC *law enforcement representatives* decided not to convert the manual rap sheet to computer usage but rather to design a more accurate and complete record called CCH to be offender history as reported by the entire criminal justice system (not just police). It was the one file to be shared across criminal justice agencies, even though each criminal justice element (police, prosecution, courts, and corrections) had its own internal functional information requirements.

In 1969, NCIC proposed to the Law Enforcement Assistance Administration a pilot test to demonstrate the interstate exchange of criminal history records. This became known as Project *Search*. The National Crime Information Center continued to design a more complete and accurate criminal history record, as well as to plan the decentralization of criminal history record-keeping and fingerprint identification processing to state level.

The abuses of criminal history records (rap sheets) are well known. Thus, an attempt was made to improve the information (NCIC–CCH). It was well established that the manual criminal history (rap sheet) was inaccurate, incomplete, lacked standardization, provided an untimely response, lacked state control, and was unmanageable at the national level. This situation still exists, since little progress was made in the 1970s, due largely to misconceptions, misunderstanding, and lack of national leadership. Criminal justice agencies, by and large, can properly interpret and wisely act on criminal history records; the problem lies with non-criminal-justice agencies that have access by law. Education of non-criminal-justice users is an alternative; but more realistic are privacy laws that prevent certain dissemination to non-criminal-justice users for frequently bad decisions. Such bad decisions do not happen every day; but they do occur often enough for us to consider these alternatives.

Westin states that he has doubts about some "police intelligence systems." My experience identifies intelligence systems as being basically internal investigative operations developing information for internal use and/or exchange with appropriate agencies. Like statistics, intelligence information will largely be gathered from day-to-day patrol and investigative operations. As an example, the New York Intelligence and Information System (NYIIS) was a classic plan and design for a total system before any execution. The more reasonable and cost-effective approach in the 1960s was "to do the possible" with flexibility for growth.

The bright, new, high-technology programs in law enforcement agencies were not planned to supplant basic patrol or investigation as suggested by Westin. They were designed to *support* basic police services, and this they have by and large accomplished, not only in the field but also at the management level. There is a tendency to measure success of law-enforcement systems solely on "hits"—a apprehension of criminals or recovery of stolen property. A "no record" timely response is a valuable communcation for user decision-making on the "street" and an innocent citizen's freedom from unnecessary detention.

It is not reasonable to state that computers will be of only marginal help to the police, as were other hopeful new technologies of the past, such as fingerprint identification and two-way radio communications in police cars. Of course computers will not eliminate the causes of crime, but they have and will contain crime, arrest and convict offenders, and support the cause of public safety.

Westin recommends and predicts a national exchange system of computerized criminal history records managed by a state consortium or an independent federal criminal justice information agency *but not the FBI.*

Our goal is an effective national telecommunications system for law enforcement–criminal justice wherever management is located. Historically, the FBI has furnished information support services to local, state, and federal criminal justice agencies. This experience is not easily replaced by a consortium, that is, management by committee or some new "independent" federal criminal justice agency. The FBI's long-standing relationship with local, state, and federal criminal justice agencies in training, identification, laboratory work, and statistical and information systems makes the FBI unique among federal agencies.

It is certainly possible that these support services provided by the FBI may in the future seriously conflict with internal investigative requirements. In recent years, with respect to NCIC, it has been "benign neglect" by FBI management not misuse of the information for ulterior purposes. However, any new agency management (and I reject a consortium for very practical reasons) must be planned with caution and have immediate credibility with local and state users or otherwise all support services will rapidly degrade. If such an agency can be created with some guarantee that better and more objective support service to criminal justice can be provided, then it should be done. Any alternative, however, should be considered very carefully.

Fear of FBI abuse of a national criminal history exchange system because of a central management role is not realistic. As a participating law-enforcement agency, the information would be available to the FBI whether it had a management role or not. Second, the information we are concerned about is public record. More importantly, central national management is subject to oversight by Congress, independent audit, and a policymaking board. The National Crime Information Center has been operating for 12 years under FBI management. There has been no criminal justice community expression for change, in fact, the opposite is true—namely, continued support for FBI management.

Projections, at any time, are risky at best; but it seems very clear that there is no "turning back" from the use of computer technology in the 1980s, especially for criminal justice organizations. Of course, it should be applied more wisely and more cost effectively—not just because we have learned from experience but also because top management should be better educated to the optimum use of computer-based systems. This is American technology, and we should learn to use it well.

Westin looks forward to an era which will "supply heretofore unavailable bodies of data that could be processed and used to expand our knowledge of crime patterns and causes." We already have "mountains" of usable data in computer form, which has few research users. Although more data elements may need to be collected for more effective analysis, the goal of the 1980s is more structured and consistent research of the data available—government and private. Do we really know what additional data are needed to "expand our knowledge of crime patterns and causes" or can we better use the data now available?

In my opinion the 1980s will bring even greater demands for fair and timely justice ("Bell and Burger Call for Stiff Bail Laws," *Washington Post*, 12 February 1979). Fair and timely justice nationally depends on many things, including effective computer-based information systems that provide more timely, more complete, and more accurate information.

The 1980s will see the decentralization to the states of criminal history record-keeping and fingerprint identification processing. This was proposed in 1969; however, most states were not ready to assume the responsibility. In the 1970s little was done to assist or to encourage the state agencies, either from federal executive agencies, national legislative committees, or criminal justice associations. This lack of progress may have been the result of "Watergate fever," but nonetheless, it is extremely costly in duplication and criminal justice system ineffectiveness on a national scale (The Need for a Nationwide Criminal Justice Information Interchange Facility, U.S. Department of Justice, 6 March 1978). Main frame, mini-, and microcomputers are well founded in public safety-criminal justice agencies at all levels of government and will continue to increase.

The objective of a common national communications system for law enforcement–criminal justice will be achieved in the 1980s. Today, we have cooperative systems, such as the NCIC; the National Law Enforcement Telecommunications System (NLETS); and state, regional, and local systems. Also, at the federal level we have a national network (JUST) supporting U.S. Attorneys, U.S. Marshalls, Drug Enforcement Administration, to name a few. Then there is the Treasury Enforcement Communications System (TECS) which is vital to a national system through its border coverage by the U.S. Customs Service. These individual systems have achieved a relative milestone but greater effectiveness can only be realized through a common objective to meet national information needs.

Protection of individual privacy and enhancement of public order are compatible. The balance must come from careful scrutiny of the systems management and audit of the users. Traditionally, this was always so; people are vigilant of their liberty.

Comment on "The Long-Term Implications of Computers for Privacy and the Protection of Public Order"

Carol G. Kaplan

Professor Westin's presentation raised a number of interesting issues related to privacy and criminal justice information systems. In his closing remarks, Professor Westin gave his opinion that "it [is] all the more important that we complete the unfinished work of enacting strong and clear rules for criminal justice information systems, including the intelligence types." You may be interested to know that the Law Enforcement Assistance Administration (LEAA) last year specifically addressed the area of criminal intelligence systems. Following an in-depth review of existing policies regarding the LEAA-funded intelligence systems, the agency prepared "Criminal Intelligence Systems Operating Policies." A draft was published for comment in the *Federal Register* on February 8, 1978. After reviewing the comments submitted, LEAA published the final *Guidelines* on June 30, 1978. The guidelines follow.

```
              FINAL INTELLIGENCE SYSTEMS OPERATING
                           POLICIES

                  Adoption of Final Policy Standards

AGENCY: Law Enforcement Assistance Administration, Justice.
ACTION: Adoption of Final Policy Standards.
SUMMARY: LEAA is adopting funding and operating principles for LEAA Dis-
     cretionary Funded Intelligence Systems.  The Operating Principles
     (sec. I) are to be followed in all discretionary grants awarded in-
     volving the collection and exchange of intelligence information.  Sec-
     tions II and III deal specifically with the funding of intelligence
     systems and set forth the funding criteria and internal LEAA monitoring
     and audit procedures for such grants.
EFFECTIVE DATE: June 30, 1978.
FOR FURTHER INFORMATION CONTACT: Thomas J. Madden, General Counsel, LEAA
     202-376-3691.
```

193

SUPPLEMENTAL INFORMATION: On February 8, 1978, LEAA published in the *Federal Register* proposed funding and operating principles for LEAA Discretionary Funded Intelligence Systems. The public was invited to comment. Responses were received from various organizations, State governments, and individuals. Most of the comments reflected a concern that strict controls be adopted to prevent infringement upon constitutionally protected political activities. The guidelines in section I.B. have, accordingly, been revised to more fully address this concern.

Other commenters were concerned that the collection and maintenance of intelligence information should only be triggered by a reasonable suspicion that an individual is involved in criminal activity. The language in section I.A. has, therefore, been revised to require this criteria as a basis for collection and maintenance of intelligence information.

These operating principles are effective immediately; however, where a system is presently being funded by LEAA and needs an additional period of time to come into compliance or seek funds from other sources, the Administrator, for good cause, may extend the period for compliance by 6 months.

A number of commenters asked that the term "need to know/right to know" be further defined. This concept "need to know/right to know" has an understood meaning to the law enforcement community; it would therefore be inappropriate to redefine the phrase. In general, the phrase means that a criminal justice official requesting access to an intelligence file must establish that he is conducting an investigation pursuant to his official duties and that he needs the information in connection with the investigation. The word "official" has been added before "law enforcement" therefore in order to emphasize that information must be required for authorized purposes. Changes were also made to require that dissemination logs be kept and that recipient agencies be advised of changes to files being maintained.

A number of commenters appeared to view the guidelines as proposing to create a national data bank. In fact, this is not the intention of the guidelines. LEAA has awarded grants for intelligence gathering pursuant to a statutory mandate which required that special emphasis was to be given to intelligence operations designed to expose organized crime and control civil disorders. (The civil disorder provision was removed from the statute in 1976.) The purpose of the guidelines is to establish LEAA policy to ensure that grants for intelligence activities are not used in violation of the privacy and political rights of citizens. It is believed that by tightening the provisions dealing with the first amendment rights as suggested by a number of commenters, this policy is now firmly established.

While these guidelines presently apply to discretionary grants awarded directly by LEAA, it is strongly encouraged that state and local governments, awarding grants under the block grant program, adopt these or similar policy guidelines.

Background

LEAA recognizes that certain criminal activities including but not limited to, loan sharking, narcotics, trafficking in stolen property, gambling, extortion, smuggling, bribery, and corruption of public officials often involve some degree of regular coordination and permanent organization involving a large number of participants over a broad geographical area. The exposure of such ongoing networks of criminal activity can be aided by the pooling of information about such activities. In recognition of the fact, however, that the collection and exchange of intelligence data necessary to support control of serious criminal activity may represent potential threats to the privacy of individuals to whom such data relates, the following LEAA policies shall be applicable to all projects in which LEAA discretionary funds are to be used for the collection and exchange of intelligence data. As used in these policies, "Intellience Systems" means the arrangements, equipment, facilities, and procedures used for the continuing storage, exchange and analysis of criminal intelligence data, however, the term does not include modus operandi files; 'Interjurisdictional Intelligence Systems' means those systems for the continuing exchange of criminal intelligence data between local, county, or larger political subdivisions, including the exchange of data between State or local agencies and units of the Federal Government.

I. Operating Principles for LEAA-Discretionary Grants Involving the
    Collection and Exchange of Intelligence Information

   A. Criminal intelligence information concerning an individual shall be collected and maintained only if it is reasonably suspected that the individual is involved in criminal activity and that the information is relevant to that criminal activity.
   B. No records shall be maintained or collected about political, religious or social views, association or activities of any individual, group, association, corporation, business or partnership unless such information directly relates to an investigation of criminal activities, and there are reasonable grounds to suspect the subject of the information is or may be involved in criminal conduct.
   C. No information which has been obtained in violation of any applicable Federal, State or local law or ordinance shall be included in any criminal intelligence system.
   D. Intelligence information shall be disseminated only where there is a need to know/right to know the data in the performance of a law enforcement activity.
   E. (1) Except as noted in (2) below, intelligence information shall be disseminated only to other law enforcement authorities who shall agree to follow procedures regarding data entry, maintenance, security, and dissemination which are consistent with these standards.
       (2) Paragraph (1) above shall not limit the dissemination of an assessment of criminal intelligence information to a Government official or to any other individual, when necessary, to avoid imminent danger to life or property.
   F. Agencies maintaining criminal intelligence data shall adopt administrative, technical, and physical safeguards (including audit trails) to insure against unauthorized access and against intentional or unintentional damage. A written record indicating who has been given data, reason for release and date of each dissemination outside the agency is to be kept. Information shall be labeled to indicate levels of sensitivity, levels of confidence, and the identity of control agencies and officials. Each agency must establish written standards for need to know/right to know under section I.D. above.
   G. Periodic review shall be made, no less than every 2 years, to assure that all information which is retained has relevancy and importance. Any information retained through a 2-year interval shall reflect name of reviewer, date of review, and explanation of decision to retain. Any information which is misleading, obsolete, or otherwise unreliable must be destroyed and recipient agencies advised of such changes.

H. If automated equipment for use in connection with a criminal intelligence system is to be obtained with funds under the grant, then:

Direct remote terminal access to data shall not be made available to system users; and

No modifications to system design shall be undertaken without prior LEAA approval.

I. LEAA shall be notified prior to initiation of formal information exchange procedures with any Federal, State, regional, or other information systems not indicated in the grant documents as initially approved at time of award.

J. Assurances shall be made that there will be no purchase or use in the course of the project of any electronic, mechanical, or other device for surveillance purposes that is in violation of the provisions of Title III of Pub. L. 90-351, as amended, or any applicable State statute related to wiretapping and surveillance.

K. Assurances shall be made that there shall be no harassment or interference with any lawful political activities as part of the intelligence operation.

L. Sanctions shall be adopted to control unauthorized access, utilization, or disclosure of information contained in the system.

II. Funding Guidelines

LEAA shall apply the following funding guidelines to all discretionary grant applications, the principal purpose of which is the funding of intelligence systems. Systems shall only be funded where a grantee agrees to adhere to the principles set forth above and the project meets the following criteria:

A. The proposed collection and exchange of data has been coordinated with and will support ongoing or proposed investigatory or prosecutorial activities relating to specific areas of criminal activity.

B. The areas of criminal activity in connection with which intelligence data are to be utilized represents a significant and recognized threat to the population and: (1) is either undertaken for the purpose of seeking illegal power or profits or poses a threat to the life and property of citizens; (2) involves a significant degree of permanent criminal organization; and (3) is not limited to one jurisdiction.

C. Control and supervision of information collection and dissemination will be retained by the head of a governmental agency or by an individual with general policymaking authority who has been expressly delegated such control and supervision by the head of the agency. This official shall certify in writing that he takes full responsibility and will be accountable for the information maintained by and disseminated from the system and that the operation of the system will be in compliance with the standards set forth in Section I.

Where the system is an interjurisdictional system: (1) the governmental agency which exercises control and supervision over the operation of the system shall have the head of that agency or an individual with general policymaking authority who has been expressly delegated such control and supervision by the head of the agency officially responsible and accountable for actions taken in the name of the joint entity; and (2) the head of each member agency or an individual with general policymaking authority who has been expressly delegated such control and supervision by the head of the agency shall certify in writing that he takes full responsibility and will be accountable for ensuring that the information transmitted to the interjurisdictional system or to other agencies will be in compliance with the standards set forth in section I.

D.   Intelligence data will be collected primarily for State and local law enforcement efforts— exceptions being made only for cases involving joint State-Federal efforts.

III.   Monitoring and Audit of Grants for the Funding of Intelligence
   Systems

A.   Grants for the funding of intelligence systems will receive specialized monitoring and audit in accordance with a plan designed to ensure compliance with operating principles as set forth in section I of this document.   Such plans shall be approved prior to award of funds.

B.   All such grants shall be awarded subject to a Special Condition requiring compliance with standards set forth in Section I of this document.

C.   An annual notice will be published by LEAA which will indicate the existence and objective of all systems for the continuing interjurisdictional exchange of intelligence data which are funded with LEAA discretionary funds.

James M. H. Gregg,
Assistant Administrator,
Office of Planning and Management
(FR Doc. 78-18196 Filed 6-29-78; 8:45 am)

Biographical Sketches of Contributors

Paul Armer

Charles Babbage Institute
701 Welch Road, Suite 224
Palo Alto, California 94304

Paul Armer is Excutive Secretary for the Charles Babbage Institute, a foundation devoted to the history of information processing. He was educated at UCLA, receiving an A.B. in Meteorology in 1946. He did additional work in statistics and economics and in 1960 was a graduate of the Executive Program of the UCLA Graduate School of Business Administration.

He was with the RAND Corporation from 1947–1968. Ten of those years were spent as head of the Computer Sciences Department.

In 1968, Mr. Armer left RAND to become director of the Stanford University Computation Center. In 1970 he joined Harvard University's Program on Technology and Society as a research associate and as a lecturer in the School of Business.

Mr. Armer returned to Stanford in 1972 where he was a fellow and program coordinator of the Program on Science and Technology of the Center for Advanced Study in the Behavioral Sciences. In 1976 Mr. Armer became assistant to the president of On-Line Business Systems, Inc. He left On-Line in March 1978 to join the Charles Babbage Institute.

Mr. Armer has been active in professional societies in information processing. He has served on the Council of the Association for Computing Machinery and was president of the American Federation of Information Processing (AFIPS). He was a founder of SHARE and served on its Executive Board.

Mr. Armer has on three occasions been an invited witness before committees of the U.S. Congress. He has testified before and/or been a consultant to four presidential commissions. He was a member of the U.S. Computer Delegation to the U.S.S.R. in 1959.

Carole Parsons Bailey

5 Squirrel Hill Lane
West Hartford, Connecticut 06107

Carole Parsons Bailey is currently a consultant to several agencies of the U.S. government and to the National Academy of Engineering. She is a recent fellow of the Institute of Politics at Harvard University, and from August 1975 to September 1977 she served as executive director of the U.S. Privacy Protection Study Commission. Prior to that time, she was associate executive director of the Domestic Council Committe on the Right of Privacy, chaired by Vice Presidents Ford and Rockefeller, and associate executive director of the Secretary's Advisory Committee on Automated Personal Data Systems established by then Health, Education, and Welfare Secretary, Elliot L. Richardson.

Mrs. Bailey was educated at Bryn Mawr College and Columbia University, and began her professional career as a member of the Behavioral and Social Sciences staff of the National Research Council.

Robert Lee Chartrand
Science Policy Research Division
Congressional Research Service
Library of Congress
Washington, D.C. 20540

Robert Lee Chartrand is senior specialist in information sciences, Congressional Research Service, Library of Congress. For the past 13 years, he has been advisor to the United States Congress concerning information policy and the application of information science and its related technology to the problems of government and society. In addition, he is the author or editor of a dozen books and major congressional studies including *Computers in the Service of Society, Systems Technology Applied to Social and Community Problems,* and *Scientific and Technical Information (STI) Activities: Issues and Opportunities.* Listed in *Who's Who in America,* he is an AAAS Fellow and an adjunct professor at The American University.

Jerome J. Daunt
7506 Allan Avenue
Falls Church, Virginia 22046

Mr. Daunt has 25 years of experience in the field of law enforcement as a member of the FBI. Nationally recognized as lecturer and author in specialized fields of crime statistics, data processing systems and telecommunications for law enforcement, from 1965 to 1972 he was inspector-in-charge of the nationwide planning, coordination, implementation, and development of the National Crime Information Center (NCIC). From 1973 to 1976 he served as executive vice president of a major consulting firm managing the installation of national, state, and local computer-based information and telecommunication systems. Since 1976 Mr. Daunt has been providing consulting services to local, state, and federal law enforcement agencies with respect to information system design. He is presently chairman of the board, HMB Associates, a Virginia firm.

Gordon C. Everest
Department of Management Sciences
University of Minnesota
Minneapolis, Minnesota 55455

Gordon C. Everest is an associate professor of management information systems in the Graduate School of Business Administration at the University of Minnesota. Previously a consultant with Auerbach Corporation concentrating on the design, implementation, and evaluation of DBMS, and having several publications relating to data base management systems, he is completing a comprehensive text entitled *Database Management: Objectives, Systems Functions, and Administration,* forthcoming from McGraw-Hill. He is a member of the CODASYL Systems Committee (since 1969) and of the recently formed ANSI/X3/SPARC Database Systems Study Group to investigate and make recommendations on the development of standards relating to data base systems. He was involved in developing the Minnesota Privacy Act passed in April 1974, the first omnibus, public-sector privacy law in the nation. Currently he is vice chairman of the AFIPS Special Committee on the Right to Privacy.

Oswald H. Ganley

Information Resources Program
Harvard University
Cambridge, Massachusetts 02138

Oswald H. Ganley is a research associate at the Harvard University John F. Kennedy School of Government and is associated with Harvard's Program on Information Resources Policy. He was deputy assistant secretary of state for advanced and applied technology affairs from 1975 to 1978 (and chairman of the NSC Task Force on Transborder Data Flow) and was previously director of the Office of Soviet and Eastern European Scientific and Technological Affairs, Bureau of Oceans and International Environmental and Scientific Affairs.

Dr. Ganley was appointed as special assistant to the science director of the Agency for International Development in 1965, following extensive experience in the medical sciences and in the pharmaceutical industry. He joined the Bureau of International Scientific and Technological Affairs, Department of State in 1966 as chief of the Technology Division. In 1967 he became head of the European Affairs Section of that bureau until his appointment as scientific attaché to the American embassies in Rome and in Bucharest during the period 1969-1973.

Dr. Ganley earned his Ph.D. from the University of Michigan in 1953 (in bacteriology and physiology), and the degree of Master of Public Administration from Harvard in 1965 (in economics and foreign affairs) following a Harvard fellowship in science and public policy. He is an elected fellow of the American Academy of Microbiology, and a member of the American Physiological Society, among other professional organizations.

Hans Peter Gassmann

Directorate for Science, Technology, and Industry
Organization for Economic Cooperation and Development
2 Rue André Pascal
75775 Paris, France

Hans Peter Gassmann is head of the Information, Computer and Communication Policy Programme of the Organization for Economic Cooperation and Development (OECD) in Paris. Since 1969, he has developed the organization's work on computer utilization, computer and telecommunications policy, their social impacts, protection of privacy, transborder data flows and on policy issues of major new information systems in central government administration and urban management. He is also responsible for the organization's work in scientific and technological information policy.

His educational backround is in economics and engineering. He is the author of many articles on computer and telecommunications policy, protection of privacy, transborder data flows and has directed the 12-volume OECD series oof publications "OECD Informatics Studies" and the new "OECD Information, Computer and Communications Policy Reports."

Robert C. Goldstein

Faculty of Commerce
University of British Columbia
Vancouver, B.C., Canada V6T 1W5

Dr. Goldstein is an associate professor of Accounting and Management Information Systems in the Faculty of Commerce and Business Administration at the University of British Columbia in Vancouver. He holds a B.S. degree in physics from the Massachusetts Institute of Technology, and a D.B.A. from the Harvard Business School. Prior to joining U.B.C. he held information systems research positions at MIT's Project MAC and the Lawrence Livermore Laboratory of the U.S. Atomic Energy Commission.

For the past several years, Dr. Goldstein's research has been in the general area of computerized data management, and, in particular, he has been concerned with the problems of protecting personal data systems. He is the author of a book, *The Cost of Privacy*, which describes a model for estimating the impact of privacy regulation on data base systems.

Lance J. Hoffman

Department of Electrical Engineering and Computer Science
The George Washington University
Washington, D.C. 20052

Lance J. Hoffman is an associate professor in the Department of Electrical Engineering and Computer Science at The George Washington University. Previously with several industrial firms and a faculty member at the University of California, Berkeley, Professor Hoffman has been a staff associate for the National Academy of Sciences Project on Computer Databanks and ACM National Lecturer on privacy and security. He currently chairs the Special Committee in the Right to Privacy of the American Federation of Information Processing Societies (AFIPS), and is an IEEE Distinguished Lecturer. Some of Dr. Hoffman's recent work includes assignments for the Social Security Administration, the Federal Trade Commission and the Office of Technology Assessment of the U.S. Congress. His most recent book is *Modern Methods For Computer Security and Privacy*.

Lucy A. Hummer

Room 4427A
State Department
Washington, D.C. 20520

Lucy A. Hummer is a deputy assistant legal advisor for management at the Department of State. In that capacity, she has had responsibility for State Department compliance with the Privacy Act of 1974. She has also represented the State Department at interagency discussions on the presidential privacy initiative, proposals for extending privacy protections to the private sector through explanation and other means. She has been deputy United States representative to the OECD Expert Group on Transborder Data Barriers and the Protection of Privacy. She serves as a member of the State Department-chaired interagency task force on transborder data flows.

Portia Isaacson
Electronic Data Systems
7171 Forest Lane
Dallas, Texas 75230

Dr. Portia Isaacson is an Electronic Data Systems Fellow. She is also co-owner of the Dallas area Micro Stores. She was conference chairperson of the 1977 National Computer Conference. She is presently chairperson of the ACM Special Interest Group on Personal Computing and ACM Council Member-at-Large. She is president of the Computer Retailers' Association. Dr. Isaacson is a contributing editor for *Datamation*, and associate of *Byte*, and technical editor for the IEEE Computer Society's *Computer* magazine. She is a member of the American Management Association Management Systems Council and the NCC Committee. Dr. Isaacson has several publications in personal computing, microprocessors, and operating systems. She was previously a member of the computer science faculty at The University of Texas at Dallas and North Texas State University and worked on the engineering staff of Xerox Corporation, Recognition Equipment, and Computer Usage Company. Dr. Isaacson holds a B.S. in Physics and Mathematics from East Central University, an M.S. in Computer Science from North Texas State University, and an MAS and Ph.D. in Computer Science from Southern Methodist University.

David A. Johnston
Legislative Service Committee
Statehouse, 5th Floor
Columbus, Ohio 43215

Dr. David A. Johston is the director of the Ohio Legislative Service Commission, a legislative agency which provides a variety of research and technical services to the Ohio General Assembly. He has served as director since August, 1966, and prior to that time as a research associate and assistant director of the commission almost 9 years, specializing in organization and management, budgetary, and welfare fields. In addition to his work with the Ohio Legislative Service Commission, Dr. Johnston also worked as a budget and management analyst in Ohio and New York state. Dr. Johnston is a native of Massachusetts, received his baccalaureate from Boston University, attended the University of Alabama doing graduate work in public administration, and received his Ph.D. degree in political science from Ohio State University. He presently serves as staff vice!president of the National Conference of State Legislatures. He is chairman of the N.C.S.L's task force to establish a computerized legislative information service.

Charles W. Joiner
ABA's Section on Individual Rights and Responsibilities
 Committe on Privacy
251 Federal Courthouse
Detroit, Michigan 48226

Charles W. Joiner is a judge of the United States District Court for the Eastern District of Michigan (Detroit). Judge Joiner chairs the American Bar Association Section of Individual Rights and Responsibilities Committee on Privacy. He is formerly a dean and professor of law at Wayne State University Law School and the University of Michigan Law School. In 1970–71, Judge Joiner was president of the State Bar of Michigan.

Carol G. Kaplan
Bureau of Justice Statistics
633 Indiana Avenue, N.W.
Washington, D.C. 20531

Carol Kaplan is presently director of the Privacy and Security Staff, Bureau of Justice Statistics (formerly known as National Criminal Justice Information and Statistics Service, Law Enforcement Assistance Administration). In this capacity she has responsibility for the administration of programs to ensure compliance with LEAA regulations relating to both the privacy and security of criminal history information and the confidentiality of research and statistical data. She has been involved with the LEAA Privacy and Security program from its inception and has participated in the original development of the LEAA regulations in the area. Ms. Kaplan has also been involved in LEAA efforts relating to NCIC–CCH development and in the recent development of LEAA guidelines relating to the operation of intelligence systems.

Ms. Kaplan has also served as an attorney with the Department of Health, Education and Welfare and with the Federal Communications Commission. Ms. Kaplan is a graduate of Columbia Law School and Radcliffe College.

Steve E. Kolodney
SEARCH Group, Inc.
1620 35th Avenue
Sacramento, California 95822

Steve E. Kolodney is Executive Director of SEARCH Group, Inc. (SGI), a consortium of governors' appointed representatives from the 50 states and U.S. territories who are organized to apply technology for the benefit of criminal justic. Mr. Kolodney is responsible for developing and coordinating the diverse programs of the consortium, and for assessing the societal issues that arise from the introduction of new technological solutions to justice system problems.

Before joining SGI, Mr. Kolodney was chief of information systems planning for the New York State Division of Criminal Justice Services where he was responsible for developing information systems plans which incorporated the data needs of the state's major justice agencies. Prior experience included consulting with federal, state, and local agencies on a wide range of criminal justice problems. In addition, Mr. Kolodney has contributed papers to numerous national conferences, journals and other publications.

Kenneth C. Laudon
Department of Sociology
John Jay College of Criminal Justice
New York, New York 10019

Kenneth Laudon is professor of sociology and statistics at John Jay College (CUNY). He is the author of *Computers and Bureaucratic Reform* (Wiley, 1974) and *Telecommunications and Democratic Participation* (Praeger, 1977), as well as numerous articles on the social impact of computers and personal data banks. Dr. Laudon has been a participant (as director, consultant, associate, and reviewer) in most of the major privacy and computer impact assessments of the last decade. These include the Harvard Program on Technology and Society (1968–1969); the National Academy of Science Project on Computer Databanks (1969–1972); the National Bureau of Standards Project on Computer Use and Citizen Rights in Personnel Administration (1976); the Office of Technology Assessment (United States Congress) Assessments of the Tax Administration System (IRS) and the FBI–NCIC System (1978–1979). He is currently engaged in social assessments of the Social Security Administration Future Process, and the FBI Criminal History System.

Abbe Mowshowitz

Department of Computer Science
University of Britsh Columbia
Vancouver, B.C., Canada V6T 1W5

Abbe Mowshowitz is associate professor of Computer Science at the University of British Columbia, Vancouver, Canada. He received his Ph.D. in Communication and Computer Science from the University of Michigan in 1967, spent a post doctoral year at the Mental Health Research Institute, University of Michigan, and then taught at the University of Toronto before coming to U.B.C.; he has also held visiting appointments at the Center for the study of Democratic Institutions and at Cornell University. For the past 7 years, Dr. Mowshowitz has been involved in research on the social impact of technology. He has authored two books — *The Conquest of Will: Information Processing in Human Affairs*, 1976 and *Inside Information*, 1977 (both published by Addison-Wesley) — and is the editor of the journal *Information Technology in Human Affairs* (published by Pergamon Press). In addition, he is a member of Working Group 9.2 (Computers and Social Accountability) of IFIP's Technical Committe 9, and was program chairman of the Second IFIP Conference on Human Choice and Computers.

Susan Hubbell Nycum

Chickering and Gregory
3 Embarcadero Center, Suite 2300
San Francisco, California 94111

Ms. Nycum is a partner of the San Francisco law firm of Chickering and Gregory, where she specializes in legal problems of computers. She is also co-principal investigator on the Stanford Research Institute's study of Computer Abuse for the National Science Foundation. In addition to practicing law in California and Pennsylvania, Ms. Nycum has been the director of the Stanford University campus Computer Facility and manager of User Services and operations at Carnegie-Mellon University Computer Center. She also served as research associate and law and computer fellow at Stanford Law School.

Ms. Nycum is currently chairman-elect of the ABA Section on Science and Technology, director of the Computer Law Association, council member and chairperson of the Standing Committee on Legal Issues of the ACM. She is a member of the board of advisors to the math and computer sciences section of the National Science Foundation and Trustee of EDUCOM.

Ms. Nycum has had numerous articles published in the computer law field and is the co-author with Robert P. Bigelow of *Your Computer and the Law*. She has lectured extensively in the United States and Canada.

She is a member of the Bar of California, Pennsylvania and the United States Supreme Court. Ms. Nycum is a graduate of Ohio Wesleyan University and Duquesne University Law School.

Elmer R. Oettinger
Institute of Government
University of North Carolina
Chapel Hill, North Carolina 27514

Elmer R. Oettinger, Jr. is professor of Public Law and Government and Assistant Director of the Institute of Government at the University of North Carolina at Chapel Hill. Dr. Oettinger is the chairman of the Drafting Committee on Uniform Privacy Act of the National Conference of Commissioners on Uniform State Laws. He is also a member of the American Bar Association Privacy Committee in the section of Rights and Responsibilities and the ABA Adjunct Committee on Fair Trial-Free Press (in the section of Criminal Justice). He is currently working with the ABA Committee on recommendations to permit controlled use of cameras in the courtroom. He has participated as chairman, speaker, panelist, and commentator in privacy meetings and conferences in the United States and in England. A teaching attorney who has published extensively, Dr. Oettinger's primary field is Communication Law, working extensively with government officials. In addition to a law degree (J.D.), he has an M.A. in Dramatic Arts and a Ph.D. in English at the University of North Carolina and has taught and published in those areas. He was a Navy officer in World War II on the CINCPAC staff at Pearl Harbor and at one time did radio and television news commentary.

James B. Rule
Department of Sociology
SUNY—Stony Brook
Stony Brook, New York 11794

James Rule was born in Northern California, where he lived until his undergraduate years, which he spent at Brandeis University. He did his Ph.D. at Harvard, where he carried out research on civil disorder and social change in France and personal data systems. He taught and did research at the Universities of Oxford, Cambridge and Bordeaux before coming to the State University of New York at Stony Brook, where he now teaches. He is the author of *Private Lives and Public Surveillance, Insight and Social Betterment: A Preface to Applied Social Science*, and, with the other authors of his contribution to this book, *The Politics of Privacy*, forthcoming from Elsevier

Irwin J. Sitkin
Aetna Life & Casualty
Corporate Data Processing and Administrative Services
151 Farmington Avenue
Hartford, Connecticut 06156

Irwin Sitkin is vice president, Corporate Data Processing and Administrative Services, at Aetna Life and Casualty. A graduate of Cornell University (B.S. in Economics, 1952), he joined Aetna's data processing department in 1954, following 2 years in the Air Force. He was named superintendent in 1958, assistant secretary in 1960, secretary in 1965, assistant vice president, D.P. development in 1968, and assistant vice president, corporate D.P. development the following year. He was appointed vice president, corporate D.P. in 1972, and assumed his present position in 1976. Mr. Sitkin has been actively involved in LOMA's (Life Office Management Association) Operations and Systems Council and currently serves as council chairman and as a member of the LOMA Board of Directors; both the AIA (American Insurance Association) and ACLI (American Council of Life Insurance) Privacy Committees as well as the chairman of Aetna's Privacy Council; the NCCC (National Computer Conference Committee) with liaison responsibility for NCC, 1979; and the Data Processing Management Association (Hartford Chapter) as a past president and international director. Irv was the 1978 recipient of the DPMA's Computer Sciences Man of the Year award.

Oliver R. Smoot
Computer and Business Equipment
Manufacturers' Association
1828 L Street, N.W.
Washington, D.C. 20036

Oliver R. Smoot is vice president and treasurer of the Computer and Business Equipment Manufacturers'Association, where he is responsible for the direction and administration of the association's internal activities. He is a lawyer with a background in systems programming. Prior to joining CBEMA, Ollie served in computer management and technical positions with the Institute for Defense Analyses and the Lambda Corporation. He is active in the American Bar Association, the Association for Computer Machinery, the Institute for Certification of Computer Professionals and the Computer Law Association. Ollie holds a BS from M.I.T. and a JD from Georgetown University.

Theodore D. Sterling
Computing Science Department
Simon Fraser University
Burnaby, B.C., Canada V5A 156

Theodore Sterling received his B.A. and M.A. from the University of Chicago and his Ph.D. from Tulane. He has taught applied mathematics, statistics, and computer science at Alabama, Michigan State, Washington (where he also held a courtesy appointment in sociology), Hebrew Union College (where he also held a visiting appointment in philology), Princeton, and Simon Fraser University. He held the position of computer ombudsman with CIPS—Vancouver, and is president of the Computer Science Association. Now, and in the past, he has served an a consultant to the Nation Science Foundation, the Enviromental Protection Administration, SRA, the Federal Trade Commission. He has published eight books and over 180 scientific articles. Professor Sterling has done empirical research on the impact of technology on human qualities.

George B. Trubow
John Marshall Law School
315 South Plymouth Court
Chicago, Illinois 60604

Since 1976, George B. Trubow has been professor of information law and policy at John Marshall Law School in Chicago. Prior to that time he served as general counsel to the White House Privacy Committee established under then Vice President Ford (Domestic Council Committee on the Right to Privacy). Professor Trubow has also been deputy counsel to a subcommittee of the U.S. Senate Judiciary Committee, and was with the Law Enforcement Assistance Administration of the U.S. Department of Justice. Professor Trubow has been a consultant on privacy to the Law Enforcement Assistance Administration, the American Bar Association, SEARCH Group, Inc., and the National Telecommunication and Information Administration of the U.S. Department of Commerce.

Rein Turn
Computer Science Department
California State University
Northridge, California 91330

Dr. Rein Turn is professor of computer science at California State University, Northridge where he lectures on computer design and programming and on societal impacts of computer technology. Previously he was employed by TRW Defense and Space Systems Group, and earlier by the Rand Corporation. He is continuing his association with TRW. His research interests and contributions are in the areas of computer security, protection of individual privacy in personal information record-keeping systems, advanced computer architectures, and technology assessment.

Dr. Turn is chairperson of AFIPS Panel on Transborder Data Flows, vice-chairperson of IEEE Computer Society's Technical Committee on Security and Privacy, secretary-treasurer of the ACM Special Interest Group on Computers and Society, and member of AFIPS Committees on Privacy and on EFTS. He was a consultant on technology to the U.S. Privacy Protection Study Commission.

Willis H. Ware
The Rand Corporation
1700 Main Street
Santa Monica, California 90406

Formally educated in engineering, Dr. Ware has long been concerned with the impact of computers and information technology upon society, and as early as the mid 1960s had begun writing and discussing his views on computers as a growing social force. As chairman of the HEW Secretary's Advisory Committee on Automated Personal Data Systems, he presented a definitive document on privacy problems and proposed solutions to Secretary Weinberger and Attorney General Richardson. In 1974 Dr. Ware was appointed chairman of the AFIPS Committee on Privacy. In the same year he attended privacy conferences in Tokyo, Paris and Vienna, giving key talks at each.

In 1975 Dr. Ware was appointed by the White House to the Privacy Protection Study Commission created by the Privacy Act of 1974. He spent the next 2 years with the commission studying data banks and information systems, public and private, across the country. Findings and recommendations were reported to the president and Congress in July 1977. His efforts on behalf of individual privacy in the age of electronic information processing earned him DPMA's Computer Sciences Man of the Year award in June 1975.

Alan F. Westin
Department of Public Law and Government
Columbia University
New York, New York 10027

Alan F. Westin is professor of public law and government at Columbia University in New York City. Born in 1929, he earned his B.A. in political science at the University of Florida, his law degree from Harvard Law School, and his Ph.D. in political science at Harvard University. He is a member of the District of Columbia Bar. Dr. Westin is author or editor of dozens books on privacy, including: *Privacy and Freedom* (1967); *Databanks in a Free Society* (1972); *Information Technology in a Democracy* (1971); *The Impact of Computer-Based Information Systemson Civil Liberties in the Advanced Industrial Nations* (with David Martin and Daniel Luskin) (1973); *Computers, Health Records, and Citizen Rights* (1976); *Computers, Personnel Administration,and Citizens' Rights* (1979)

He has served as a consultant on privacy to a wide range of organizations, such as the New York State Identification and Intelligence System, the IBM Corporation, Monsanto Chemical, Project SEARCH (criminal justice systems), Nabisco, Sentry Insurance Co., Allied Chemical, Equifax, and the New York State Assembly. In 1977, Professir Westin was appointed by Governor Brendon Byrne as a member of the New Jersey State Commission on Individual Liberty and Personal Privacy, and now serves as vice-chairman of the commission.

Subject Index